CW00503931

CONSTITUTIONAL POLI'
MIDDLE EAS1

This book is the first comparative and interdisciplinary study of constitutional politics and constitution making in the Middle East. The historical background and setting are fully explored in two substantial essays by Linda Darling and Saïd Amir Arjomand, placing the contemporary experience in the contexts, respectively, of the ancient Middle Eastern legal and political tradition and of the nineteenth and twentieth century legal codification and political modernisation. These are followed by Ann Mayer's general analysis of the treatment of human rights in relation to Islam in Middle Eastern constitutions, and Nathan Brown's comparative scrutiny of the process of constitution making in Iran, Afghanistan and Iraq with reference to the available constitutional theories which are shown to throw little or no light on it. The remaining essays are country by country case studies of Turkey, Afghanistan and Iraq, the case of Iran having been covered by Arjomand as the special point of reference. Mehmet Fevzi Bilgin examines the making and subsequent transformation of the Turkish Constitution of 1982 against current theories of constitutional and deliberative democracy, while Hootan Shambayati examines the institutional mechanism for protecting the ideological foundations of the Turkish Republic, most notably the Turkish Constitutional Court, which offers a surprising parallel to the Iranian Council of Guardians. Arjomand's introduction brings together the bumpy experience of the Middle East along the long road to political reconstruction through constitution making and constitutional reform, drawing some general analytical lessons from it. He also shows the consequences of the fact that the constitutions of Turkey and Iran had their origins in revolutions, and of Afghanistan and Iraq, in war and foreign invasion.

Oñati International Series in Law and Society

A SERIES PUBLISHED FOR THE OÑATI INSTITUTE
FOR THE SOCIOLOGY OF LAW

General Editors

William LF Felstiner   Johannes Feest

Board of General Editors

Rosemary Hunter, University of Kent, United Kingdom
Carlos Lugo, Hostos Law School, Puerto Rico
David Nelken, Macerata University, Italy
Jacek Kurczewski, Warsaw University, Poland
Marie Claire Foblets, Leuven University, Belgium
Roderick Macdonald, McGill University, Canada

Titles in this Series

Social Dynamics of Crime and Control: New Theories for a World in Transition edited by Susannah Karstedt and Kai Bussmann

Criminal Policy in Transition edited by Andrew Rutherford and Penny Green

Making Law for Families edited by Mavis Maclean

Poverty and the Law edited by Peter Robson and Asbjørn Kjønstad

Adapting Legal Cultures edited by Johannes Feest and David Nelken

Rethinking Law Society and Governance: Foucault's Bequest edited by Gary Wickham and George Pavlich

Rules and Networks edited by Richard Appelbaum, Bill Felstiner and Volkmar Gessner

Women in the World's Legal Professions edited by Ulrike Schultz and Gisela Shaw

Healing the Wounds edited by Marie-Claire Foblets and Trutz von Trotha

Imaginary Boundaries of Justice edited by Ronnie Lippens

Family Law and Family Values edited by Mavis Maclean

Constitutional Politics in the Middle East

With special reference to Turkey, Iraq, Iran and Afghanistan

Edited by
Saïd Amir Arjomand

Oñati International Series in Law and Society

A SERIES PUBLISHED FOR THE OÑATI INSTITUTE
FOR THE SOCIOLOGY OF LAW

·HART·
PUBLISHING

OXFORD AND PORTLAND OREGON
2008

Published in North America (US and Canada)
by Hart Publishing
c/o International Specialized Book Services
920 NE 58th Avenue, Suite 300
Portland, OR 97213-3786
USA
Tel: +1 503 287 3093 or toll-free: (1) 800 944 6190
Fax: +1 503 280 8832
E-mail: orders@isbs.com
Website: www.isbs.com

© Oñati IISL 2007

Hart Publishing, 16c Worcester Place, Oxford, OX1 2JW
Telephone: +44 (0)1865 517530 Fax: +44 (0)1865 510710
E-mail: mail@hartpub.co.uk
Website: http://www.hartpub.co.uk

British Library Cataloguing in Publication Data
Data Available

ISBN-13: 978-1-84113-774-2 (hardback)
ISBN-13: 978-1-84113-773-5 (paperback)

Typeset by Compuscript, Shannon
Printed and bound in Great Britain by
TJ International, Padstow, Cornwall

Acknowledgement

An earlier version of the chapter by Barnett R Rubin was published as 'Crafting a Constitution for Afghanistan' (2004) 15(3) *Journal of Democracy* 5. © National Endowment for Democracy and The Johns Hopkins University Press. We are grateful for the kind permission to reproduce the material by The Johns Hopkins University Press.

Contents

List of Contributors

Andrew Arato (PhD, University of Chicago, 1975) is Dorothy Hirshon Professor in Political and Social Theory, New School for Social Research and Editor of *Constellations*. He is currently Fullbright Distinguished Professor in American Studies, JW Goethe Universität, Frankfurt/M (2007–8), and his forthcoming book is The Imposed Revolution and its Constitution: Iraq 2003–2006 (New York, Columbia University Press).

Saïd Amir Arjomand (PhD, University of Chicago, 1980) is Distinguished Service Professor of Sociology at the State University of New York at Stony Brook. He is the founder and President (1996–2002, 2005–08) of the Association for the Study of Persianate Societies. His latest edited book is *Constitutionalism and Political Reconstruction* (Leiden, E J Brill, 2007).

Mehmet Fevzi Bilgin (PhD, University of Pittsburgh, 2004) is Assistant Professor of Political Science at Sakarya University, Turkey. He has published several articles on religion and politics and recently translated John Rawls's *Political Liberalism* into Turkish (Istanbul, Bilgi University Press). He is currently working on the constitutional aspects of democratisation in Turkey and the Middle East.

Nathan J Brown is Professor of Political Science and International Affairs and Director of the Institute of Middle Eastern Studies at George Washington University. He also serves as a senior associate at the Carnegie Endowment for International Peace. His books include *Constitutions in a Nonconstitutional World. Arab Basic Laws and the Prospects for Accountable Government* (Albany, SUNY Press, 2002).

Linda T Darling (PhD, University of Chicago 1990) is Associate Professor of History at the University of Arizona. She has written extensively on the fiscal administration of the Ottoman Empire and her publications include *Revenue-Raising and Legitimacy: Tax Collection and Finance Administration in the Ottoman Empire, 1560–1660* (Leiden, E J Brill, 1996).

Ann Elizabeth Mayer is an Associate Professor of Legal Studies at the Wharton School of the University of Pennsylvania. She has published extensively on topics such as Islamic law in contemporary Middle Eastern countries and cultural particularism and international human rights. Her book *Islam and Human Rights. Tradition and Politics* (Boulder, CO, Westview Press, 2006) is now in its fourth edition.

Barnett R Rubin is Director of Studies at the Center on International Cooperation of New York University. Dr Rubin served as adviser to the UN Special Representative of the Secretary-General to Afghanistan and Director of the Center for Preventive Action at the Council on Foreign Relations. He has taught political science at Yale and Columbia Universities and written numerous books and articles on Afghanistan, conflict prevention, state formation and human rights.

Hootan Shambayati is Assistant Professor of Political Science at Bilkent University, Ankara. He has previously published in *Comparative Politics* and the *International Journal of Middle East Studies*. He is interested in the study of democratisation and accountability.

Introduction

SAÏD AMIR ARJOMAND

T HE FIRST REQUIREMENT for a comparative approach to constitutional politics—politics of the creation and reconstruction of political order—is to broaden its scope by shifting the focus of analysis from constitutionalism to constitution-making. I have argued elsewhere that constitution-making often has little to do with constitutionalism.[1] Although it still retains its association with the original eighteenth-century idea of the constituent power of the representatives of the people, constitution-making has performed different functions in different historical periods, and it should be added, in different regions of the world in the same period. In this broadened perspective, Nathan Brown has identified the distinctive novel feature of the Middle Eastern historical experience. Since the Tunisian Constitution of 1861, Middle Eastern constitutions have typically been documents for organising power and rationalising the structure of the state, with the objective of making government more efficient rather than limiting its power.[2]

Although we can talk of a global, post-1989 wave of constitution-making, we should not ignore variations within this wave in Eastern and Central Europe, East Asia, the Middle East and Africa. Central and Eastern Europe have been the trendsetters in this wave of constitution-making, and they have been the focus of attention in the literature. Africa and the Middle East, however, have not received much attention. The purpose of the essays in this volume, and of the Workshop at the International Institute for the Sociology of Law at which they were first presented in April 2005, is to remedy the situation with regard to the Middle East.

It goes without saying that the most hotly debated subject in the constitutional politics of the Middle East is the vexing relation between Islam and democracy. This relation is very poorly understood, however, because of ahistorical, ideological and essentialist readings of Islam on all sides. The debate on Islam and democracy and their alleged incompatibility was already wrapped in thick ideological clouds long before 9/11. There are

---

[1] SA Arjomand, 'Law, Political Reconstruction and Constitutional Politics' (2003) 18(1) *International Sociology* 7.
[2] NJ Brown, *Constitutions in a Nonconstitutional World: Arab Basic Laws and the Prospects for Accountable Government* (Albany, SUNY Press, 2002).

two mutually reinforcing reasons for this: an astonishing lack of historical, institutional perspective in legal scholarship, and a curious textualist
convergence between Orientalism and fundamentalism. As evidence for
this convergence, let me quote what was actually written in 1970 by HAR
Gibb at Harvard, but could just as easily have been written by Mawdudi in
Lahore or Khomeini in Najaf:

> The community exists to bear witness to God amid the darkness of this world,
> and the function of its government is essentially to act as the executive of the Law
> [meaning, the *shari'a*].[3]

The confusion is widely shared. The President of the Egyptian People's
Assembly, for instance, would state during the discussion of projects for the
codification of the Islamic *shari'a* in 1982 that 'until the end of the nineteenth century, Islamic *shari'a* alone governed Arab states!'[4] Furthermore,
both Gibb and Mawdudi confuse the community of believers (*umma*) with
the political community—the term for which in traditional public law and
statecraft literature was the *ra'iyya[t]*, or subjects of the kingdom. The term
literally means the flock, with the king as its shepherd, and belongs to the
traditional pre-Islamic Middle Eastern political ethic.

   The first two essays in this volume therefore seek to remedy the lack of
attention to the historical background of the current constitutional crisis in
the Muslim world. Linda Darling analyses the fundamental idea of justice
as the underlying principle of government in pre-modern Middle Eastern
monarchies. She shows that the Middle Eastern conception of the circle of
justice, as the core of political ethic and basic norm of statecraft, indeed
predates Islam, and was integrated with Islamic concepts of governance in
the medieval period. Furthermore, the historical picture of the normative
principles of government she offers bears no resemblance to the 'Islamic
state' as depicted by the Islamic fundamentalist ideologues and some
Orientalist scholars. Rather, these principles were based on the agrarian
state's dependence on its tax-paying subjects and its corresponding need to
deliver justice to them. This notion of the state's dependence on its people
animated the first Ottoman constitution-makers in the 1860s and 1870s.

   My own essay examines the public law and political ethic of the Ottoman
empire and Iran as the historical context of the construction of legal codes
and advent of modern constitutionalism. It proceeds to discuss the place
of Islam in the old and new Iranian Constitutions, of 1906 (supplemented
in 1907) and 1979 (amended in 1989). This historical and comparative

---

[3] HAR Gibb, 'The Heritage of Islam in the Modern World (I)' (1970) 1 *International
Journal of Middle East Studies* 11.

[4] Cited in B Botiveau, 'Contemporary Reinterpretations of Islamic Law: the Case of Egypt'
in Ch Mallat (ed), *Islam and Public Law: Classical and Contemporary Studies* (London,
Graham & Trotman, 1993) 265.

perspective also enhances our understanding of the place of Islam in the Afghan Constitutions of 1964 and 2004. I argue that the case of Iran is particularly significant for showing that the questions about the relation between Islam and constitutionalism in the first decade, the middle and the end of the twentieth century were not the same, but varied enormously. Again, the notion of the Islamic state stands out as a modern ideological construct that does not correspond to any historical reality embedded in the political and legal institutions of the Muslim Middle East.

In the first stage of constitutional history, the *shari'a* (Islamic law) appeared as a *limitation* to government and legislation. There was never a presumption that it should be the basis of the constitution itself. In this period, Islam is considered a part of the larger issue of constitutional governance and not as the basis of the constitution. The impact of Islam on constitutionalism with the late coming of the age of ideology in the Middle East was radically different from the first, and far more destructive. In this wave of ideological constitution-making, Islam increasingly appears as the *basis* of the constitution and the state rather than a *limitation* to them. This makes current constitutional problems especially intractable but it should be attributed to the ideological character of the constitutional model now taken over by the Islamists, rather than to Islam per se.

The constitutional implications of late arrival of the age of ideology in the Middle East are striking. Like those who had drafted the Ottoman Fundamental Law of 1876, the makers of the Iranian Fundamental Laws of 1906 and 1907 had recognised the fundamental dualism of temporal and religious law in the politico-legal system they were living under. Both groups used the term *qānun* for the fundamental law, and identified the legislative power as *muqannina* from the same root, ie the power to make public law. For them, the transfer of the legislative power—the right to make public laws—from the monarch to the people, which was the culmination of a gradual and arduous amplification of the ruler's duty of consultation (*shurā*), was conceptually non-problematic; and it did *not* involve the *shari'a*. It took the arrogance of Atatürk's militant secularists to use the term *teshri'iyye* (derived from the *shari'a*) for the legislative power, thereby confusing, by appropriation, the people's newly acquired right to make public laws with the divine inspiration of the sacred law. The first generation of constitutionalists had no conceptual difficulty in recognising that what they were seeking to transfer to the people was not any divine prerogative but the ruler's right, be he the Sultan or the Shah, to make public laws.

The same cannot be said about the constitution-makers of Pakistan a century after the replacement of the Mughal empire by the British Raj. Only in the absence of an actual Muslim monarch could the notion of national sovereignty evoke, in the minds of the Islamic ideologues such as Mawdudi, the superiority of God over the nation and result in the declaration of God's sovereignty in the 1956 Constitution of the Islamic Republic of Pakistan, the first state ever to be so designated in history. With this declaration and designation, ideological elements were grafted upon the liberal, 'Westminster' constitutional model that were to grow cancerously and deform its character. Only thereafter, with the elaboration and spread of Islamic ideology, would Gibb's ahistorical model of an Islamic state that exists primarily for the implementation of the *shariʿa* become a social force in the Muslim world. The term *umma* for political community had meanwhile made its first modern appearance in the five-article 1938 Constitution of Kuwait, the first of which derives the powers of the government from the *umma*, meaning the nation. The Kuwaiti Constitution of 1962 was more elaborate and adopted much of the Ottoman Constitution of 1876.[5] It did, however, graft another ideological item that had been anticipated by the short-lived and forgotten Syrian Constitution of 1950 but was now destined to become a staple element in Islamic constitution-making. Its Article 2 declared the principles of the *shariʿa* 'a main source of legislation'. Egypt eagerly followed this method of pre-emptive appropriation of fundamentalist ideological notions by Muslim authoritarian regimes, and incorporated the phrase into Article 2 of its Constitution of 1971, thus adding Islam to the syncretic socialist-liberal-nationalist ideological foundations. The same Article 2 was once more preemptively amended in 1980, changing 'a' to 'the' to read in translation: 'the principles of the Islamic *shariʿa* are the chief source of legislation'.[6] The gambit was followed by one country after another, and by 2000, constitutions of some 24 Muslim states had declared *shariʿa* (or its principles) 'a' or 'the' source of legislation. And the new millennium opened with the stampede of the 12 northern federal states of Nigeria declaring the *shariʿa* the state law.

In contrast to this peculiarly Islamic late ideological turn, the constitutional implications and ramifications of the centrality of religion to collective identity is not confined to the Muslim world but have interesting parallels in the Middle East's Jewish state, Israel. Two of the first new postcolonial states, namely Pakistan and Israel, were created in 1947 and 1948 respectively. Both these new states emerged out of the legal tradition of the British empire as respective results of the Partition of India and the ending of the Palestinian Mandate. New governments in both countries were given the mandate to prepare written constitutions. Ideology had played a powerful role in the creation of both states as homelands for Muslims of India and the Jewish people, respectively, and could be expected to have a strong impact on the making of these constitutions. The debate on the constitutional implications of Islam contributed to the long delay in the making of the 1956 Constitution of the Islamic Republic of Pakistan, which

---

[5] Kuwait became independent in 1961 and made the Ottoman codification of the Hanafi law, the Majalla, its civil code.

[6] Brown, above n 2, at 30, 56, 82–4. The word for 'legislation' itself is derived from *shariʿa* in Arabic, unlike the Persian word which stems from *qānun*, so the Arabic text reads: *mabadi al- shariʿa al-islamiyya al-masdar al-raʾsi liʾl-tashriʿ*.

is briefly discussed in my own chapter. In Israel, the Zionist ideology was embodied in the Law of Return which entitled every Jew to return to the homeland and to automatic citizenship in the state of Israel. The religious component of the Jewish identity, however, prevented Ben-Gurion from ever carrying out the task of preparing a written constitution. Even though the religious parties were a tiny minority, Ben-Gurion and other secular Zionists could not bring themselves to contradict the slogan, 'the Torah is our Constitution!' As a result, the Constituent Assembly elected in January 1949 became a parliament, the Knesset, and in June 1950, passed the Harari resolution that there would be no constitution of Israel but only a series of basic laws.[7]

The discussion of the place of Islam in the constitutional order of contemporary Middle East would be incomplete without an investigation of the problem of defining the respective roles of Islam and human rights. Ann Mayer's chapter examines the human rights provisions of a representative selection of constitutions of Muslim countries, all set forth in explicit or implied relationship to Islam, with qualifications on human rights ranging from the general 'principles of Islam' to the specific provisions of the *shari'a*. The analysis highlights unresolved tensions, showing that drafters have not yet managed to devise clear and coherent constitutional principles defining this relationship.

Nathan Brown's theoretical reflections in his chapter are prompted by the process of constitution-making in Iran, Afghanistan and Iraq. He uses these examples from the Middle East to demonstrate how very remote are the current theories of constitution-making, both the liberal/Rawlsian and the rational choice variants, from the reality of constitutional bargaining and process. Nor does he find the local political traditions any better than these rarefied constitutionalist theories in giving a firmer ground for the critical role of partisan interests and political passions in constitution-writing. Constitutional bargaining is shaped by partisan interests in distribution of national power and resources among ethnic groups, and in the structuring of power among the offices of the state according to short-term partisan interests, and not by general, philosophical considerations of public welfare. Nor is there any evidence that publicity in negotiations is conducive to rational consensus building or conflict resolution. Andrew Arato's chapter offers a painstakingly detailed and penetrating account of the bargaining behind the ultimately abortive process of constitution-making in occupied Iraq. His account fully supports Brown's sobering conclusion of the inadequacy of current theories, but it also presents an alternative analytical perspective focused on the constitutional implications and requirements of state destruction and state formation or reconstruction.

---

[7] E Rackman, *Israel's Emerging Constitution: 1948–51* (New York, Columbia University Press, 1955).

An important feature of the Middle Eastern constitutional history is the ideological character of many of its constitutions. The defining character- istics of the ideal-type I have called 'ideological constitution', as originally developed in the Soviet Constitution of 1918 are (a) the conception of constitution primarily as an instrument of social transformation and only secondarily as the foundation of the political order, and (b) the nullification of civil and human rights when found inconsistent with the ideological prin- ciples underlying the constitution. An 'ideological constitution' is designed not for the limitation of government but for the transformation of the social order according to a revolutionary ideology. Limited government and civil liberties therefore have to give way as the constitution itself is now an instrument of social transformation.[8] Immediately after the Second World War, a new institution, the constitutional court, was used as an instrument for prevention of the return of the old regime through the protection of rights in the post-war political reconstruction of Germany, Japan and Italy; and in the following decades of decolonisation, the model of ideological constitution spread in the Third World.[9] The constitutional courts emerged as the key institution in the post-1989 wave of constitutionalism and tran- sition to democracy in Central and Eastern Europe.[10] In the Middle East, however, the constitutional courts and similar organs with the power of judicial review have assumed a somewhat unexpected function.

When Hans Kelsen had originally conceived a constitutional court for Austria in 1920, and when he challenged Carl Schmitt by maintaining that the constitutional court and not the President be considered the guardian of the constitution in 1928, neither Kelsen nor Schmitt paid much atten- tion to ideology in relation to the constitution.[11] The Communists and the Fascists in the interwar period had ideological constitutions but no constitutional courts. When the age of ideology spread from Europe to the Middle East, a number of ideological constitutions appeared with it—most notably the Turkish constitutional amendment of 1928, the Egyptian Constitution of 1971 and the 1979 Constitution of the Islamic Republic of Iran. Furthermore, with the global transplantation of legal institutions, con- stitutional courts were set up in Egypt in 1979 and Turkey in 1961 (reor- ganised in 1982), while the Iranian Constitution of 1979 set up a Council of Guardians modelled on the French *Conseil constitutionnel*, with more extensive powers. This briefly sketched historical background brings out

[8] SA Arjomand, 'Constitutions and the Struggle for Political Order: a Study in the Modernization of Political Traditions' (1992) 33(4) *European Journal of Sociology* 46.
[9] SA Arjomand, 'Law, Political Reconstruction and Constitutional Politics' (2003) 18(1) *International Sociology* 9.
[10] L Sólyom, 'The Role of Constitutional Courts in the Transition to Democracy, with Special Reference to Hungary' (2003) 18(1) *International Sociology* 133.
[11] D Dyzenhaus, *Legality and Legitimacy: Carl Schmitt, Hans Kelsen and Hermann Heller in Weimar* (Oxford, Clarendon Press, 1997).

the very interesting and comparatively salient connection between ideology and judicial review and constitutional interpretation by the constitutional courts in the Middle East, which is the subject of Hootan Shambayati's study. In constitutional orders with entrenched ideologies, constitutional courts are more likely to act as guardians of the ideological foundations of the regime than as protectors of rights. Adopting the notion of the guardian of the constitutional order from the Kelsen-Schmitt debate, Shambayati examines the quarter-century history of the Turkish constitutional court as one of the major institutions guarding the Kemalist, secularist foundations of the regime, and offers a concise comparison at the end with the same function performed by the Iranian Council of Guardians in the theocratic republic.

The chapter by Mehmet Fevzi Bilgin enables us to put the performance of the Turkish constitutional court in the broader context of the making of the authoritarian constitution of 1982, with its 'reserve domains' for the military elite. He examines the current Turkish aspirations to complete the transition from authoritarian constitutionalism to democracy in the light of the requirements of democratic legitimacy elaborated in relation to the current theories of deliberative democracy. His analysis of the making of the Turkish Constitution of 1982 and the means for its democratisation thus provides the indispensable background to the constitutional reforms and reconstruction since 2001 set in motion by the application of Turkey for membership in the European Union.

The Iranian and Turkish cases of constitutional review organs as guardians of the ideological foundations of regimes invite a comparison with the Supreme Constitutional Court of Egypt and its notable jurisprudence of Article 2 of the Egyptian Constitution, which was amended in 1980 to declare that 'the principles of the Islamic *shari'a* are the chief source of legislation'. The issue is of considerable importance for understanding the consequences of the ideological declaration of the *shari'a* as the source of legislation. Here, the scholarly opinion is divided. Botiveau[12] and Brown,[13] basing their sanguine opinions mainly on the earlier decisions of the Egyptian Supreme Constitutional Court, argue that it tends to meet the Article 2 challenges to laws by upholding them on the grounds of the discretionary power of the state. Lombardi and especially Vogel, on the other hand, present a more disturbing picture.[14] It appears from these

---

[12] Above n 4.

[13] NJ Brown, 'Shari'a and the State in the Modern Middle East' (1997) 29(3) *IJMES* 359; Brown, above n 2, at 180–4.

[14] CB Lombardi, 'Islamic Law as a Source of Constitutional Law in Egypt: the Constitutionalization of the Shari'a in a Modern Arab State' (1998–99) 37 *Columbia Journal of Transnational Law* 81; FE Vogel, 'Conformity with Islamic Shari'a and Constitutionality under Article 2: Some Issues of Theory, Practice, and Comparison' in Eugene Cotran and Adel Omar Sherif (eds), *Democracy, the Rule of Law and Islam* (London, Kluwer, 1999) 525–44.

accounts together that, while Egypt's Supreme Constitutional Court at first responded vigorously to the major change in the international politico-legal culture by largely demolishing the *socialist* ideological foundation of Egypt's constitution and by moderating authoritarian statism, it has more recently been increasingly responsive to the popular pressure and has tended to bring to life the *Islamic* ideological principles of their syncretic constitution to trump civil rights and women's rights.

Comparing these two bodies' exercise of the powers of judicial review and constitutional interpretation, we can say that, whereas the Iranian Council of Guardians is primarily the guardian of the *shari'a* against the constitution as well as legislation, the Egyptian Supreme Constitutional Court is primarily the guardian of the constitution. The Egyptian Constitution of 1971 recognises no guardian for the *shari'a*. Indeed, for a quarter of a century, the Supreme Constitutional Court has considered Article 2 as primarily addressed to the legislature or the ruler.[15] As the Islamist pressure mounted in the 1990s, however, it has also come to consider itself the interpreter of the 'principles of the Islamic *shari'a*' to the horror of its official guardians—the *ulema* of al-Azhar.

Post-ideological constitutional development through the jurisprudence of constitutional courts is not the only avenue for subverting ideology by the rule of law. A return to the earlier conception of the *shari'a* as a limitation on government and legislation instead of being the basis of the constitution and the source of all legislation could have the same effect. A new phase of post-ideological Islamic constitutionalism, marked by such a return to limited government according to a constitution inclusive of the principles of Islam as the established religion, is, in fact, much in evidence.[16]

Revolutions and wars can result in significant constitutional settlements. The very appearance of constitutions as rational means for the construction of a new political order in the eighteenth century followed the American and French Revolutions, and constitution-making served as a guide to the political reconstruction of Germany and Japan after the Second World War. The Kemalist revolution in the Ottoman empire and the Islamic revolution in Iran both produced significant constitutions that have shaped enduring political regimes: the Turkish Republic and the Islamic Republic of Iran, respectively. Shambayati examines one significant consequence of the revolutionary matrix, namely the later emergence of organs of constitutional review as the guardians of the heritage of respective revolutions. It may still be too early to assess the significance of the constitution-making that

---

[15] N Bernard-Maugiron, 'La Haute Cour Constitutionelle Egyptiennes et la Shari'a islamique', paper presented at the Second Joseph Schacht Conference on the Theory and Practice of Islamic Law, Granada, 16–20 December 1997, at 12–13; Brown, above n 2, at 183.

[16] See SA Arjomand, 'Islamic Constitutionalism' (2008) 3 *Annual Review of Law and Social Science* (forthcoming).

followed the American invasions of Afghanistan and Iraq, but the detailed study of these two cases in the chapters by Rubin and Arato surely invite comparison with other post-war constitutional settlements and thus merit the attention of comparative constitutionalism.

Constitution-making in Afghanistan and Iraq also invites comparison with the pattern of constitution-making in Africa rather than Eastern Europe. The experience of state failure and ensuing civil wars in post-colonial Africa has suggested a new function for constitution-making as a means for conflict resolution.[17] Although this use of constitution-making is new, it does resonate with Hobbes's idea that the purpose of the social compact was to end the war of all against all. The focus on conflict inserts inter-ethnic relations and multilingualism at the expense of the citizen-state relations in classic, liberal constitutional models, promoting group rights at the expense of individual and civil rights, and shares with the East European transition the feature of establishing negotiation as a principle of constitution-making, alongside the classical principle of the constituent power of the people.

Similarly, the background of constitution-making in Afghanistan is state failure and many-sided civil war, as well as foreign invasion and occupation. A balance therefore had to be struck in its making between the immediate requirements of conflict resolution, after two decades of civil strife, and the long-term requirements of state-building and good governance. The making of a constitution was evidently important to enhance the legitimacy of a regime installed by the American invasion in Afghanistan. So the Afghan tradition of convening a Loya Jirga with constituent powers was followed to enhance the legitimacy of the new regime, and attempts were made at popular consultation by means of questionnaires circulated by the Afghan Constitutional Commission. However, neither the answers people gave, nor a large number of memoranda provided through the United Nations Assistance Mission for Afghanistan, played much of role in the drafting of the constitution by the Constitutional Commission or its adoption by the Constituent Loya Jirga. Instead, what was decisive was the fortunate existence of a significant previous 1964 constitution, which formed the basis of the new one, and negotiations within the Loya Jirga which reflected the ethno-linguistic alignments as much as the pre-Taliban struggle of the Islamic Mujahedin against the Soviet Union. The process is traced in detail in the chapter by Barnett Rubin. Rubin analyses the three-way contention between the new government and ruling coalition, the former Mujahedin and international bodies in the making of the Afghan Constitution of 2004.

---

[17] J Widner, 'Constitution Writing and Conflict Resolution' (2005) 94(381) *Round Table: Commonwealth Journal of International Affairs* 503.

State failure in post-Saddam Iraq is also critical for understanding the rushed and messy transition from an interim to the 'permanent' constitution. Indeed, Arato's step-by-step critical assessment of this process strongly suggests that the unprincipled and excessively politicised manner of constitution-making itself was a main contributory factor to the increasingly evident state failure after the American invasion. According to him, three main factors contributed to this failure: external imposition, the attempt to bind more than to assert the sovereign constituent power of 'the Iraqi people' by the Transitional Administrative Law (TAL), and last but not least, exclusionary bargaining. The critical connection among these factors can be found in L. Paul Bremer's fateful mistake of opting for a quick fix, dictated by American domestic politics, by choosing a two track negotiating process with the Kurds and the Arabs, without making the necessary effort to include the Sunnis among the latter. This fast and bifurcated process of negotiation, in preference to the more inclusive but slower Round Table model favored by the UN, doomed the prospects for constitutional state-building and facilitated the disintegration of Iraq. The final collapse of the consensual process of constitution-making involving the Sunnis, the American insistence that the Iraqis not avail themselves of the six-month extension allowed by the TAL, the putting of the draft to vote in a referendum by executive fiat, and then the adding of a compromise article on the amendment procedure that was not in the draft distributed to the voters—all that made a complete mockery of constitution-making as an act of the foundation of democracy, the stated goal of the American invasion of Iraq.

Taken together, the essays presented in this volume seek to put the constitutional experience of the Middle East, long ignored or obscured by the presumed exceptionalism of Islam, on the cognitive map of the scholarly community. I hope the reader will be led to the conclusion that the current constitutional crisis in the Middle East deserves the same attention as other salient contemporary trends such as 'new constitutionalism', post-Communist constitutional reconstruction, the rights revolution and possible new instrumental use of constitution-making for conflict resolution and restorative justice.

1

Islamic Empires, the Ottoman Empire and the Circle of Justice

LINDA T DARLING

T HE WORDS 'ISLAMIC government' or 'Islamic politics' usually bring
to mind a politics based on Qur'anic precepts about the righteous
community or the history of the early Muslim caliphs. And there
have always been those, mainly Islamic legal scholars reasoning from the
sayings of Muhammad, who have argued that this is the only legitimate
Islamic politics. But historically, most Muslim governments have been pat-
terned not only on the example of Muhammad but also on the example
of Khusrau, the Persian emperor within whose lifetime Muhammad was
born. Pre-modern Middle Eastern states were almost uniformly monarchies
modelled on the bureaucratic empire tradition of the ancient Near East and
the Mediterranean world: the Caliphate was such a monarchy informed by
the example of Muhammad as leader of the Muslim community, while the
Turkish and Mongol sultanates retained some aspects of tribal chieftain-
ship. These monarchies preserved ancient traditions of political organisation
and ethics, adapting them to the needs of a Muslim state.

Khusrau and other emperors employed a concept of government encapsulated in the following formula: 'There can be no government without
men, no men without money, no money without prosperity, and no prosperity without justice and good administration'. That concept is often
called the 'Circle of Justice', after a longer and more elaborate version that
brought the end around to the beginning. On the ruler's justice and good
administration depended the peasants' and merchants' ability to generate
prosperity; from this wealth taxes flowed to pay the military, which supported the king and protected the realm. This ideology reflected the social
structure of the Middle East and the relationships among different social
groups, while assigning to those in power the responsibility for maintaining a just equilibrium within the system. The model of Muhammad and the
early caliphs is a model (or several models) for choosing the right ruler, on
the assumption that if the right person leads the community he can guide it
on the right path. The model of Khusrau is a model for how the ruler ought

to behave, no matter who he is or how he came to power. And there have also always been those—rulers, bureaucrats and legal scholars reasoning from God's guidance of the Muslim community—who argued that without the justice of the Circle no politics was Islamically legitimate. They were concerned not with theoretical or juridical legitimacy but with popular legitimacy, the standards to which rulers had to conform to gain acceptance by their subjects.

This discussion of the ideology of justice seeks to evaluate the salience of the Circle of Justice for describing and legitimising the relations between the historic Middle Eastern states and their people, relations which in the modern period are regulated by constitutions and the governmental institutions mandated by them. There will be no attempt here to evaluate the actual justice or injustice of any particular regime. The citation of the Circle and its concepts by rulers, propagandists or governmental critics, along with the social relations and governmental institutions through which they could be implemented, are considered as indicators of commitment to the Circle as a public posture and as a vehicle of state-society relations. The Circle's effectiveness as a formula for legitimacy depended on the perception of a congruence between its recommendations and the institutions and activities of the government and its servants. Those activities could be informal or institutionalised; they might simply conform to those laid out in the Circle (or not), or they could be consciously guided by it. The subjects' response is suggested by their echoing of these ideas and their use of these institutions, but there is little direct evidence of their attitudes until the modern period. This chapter, summarising a longer project, provides an overall history of Middle Eastern political change in the Islamic period while emphasising particular areas of congruency or tension between the ideology of the Circle and the historical relations and institutions that seem most pertinent to modern concerns about constitutional reconstruction in the Middle East. It culminates by discussing the development of constitutionalism in the Ottoman Empire and the transformation of traditional Middle Eastern political discourse couched in terms of the Circle to a modern discourse couched in Western political terms.

THE EARLY ISLAMIC ERA

The first Islamic politics, under Muhammad and the first four caliphs (622–661), was a matter of transforming tribal governing mechanisms developed in a stable condition of competition for resources to handle the new situation of a religiously-based, non-tribal polity undergoing rapid expansion. After a century of conquest, however, the Muslims found a modified tribal government inadequate to the needs of an Islamic polity attempting to govern large expanses of territory and people with their own ancient civilizations. They then shifted to an imperial system of government that lasted down to modern times and was adopted by every major conquering group, although tribal mechanisms were still used in smaller-scale politics. With imperial politics came imperial ideologies, including the Circle of Justice. The Umayyad dynasty of caliphs (661–750), and their subjects as well, employed concepts of rulership stemming from the ancient Near Eastern empires, adapting them, as earlier Muslims had adapted the concepts of tribal politics, to a religiously-based and Arab-dominated state.[1]

Poetry dedicated to the Umayyad caliphs imitated the styles of pre-Islamic Arabic poetry but expressed ideas of kingship consonant with Mesopotamian and Persian royal ideologies of the king as shepherd, protector and source of prosperity encapsulated in the Circle of Justice. The Umayyad caliphs were called 'the shepherd of God on earth', with the Muslim community as the flock for which they were responsible. Their task was to guard and keep the people: Mu'awiya was spoken of as a refuge where protection could be found.[2] Like Mesopotamian kings, the caliphs were considered to be divinely appointed to their posts; as the poet Ahwas told the caliph Sulayman, 'God has confided to you rule and authority over us; command and be just'.[3] 'Abd al-Malik, like a Babylonian or Assyrian king, was hailed as one 'whom God has made victorious, … the vicegerent of God, from him we expect rain'.[4] His successors al-Walid I and Sulayman were also expected to control fertility by bringing rain.[5] A poem by the caliph al-Walid II put his own accession in a similar light: 'The shrewd and evilbringing one is dead; the rain is already falling'.[6] Divine support, military victory, protective care, justice and the prosperity of the land were all ascribed to the Umayyads. The later Umayyad rulers themselves shared the poets' view of the caliphate as having the qualities and responsibilities of Near Eastern kingship. Al-Yazid III, to justify his seizure of the throne, claimed that he would not allow the mighty to oppress the weak, nor

---

[1] For a history of the Muslim world see Marshall GS Hodgson, *The Venture of Islam: Conscience and History in a World Civilization*, 3 vols (Chicago, University of Chicago Press, 1974).

[2] W Thomson, 'The Character of Early Semitic Sects' in Samuel Löwinger and Joseph Somagyi (eds), *Ignace Goldziher Memorial Volume*, 2 vols (Budapest, 1948; Jerusalem, Rubin Mass, 1958) 1:91–92; I Goldziher, 'Du sens propre des expressions Ombre de Dieu, Khalife de Dieu, pour désigner les chefs d'Islam' (1897) 35 *Revue de l'histoire des religions* 335.

[3] Quoted in É Tyan, *Institutions du droit public musulman*, 2 vols (Paris, Recueil Sirey, 1954) 1:442 and n 2. For an exposition of this stance within a Qur'anic context see W al-Qadi, 'The Religious Foundation of Late Umayyad Ideology and Practice' in *Saber Religioso y Poder Político en el Islam* (Madrid, Agencia Española de Cooperación Internacional, 1994) 231–73.

[4] Quoted in H Lammens, 'Le chantre des Omiades: Notes biographiques et littéraires sur le poète arabe Ahtal' (1894) 4(9) *Journal asiatique* 163.

[5] P Crone and M Hinds, *God's Caliph: Religious Authority in the First Centuries of Islam* (Cambridge, Cambridge University Press, 1986) 9.

[6] Quoted in H Ringgren, 'Some Religious Aspects of the Caliphate' in *The Sacral Kingship* (Leiden, EJ Brill, 1959) 740.

overtax the peasantry and force them to flee, nor squander the treasury on women, palaces or irrigation works, but would treat his distant subjects equally with those nearby and would pay stipends promptly.[7] By the end of the Umayyad period, the royal obligation of providing justice was solidly entrenched in the rhetoric and conceptualisation of the caliphate.

Opponents of Umayyad rule also deployed these concepts of justice in critiques of the caliphs and their deeds, emphasising the need for their fulfilment in practice. The Bihafarid movement in the late 740s demanded the elimination of economic oppression and the maintenance of roads and bridges.[8] Extremist rebels expected justice from another source: a *mahdi*, or messiah, who would similarly establish equality and bring security and prosperity. He would 'fill the world with justice and equity as it is now filled with tyranny and oppression', for in his time 'the heavens would not withhold rain; the earth would give bountiful crops and surrender her precious metals'.[9] The developing Shi'i movement looked forward to the coming of a messiah from the family of the Prophet who would 'distribute equally among the people and ... establish justice among his subjects'.[10] The figure of 'Ali, the fourth caliph and first Shi'i Imam (leader), emerged as the spokesman for the struggle against oppression.[11] The Shi'i Imam was endowed with numerous attributes from the Near Eastern tradition of kingship. He was chosen by God, a shepherd of his sheep, without whom worship and prayers could not be accepted; he was the pillar of the earth, the father of orphans, the judge, the interpreter of God's commands; he was the light towards which people walk, a raincloud of blessings and kindness and a clear spring that flows at God's command, the owner of all the land and fresh waters and the treasures of the earth.[12] The Khariji rebels stressed the practical side of the Circle of Justice over the apocalyptic, forbidding their followers to pay taxes to the Umayyad caliph because he could not provide protection and exhorting them: 'Do not allow these tyrants to oppress the weak'.[13] At that point, there was apparently little

---

[7] Crone and Hinds, above n 5, at 68; GR Hawting, *The First Dynasty of Islam: the Umayyad Caliphate, AD 661–750* (London, Croom Helm, 1986) 95.

[8] H Bailey *et al* (eds), *The Cambridge History of Iran*, 7 vols (Cambridge, Cambridge University Press, 1968–91) 4:490.

[9] Quoted in B Lewis, 'On the Revolutions in Early Islam' (1970) 32 *Studia Islamica* 225; see also I Friedlander, 'The Heterodoxies of the Shi'ites in the Presentation of Ibn Hazm' (1907) 28 *Journal of the American Oriental Society* 43.

[10] The tradition regarding the Shi'i messiah, attributed to the fifth Imam Muhammad al-Baqir, is quoted in AA Sachedina, *Islamic Messianism: the Idea of the Mahdi in Twelver Shi'ism* (Albany, State University of New York Press, 1981) 39.

[11] M Dorraj, *From Zarathustra to Khomeini: Populism and Dissent in Iran* (Boulder, Lynne Reinner, 1990) 44–66.

[12] 'The Characteristics of the Imama' from *Kitab al-Hujja*, in Muhammad b Ya'qub al-Kulayni, *al-'Usul min al-Kafi*, quoted in Sachedina, above n 10, at 188–92.

[13] Quoted in JS Meisami, *Persian Historiography: to the End of the Twelfth Century* (Edinburgh, Edinburgh University Press, 1999) 114–15.

sense that these concepts were inappropriate or foreign to the Muslim community.

In the late Umayyad period, histories and works of political thought containing these political ideas began to be translated from Greek and Persian into Arabic. Abu al-'Ala' Salim, the head of the Umayyad chancery, translated several pre-Islamic works of political thought, including the apocryphal 'Letters of Aristotle to Alexander'.[14] In addition to what this work derived from Greek political tradition, it contained a number of recommendations based ultimately on Near Eastern precedents, notably that the ruler should hold audience to hear appeals for justice on a daily basis and should ensure that the legal system redressed the grievances of the people.[15] More well known are the translations of Persian works made by the courtier Ibn al-Muqaffa', especially the *Kitab al-Taj* (*Book of the Crown*), quoting the Circle of Justice; *Kalila wa-Dimna*, a collection of political fables; the 'Letter of Tansar' and 'Testament of Ardashir,' replete with political advice; the *Shahnama* (*Book of Kings*) containing the history of the Persian kings; and *Al-Adab al-Kabir* (*Great Book of Etiquette*), addressing the needs of kings and courtiers.[16] Among his original compositions was the *Risala fi al-Sahaba* (*Essay on Royal Companions*) on the court and the army, in which he proposed a plan for a more thoroughly Persian-style Islamic monarchy.[17] The ninth century also saw a wave of translations from Greek and Syriac into Arabic; the first work translated from Greek was Plato's *Republic*, with its division of society into rulers, soldiers and the productive classes.[18] This literature associated the idea of the Circle more directly with the cultural milieu of the pre-Islamic empires of the Byzantines and Persians, an association that became somewhat problematic in the subsequent period.

[14] M Grignaschi, 'Les "Rasa'il Aristatalisa ila-l-Iskandar" de Salim Abu-l-'Ala' et l'activité culturelle à l'époque omayyade' (1965–66) 19 *Bulletin d'études orientales* 7; *idem*, 'Le roman épistolaire classique conservé dans la version arabe de Salim Abu-l-'Ala" (1967) 80 *Le Muséon* 211; SM Stern, *Aristotle on the World State* (Columbia, University of South Carolina Press, 1968) 2 and n 2.

[15] Grignaschi, 'Le roman épistolaire,' above n 14, at 9–12; *idem*, 'Un roman épistolaire gréco-arabe: la correspondance entre Aristote et Alexandre' in M Bridges and JCh Bürgel (eds), *The Problematics of Power: Eastern and Western Representations of Alexander the Great* (Bern, Peter Lang, 1996) 109 n 1.

[16] F Gabrieli, 'L'opéra di Ibn al-Muqaffa'' (1931–32) 13 *Rivista degli studi orientali* 197; G Richter, *Studien zur Geschichte der älteren arabischen Fürstenspiegel* (Leipzig, JC Hinrichs, 1932); JD Latham, 'Ibn al-Muqaffa' and Early 'Abbasid Prose' in AFL Beeston *et al* (eds), *The Cambridge History of Arabic Literature*, 3 vols (Cambridge, Cambridge University Press, 1983), vol 2, J Ashtiany *et al* (eds), *Abbasid Belles-Lettres*, 48–77; Ibn al-Muqaffa', 'Al-Adab al-Kabir' in M Kurd Ali (ed), *Rasa'il al-Bulagha'* (Cairo, Dar al-Kutub al-'Arabiyya al-Kubra, 1913) 55–114; trans J Tardy in 'Traduction d'*al-Adab al-Kabir* d'Ibn al-Muqaffa'' (1993) 27 *Annales Islamologiques* 181.

[17] Ibn al-Muqaffa', 'Risala fi al-Sahaba' in *Rasa'il al-Bulagha'*, above n 16, 120–31.

[18] AKS Lambton, *State and Government in Medieval Islam, an Introduction to the Study of Islamic Political Theory: the Jurists* (Oxford, Oxford University Press, 1981) 44.

The concept of the Circle was not the only tradition of justice in Muslim society. From the Greek philosophical heritage came the definition of justice as balance or equilibrium between unequals. This definition was repeated and expanded by Islamic philosophers, most notably Miskawayh, who saw justice as an equilibrium, a balance among potentially opposing forces, which assured the dominance of reason and the 'peaceful cooperation of the faculties' both within the human individual and in the body politic. The idea of equilibrium was equally powerful on the social level: social stability rested on a balance of interests among people of different walks of life and levels of power, and Miskawayh defined royal justice as the maintenance of that balance.[19] This idea of balance appears in the Qur'an as well, both in the form of the scales of justice and in the form of the middle way, the mean between two extremes. The Circle's concept of justice can also be found in the Qur'an as freedom from oppression.[20] But the most prominent Qur'anic definition of justice is as personal integrity, uprightness or probity, a quality of individuals rather than a quality of their acts. The assumption is that an upright individual will produce just actions. Social justice, however, the demand for care of the poor and weak and support of widows and orphans, was a key element in Muhammad's message from the beginning.[21] Despite their varied origins, these concepts of justice were assimilated into one by the beginning of the thirteenth century.

THE ABBASID ERA

The Umayyads were succeeded by the Abbasid dynasty (750–945), under whom Persian and Greek history and culture began to be better known among the Arabs. As Persian influences in the caliphal government grew stronger with the employment of officials of Persian origin such as the Barmakids, the Abbasids' imperial ways were criticised in purist circles as borrowings from foreign and pre- or un-Islamic sources. These critics

---

[19] Miskawayh, *An Unpublished Treatise of Miskawayh on Justice; or Risala fi Mahiyat al-'Adl li Miskawayh* (MS Khan (ed and trans), Leiden, EJ Brill, 1964) 28–31; M Fakhry, 'Justice in Islamic Philosophical Ethics: Miskawayh's Mediating Contribution' (1975) 3 *Journal of Religious Ethics* 247; A al-Azmeh, *Arabic Thought and Islamic Societies* (London, Croom Helm, 1986) 35. See also Miskawayh, *Tahdhib al-Akhlaq wa-Tathir al-A'raq* CK Zurayk (trans) as *The Refinement of Character* (Beirut, American University of Beirut, 1968), a Greek-influenced work of philosophical ethics, in which he discussed justice as a mean between two extremes.

[20] M Ayoub, 'The Islamic Concept of Justice' in NH Barazangi, MR Zaman and O Afzal (eds), *Islamic Identity and the Struggle for Justice* (Gainesville, University Press of Florida, 1996) 19–22.

[21] FJ Ziadeh, 'Integrity ('*Adalah*) in Classical Islamic Law' in N Heer (ed), *Islamic Law and Jurisprudence* (Seattle, University of Washington Press, 1990) 73–93; L Rosen, *The Justice of Islam: Comparative Perspectives on Islamic Law and Society* (Oxford, Oxford University Press, 2000) 155. S Qutb, *Social Justice in Islam* (Washington, DC, American Council of Learned Societies, 1953).

censured the Umayyads for having initiated a trend away from Muhammad's style of governance and blamed these organisational changes for a perceived ethical decline in political life. Imperial political structures included a class system seen as inimical to Islam's egalitarian principles and a land and tax system that ran against customs brought from the peninsula or developed early in the Muslim conquest. Persian history and literature provided a 'foreign' attribution for these systems and their ideology that was used by some to condemn and marginalise them.

Other Abbasid authorities, however, treated imperial ideologies not as foreign borrowings but as common knowledge, normal political wisdom. Among these were the author of a letter to the judge Abu Musa (attributed to 'Umar I but probably written in the late Umayyad period); the judge's instructions on court procedure echoed ancient texts from Egypt and Iran.[22] Harun al-Rashid's chief justice Abu Yusuf strengthened this trend with his authorship of the *Kitab al-Kharaj (Book of Taxation)*, which included a preface on rulership.[23] His attribution of most of his advice to Muslim sources has sometimes been interpreted as a deliberate refutation of 'the prevailing cult of the Sasanian tradition',[24] but that assessment is overstated; advice that could not be supported directly by quotations from Muslim authorities was not rejected but simply presented as the jurist's own idea, even if it had Sasanian origins. Abu Yusuf linked the caliph's dispensation of justice with accuracy and fairness in taxation, employing the concepts of shepherd over the flocks of God, the light or illumination given to rulers by God, the responsibility of rulers for the welfare of their people and the resulting increase of the yield of the land tax (*kharaj*), and the prosperity of the subjects which came from the prevention of oppression and injustice. The Circle of Justice clearly lay behind these ideas, even though they were not explicitly attributed to the Persians. Abu Yusuf presented the concept of the Circle as the normal ethic of an imperial state, Islamic or otherwise, not as a foreign borrowing. That it could be supported by verses from the Qur'an and references to Islamic concepts rather than allusions to Persian statecraft indicates how thoroughly it had been assimilated into Islamic political thought.

When the well-known formulas of the Circle of Justice appeared in the ninth and tenth centuries, they were quoted as common knowledge. The

---

[22] Quoted in DS Margoliouth, 'Omar's Instructions to the Kadi' (1910) *Journal of the Royal Asiatic Society* 311.

[23] Abu Yusuf, *Kitab al-Kharaj*, A Ben Shemesh (ed and trans), *Taxation in Islam*, vol 3, *Abu Yusuf's Kitab al-Kharaj* (Leiden, E. J. Brill, 1969) 35–9; B Lewis (trans) in *Islam: from the Prophet Muhammad to the Capture of Constantinople*, 2 vols (New York, Harper Torchbooks, Harper & Row, 1973), vol 1, *Politics and War*, 152–5.

[24] HAR Gibb, 'The Evolution of Government in Early Islam' (1955) 4 *Studia Islamica* 1, rpt in SJ Shaw and WK Polk (eds), *Studies on the Civilization of Islam* (Boston, Beacon Press, 1962) 45.

first appearance of the Circle of Justice in extant literature was in *'Uyun al-Akhbar* (*Fountains of Information*) by Ibn Qutayba, where a chapter entitled 'Authority', a collection of 'quotable quotes' and anecdotes on good government, contained the four-part version of the Circle quoted above. A more complex eight-part version appeared in the tenth-century *Sirr al-Asrar* (*The Secret of Secrets*).[25] In both cases the manner of quotation indicates that it was already a common saying, existing in multiple versions not attributable to any one author. Whether or not it had been known to the peninsular Arabs, many of whom prided themselves on not following a king and being unfamiliar with imperial thought and administration, it was certainly part of the intellectual furniture of Muslims from the Fertile Crescent. This conclusion is reinforced by the fact that it resonates with a number of images that are widespread in Middle Eastern cultures.

The Circle's eight-line version, supposed to have been composed by Aristotle for Alexander the Great, was sometimes actually written in a circle:

> The world is a garden hedged in by sovereignty
> Sovereignty is lordship, preserved by the law
> Law is administration, governed by the king
> The king is a shepherd, supported by the army
> The army are soldiers (in one version dragons) fed by wealth
> Money is livelihood, gathered by the people
> The people are servants, enfolded by justice
> Justice is harmony, the wellbeing of the world. The world is a garden, etc.[26]

This version of the Circle paints a picture of the realm as a 'hedged garden' where people likened to sheep are at pasture, while an army of hungry dragons (bringers of famine) is satisfied by the prosperity made possible by the ruler's justice. This portrait of the realm as a garden flourishing by justice coincided in time with the similar portrait painted by Firdawsi in his *Shahnama* (*Book of Kings*), and it became a stock image in Islamic art and poetry. It also underlaid the creation of actual royal gardens in Mesopotamian, Persian and Islamic palaces; some rulers even rotated among their gardens like the sun.[27] Present also is the image of the king as a shepherd, feeding his flock in rich pastures and protecting them in walled enclosures; this image appears, of course, in the Bible as well as in numerous

[25] Ibn Qutayba, *Kitab 'Uyun al-Akhbar*, 10 pts in 4 vols (Cairo, Dar al-Kutub al-Misriyya, 1925–30) 1:9; Lewis, above n 23, at 1:185; R Steele (ed), *Opera hactenus inedita Rogeri Baconi*, vol 5, *Secretum Secretorum* (I Ali (trans), Oxford, Clarendon Press, 1920).

[26] Steele, above n 25, at 224–7; A Badawi (ed), *Fontes Graecae Doctrinarum Politicarum Islamicarum*, pt 1, *Testamenta Graeca (Pseudo-) Platonis, et Secretum Secretorum (Pseudo-) Aristotelis* (Cairo, Matba'a Dar al-Kutub al-Misriyya, 1954) 126–8; M Gaster, 'The Hebrew Version of the "Secretum Secretorum" with an Introduction and an English Translation' (1907) *Journal of the Royal Asiatic Society* 901.

[27] S Redford, 'Just Landscape in Medieval Anatolia' (2000) 20 *Studies in the History of Gardens and Designed Landscapes* 314–15.

inscriptions of Mesopotamian kings and in poetry dedicated to Islamic caliphs. The harmony of the spheres and the security gained by following the right path are also referenced. A number of these images have circles embedded in them, reinforcing the intrinsic circularity of this concept of justice. These circles figure the interdependence of social groups in Middle Eastern society. The modern image of autocratic rulers and downtrodden peasants must be modified, because ancient and medieval rulers were well aware of their dependence on the peasants and their productive capacity; they knew that when the treading grew too heavy-footed the revenues would stop flowing. Peasants refused to pay taxes or fled the land or took up banditry, nomadism or new religions; irrigation systems decayed; sometimes whole villages moved off the road and resettled on mountaintops inaccessible to tax collectors. Or local or rival lords might take advantage of the peasants' disaffection to provide the protection that peasants needed, turning the revenue flow in their direction.

The Circle of Justice was not merely a literary device or a propaganda tool; members of the Muslim clergy, the '*ulama*', also used it in analysing Islamic politics. The most important thinker in this vein is al-Mawardi, who laid down what became the canonical view of the caliph's qualifications and responsibilities in his book, *al-Ahkam al-Sultaniyya* (*The Rules of Government*). He drew the caliph's qualifications from the Qur'an and the history of the early Muslim community, but most of the caliph's responsibilities came directly from the Circle of Justice, including defence of the realm, provision of security, appointment of capable officials, proper tax collection and disbursement, execution of justice and good administration.[28] Al-Mawardi also emphasised the caliph's role in *mazalim*, the ruler's provision of justice outside the regular legal system.

The *mazalim* court was the setting in which the ruler exercised his duty to right wrongs of oppression, especially those committed by himself or his officials.[29] People presented petitions to the ruler either orally or in writing, and petitions and responses survive from Fatimid Egypt to show how a petition was written and handled.[30] Rulers also accepted petitions when

---

[28] al-Mawardi, *al-Ahkam al-Sultaniyya*, WH Wahba (trans) as *The Ordinances of Government* (Reading, Garnet Publishing, 1996) and by E Fagnan (trans) as *Les statuts gouvernementaux, ou Règles de droit public et administratif* (Algiers, Librairie de l'Université, 1915).

[29] al-Mawardi/Wahba, above n 28, at 90.

[30] H Massé, 'Ibn el-Çaïrafi, Code de la chancellerie d'état (Période fatimide)' (1914) 11 *Bulletin de l'Institut français d'archéologie du Caire* 113; SD Goitein, 'Petitions to Fatimid Caliphs from the Cairo Geniza' (1954/55) 45 *Jewish Quarterly Review* 30; SM Stern, 'Three Petitions of the Fatimid Period' (1962) 15 *Oriens* 172; SM Stern, *Fatimid Decrees: Original Documents from the Fatimid Chancery* (London, Faber and Faber, 1964); G Khan, 'The Historical Development of the Structure of the Medieval Arabic Petition' (1990) 52 *Bulletin of the School of Oriental and African Studies* 8; *idem, Arabic Legal and Administrative Documents in the Cambridge Genizah Collections* (Cambridge, Cambridge University Press, 1993) 321–76, 451.

they rode through the city or went out hunting. The idea that the duties of kingship centred around justice became a theme in popular literature, such as the *Thousand and One Nights*.[31] Caliphs and governors saw the need to be (or at least to appear) just, so they paid for irrigation works and food distribution, gave tax remissions in times of need, protected people and their property from abuse, made themselves accessible to petitioners and answered their requests. Ordinary people well understood that the caliphs were supposed to dispense justice and petitioned frequently to get what they wanted.

THE TURCO-MONGOL ERA

The entry of nomadic Turks and Mongols into the Middle East forced Muslims to justify rule with no claim but conquest, and the provision of justice became still more central to political legitimacy. The sultans of the Seljuk Turks (1055–1194) had numerous advisors, both Persian administrators and members of the *'ulama'*, who wrote works of advice built around the concepts of the Circle of Justice. The most famous of these was the vizier Nizam al-Mulk, but they also included the historians al-Nisaburi and al-Ravandi.[32] A surprising number were men of religion: al-Ghazali, of course, but also Imam al-Haramayn al-Juvayni, the anonymous author of the *Bahr al-Fava'id* (*The Sea of Virtues*), the imam al-Turtushi, and the mystics al-Harawi, al-'Attar and Najm al-Din Razi.[33] These men integrated the idea of the Circle with Islamic concepts of state, helping to overcome the objections of religious scholars to government service. Poets like the Persian Nizami and the Turk Yusuf Khass Hajib merged the Circle with their own cultural

---

[31] V Chauvin, *La récension égyptienne des Mille et Une Nuits* (Brussels, Faculté de Philosophie et Lettres de L'Université de Liège, 1899) 61–2; MJ de Hammer, *Contes inédits des Mille et Une Nuits* (MG-S Trébutien (trans), Paris, Librairie Orientale de Dondey-Dupré Père et Fils, 1828) 421–2 (672nd-673rd nights); M al-'Adawi (ed), *Kitab Alf Layla wa-Layla* (*Bulaq, Matba'a 'Abd al-Rahman Rushdi Bey*, 1862–63) 2:393 (465th night).
[32] Nizam al-Mulk, *The Book of Government or Rules for Kings: the Siyar al-Muluk or Siyasat-nama* (H Darke (trans), 2nd edn, London, Routledge and Kegan Paul, 1978) 9; Zahir al-Din Nishapuri, *The History of the Seljuq Turks, from the Jami' al-Tawarikh: an Ilkhanid Adaption of the Saljuq-nama* (KA Luther (trans), CE Bosworth (ed), Richmond, Curzon Press, 2001); Muhammad b 'Ali b Sulayman al-Ravandi, *Rahat-üs-Sudur ve Ayet-üs-Sürur*, 2 vols (A Ateş (trans), Ankara, Türk Tarih Kurumu Basımevi, 1957–1960) 1:68–1:82.
[33] al-Ghazali, *Ghazali's Book of Counsel for Kings (Nasihat al-Muluk)* (FRC Bagley (trans), London, Oxford University Press, 1971) 56; anon, *The Sea of Precious Virtues (Bahr al-Fava'id): a Medieval Islamic Mirror for Princes* (JS Meisami (trans), Salt Lake City, University of Utah Press, 1991) 295, 297; al-Turtushi, *Flambeau of Kings (Siraj al-Muluk)* (J al-Bayati (ed), London, Riad El-Rayyes Books, 1990) 169–70; Lewis, above n 23, vol 2, *Religion and Society*, 134; J Sourdel-Thomine, 'Les conseils du Šayh al-Harawi à un prince ayyubide' (1961–62) 17 *Bulletin d'études orientales* 219, 263; Farid al-Din 'Attar, *Pend-Nameh, ou, Le livre des conseils* (S de Sacy (trans), Paris, Imprimerie Royale, 1819) 31; Najm al-Din Razi, *The Path of God's Bondsmen from Origin to Return* (H Algar (trans), Delmar, NY, Caravan Books, 1982) 413, 434, 440.

traditions.[34] It is difficult to tell the extent to which the Turkish rulers acted out this integrated tradition, because their government documents have perished, but we do have copies of orders to provincial administrators that refer to the Circle of Justice and make it the standard by which officials' behaviour should be judged.[35] As for putting it into practice, there is the meagre evidence of anecdotes such as Tughril Bey's setting up a *mazalim* court or Sultan Sanjar's giving justice to an old woman while out hunting.[36]

The concept of the just ruler who protected the peasants and listened to complaints gained a new urgency during the Mongols' Ilkhanid regime (1258–1335), even though the Mongols were not initially Muslims. The story of Alexander the Great, that world-conquering outsider who became a Middle Eastern ruler, became important to Ilkhanid legitimacy, and every reference to Alexander implied a reference to Aristotle and his eight sentences. The historians and imperial advisors Juvayni and Rashid al-Din included the concept of the Circle of Justice in their works. The reform edicts of Ghazan Khan, who converted the regime to Islam, referred to the Circle as well as Qur'anic quotations and *hadith* in justifying the changes they commanded.[37] The concepts of the Circle were also an important element in works of ethics and imaginative literature.[38] Its most important representation, however, was in artwork, as sultans dispensing justice appeared on ceramics, metalwork and tiles, and in Persian miniatures, invented under the Ilkhanids.[39] The Ilkhanids' successor states continued to read the same

---

[34] *Cambridge History of Iran*, 5:582–83; JS Meisami, 'Kings and Lovers: Ethical Dimensions of Medieval Persian Romance' (1987) 1 *Edebiyat* 3; Nizami Ganjavi, *Makhzanol Asrar, The Treasury of Mysteries* (GH Darab, London, Arthur Probsthain, 1945) 217–19, 167–9, 157–60; Yusuf Khass Hajib, *Wisdom of Royal Glory (Kutadgu Bilig): a Turko-Islamic Mirror for Princes* (R Dankoff (trans), Chicago, University of Chicago Press, 1983) 107.

[35] Atabak al-Juvayni, *Kitab-i 'Atabat al-Kataba* (M Qazvini and A Iqbal (eds), Tehran, Shirkat Sami Chap, 1950); Muhammad al-Baghdadi, *al-Tavassul ila al-Tarassul* (A Bahmanjar and M Qazvini (eds), Tehran, Shirkat al-Sahami, 1937); J Paul, '*Insha*' Collections as a Source on Iranian History' in BG Fragner *et al* (eds), *Proceedings of the Second European Conference of Iranian Studies* (Rome, Istituto Italiano per il Medio ed Estremo Oriente, 1995) 539, 544–7.

[36] CE Bosworth, *The Ghaznavids: their Empire in Afghanistan and Eastern Iran, 944–1040* (2nd edn, Beirut, Librairie du Liban, 1973) 256; Nizami, above n 34, at 167–9.

[37] 'Ala al-Din 'Ata-Malik Juvayni, *The History of the World-Conqueror*, 2 vols (JA Boyle (trans), Cambridge, Harvard University Press, 1958); rpt as *Genghis Khan: the History of the World-Conqueror*, introduction and bibliography by DO Morgan (Manchester, Manchester University Press, and Seattle, University of Washington Press, 1997) 557; Rashid al-Din, *Jami'u't-Tawarikh: Compendium of Chronicles* (WM Thackston (trans), Cambridge, Harvard University Department of Near Eastern Languages and Civilizations, 1998–99) 3:692.

[38] Nasir ad-Din Tusi, *The Nasirean Ethics* (GM Wickens (trans), London, George Allen & Unwin Ltd, 1964) 95–7, 100–1; M Minovi and V Minorsky, 'Nasir al-Din Tusi on Finance' (1940–42) 10 *Bulletin of the School of Oriental and African Studies* 769; Ibn al-Tiqtaqa, *Al Fakhri: On the Systems of Government and the Moslem Dynasties* (CEJ Whitting (trans), London, 1947; rpt Karachi, Indus Publications, 1977) 30–1; O Grabar and S Blair, *Epic Images and Contemporary History: the Illustrations of the Great Mongol Shahnama* (Chicago, University of Chicago Press, 1980).

[39] AS Melikian-Chirvani, 'Le *Shah-name*, la gnose soufie et le pouvoir mongol' (1984) 272 *Journal asiatique* 249.

books and look at the same pictures; they copied each other and gave each other books (or stole them), and art historians have traced the movement of these books across the Middle East. This cultural development climaxed in the production of key literary works that transmitted the Circle of Justice to later generations: gorgeously illustrated copies of the *Shahnama*, a book of ethics and politics written by Davvani in Iraq, and the famous *Introduction to History*, or *Muqaddimah*, of Ibn Khaldun, who based his analysis of society on the Circle of Justice, which he quoted in three versions.[40]

The early modern Ottoman (1299–1923), Safavid (1501–1722) and Mughal (1526–1867) dynasties were the inheritors of this process. For these later dynasties, the Circle of Justice was an integral part of the heritage of Islamic rulership which they had from prior regimes; they began their rule with the concept of the Circle rather than having to learn it later from their advisors like the earlier Turks and Mongols. It already appeared in works written or translated in Ottoman Anatolia in the fourteenth century, and in the poet Ahmedi's *Iskendername* (*Book of Alexander*) of 1402 this justice formed one of the criteria for the Ottoman sultans' good rulership, along with *ghaza* ('holy war').[41] The eight-part Circle was presented by Kınalızade in his *'Alian Ethics*, in a section suggesting that the religious, administrative and social perfection of the empire reached in the reign of Süleyman the Magnificent was worthy to be compared with Plato's utopian vision of the Virtuous City.[42] The Ottomans institutionalised the Circle's concept of justice in the functioning of the Islamic law courts, whose judges administered both Islamic law (*shari'a*) and ruler's law (*kanun*). The sultan's imperial court handled land and tax issues and also executed the *mazalim* function, serving as a court of appeal open to all.[43]

[40] Grabar and Blair, above n 38; BW Robinson, 'A Survey of Persian Painting (1350–1896)' in C Adle (ed), *Art et Société dans le Monde Iranien* (Paris, Éditions Recherche sur les Civilisations, 1982) 13–80; E Sims, 'The Illustrated Manuscripts of Firdausi's *Shahnama* Commissioned by Princes of the House of Timur' (1992) 22 *Ars Orientalis* 44; Davvani, *Akhlaq-i Jalali* (Lucknow, Matba'a-i Munshi Naval Kishur, 1866) 331; Ibn Khaldun, *The Muqaddimah: an Introduction to History*, 3 vols (F Rosenthal, New York, Pantheon Books, 1958) 3:81–3:82.
[41] Ebu'l-Hayr Rumi, *Saltuk-name: The Legend of Sarı Saltuk*, 7 vols (F İz (ed) Cambridge, MA, Orient Press, 1974–84); MF Köprülü, *Türk Edebiyatı Tarihi* (Istanbul, Milli Matbaa, 1926; rpt Istanbul, Ötüken, 1984) 340–2; AS Levend, 'Ümmet Çağında Ahlak Kitaplarımız' (1963) *Türk Dili Araştırmaları Yıllığı Belleten* 107; A Ateş, 'Hicri VI–VIII. (XII–XIV.) Asırlarda Anadolu'da Farsça Eserler' (1945) (7–8) *Türkiyat Mecmuası* 105, 111, 120, 123; P Fodor, 'State and Society, Crisis and Reform, in 15th–17th Century Ottoman Mirrors for Princes' (1986) 40 *Acta Orientalia Academiae Scientiarum Hungarica* 220; E Birnbaum, *The Book of Advice by King Kay Ka'us ibn Iskander: the Earliest Old Ottoman Turkish Version of His Kabusname* (Cambridge, Harvard University Printing Office, 1981); Ahmedi, 'Dastan ve Tevarih-i Al-i Osman' in CN Atsız (ed), *Osmanlı Tarihleri* (Istanbul, Türkiye Basımevi, 1949) 3–35; K Silay (trans), 'Ahmedi's History of the Ottoman Dynasty' (1992) 16 *Journal of Turkish Studies* 129.
[42] Kınalızade 'Ali Çelebi, *Ahlak-i 'Ala'i* (Bulaq: n.p., 1228/1832–33) 3:49.
[43] H İnalcık, 'Süleiman the Lawgiver and Ottoman Law' (1969) 1 *Archivum Ottomanicum* 105; rpt in H İnalcık, *The Ottoman Empire: Conquest, Organization and Economy* (London, Variorum Reprints, 1978) vii.

By the end of the sixteenth century, there was a shift in emphasis from the Circle of Justice as a model for government to the Circle of Justice as a critique of government; it formed a central motif in the vast literature of advice generated by the 'time of troubles' at the end of the sixteenth century. For authors like Akhisari, Koçi Bey and Katib Çelebi, the Circle of Justice became an analytical tool to pinpoint locations of weakness in the state and a call to action.[44] However, changes in global technology and in world economic and political systems rendered their advice incapable of fending off defeat, and during the eighteenth and nineteenth centuries most of the Muslim lands became colonies of the West.

THE ERA OF OTTOMAN REFORM AND CONSTITUTIONALISM

During the nineteenth-century era of modernisation, the Circle of Justice took on yet another new role, that of legitimising the changes and reforms introduced into the Ottoman political system. The Gülhane Rescript of 1839, the imperial order initiating the Tanzimat reform period (1839–1876), has been interpreted as both a Westernisation and an Islamisation of Ottoman politics, but it also justified the reforms it introduced with the traditional formula for state centralisation: the connection between justice, popular prosperity and the strength of the state:

> A state certainly needs armies and other necessary services in order to preserve its lands; and this is done with money, and money is obtained from the taxes of the subjects ... [thus] henceforth each of the empire's people should be assessed a tax in proportion to his wealth and possessions, and it should be impossible for anything more to be exacted from him.[45]

Subsequent proclamations by Sultan Abdülmejid conveyed the idea that a new era of justice and equity had commenced with the reform edict:

> The basic purpose of the Tanzimat was the application of the foundations of justice ... and the guaranteeing of the good order of land and people.[46]

---

[44] G de Tassy, 'Principes de Sagesse, touchant l'art de gouverner' (1824) 4 *Journal asiatique* 219; Kochi Bey, *Koçi Bey Risalesi* (AK Aksüt (ed), Istanbul, Vakıt Gazetesi Matbaa Kütüphane, 1939); Katip Çelebi, *Bozuklukların Düzeltilmesinde Tutulacak Yollar = Düsturu'l-Amel li-İslahi'l-Halel* (Ankara, Kültür ve Turizm Bakanlığı, 1982).

[45] Ahmed Lütfi, *Tarih-i Lütfi*, 8 vols in 3 (Istanbul, Mahmud Bey Matbaası, 1302/1885–86) 6:62, M Ma'oz (trans) in *Ottoman Reform in Syrian and Palestine, 1840-1861: the Impact of the Tanzimat on Politics and Society* (Oxford, Clarendon Press, 1968) 69; *cf* SJ Shaw and EK Shaw, *The History of the Ottoman Empire and Modern Turkey*, 2 vols (Cambridge, Cambridge University Press, 1976) 2:60; JC Hurewitz, 'The Hatti Şerif of Gülhane, 3 November 1839' in *Diplomacy in the Near and Middle East: a Documentary Record, 1646–1914*, 2 vols (Princeton, D Van Nostrand, 1956) 1:114.

[46] B Abu-Manneh, 'The Islamic Roots of the Gülhane Rescript' (1994) 34 *Die Welt des Islams* 196.

Generally, however, although the reforms introduced by the rescript could be legitimated by traditional formulas, they did not follow traditional political models. Tax reforms shifted part of the burden to urban wealth and eliminated outmoded exceptions, and the Ottomans tried to abolish tax farming. The state was attempting the modern political task of exerting control directly over its subjects as individuals rather than dealing with groups through intermediaries, and this control was aided by new means of communication, new methods of funding and the reconsolidation of law-making and administration in official hands. Because of the systematisation and control required for reform, a highly centralised modern bureaucracy soon became the most powerful element in the state. A number of state councils were established to make new laws, administer taxation and budgets, control the army and navy and exercise governmental oversight both at the capital and in the provinces. Besides working to restore the empire's former order and strength, these councils gave participation and power to a variety of new social groups, such as bureaucrats, wealthy provincial families and non-Muslims.[47]

These changes altered the social classes and their relationships, bringing into power groups that had never had the responsibility for maintaining social equilibrium and creating new tensions between the ideology of just rule and the organisation of the state. Together with the elimination of old elites and increased regulation and taxation, the state councils came to be seen as overturning the social order, intensifying oppression and violating the state's traditional role as preserver of order and protector of its subjects.[48] That role was reasserted in the second reform rescript of 1856 in the form of promises of judicial reform and commercial and agricultural improvement.[49] Despite the reforming government's claims to end corruption, however, many of its officials were found to be milking the system, and public opinion turned against them. The social upheavals created by

---

[47] SJ Shaw, 'The Nineteenth-Century Ottoman Reforms and Revenue System' (1975) 6 *International Journal of Middle East Studies* 421; Ş Mardin, 'Center-Periphery Relations: a Key to Turkish Politics?' (1973) 102(1) *Daedalus* 180; C Issawi, *The Economic History of Turkey, 1800–1914* (Chicago, University of Chicago Press, 1980) 353; SJ Shaw, 'Some Aspects of the Aims and Achievements of the Nineteenth-Century Ottoman Reformers' in WR Polk and RL Chambers (eds), *Beginnings of Modernization in the Middle East: the Nineteenth Century* (Chicago, University of Chicago Press, 1968) 33.

[48] B Lewis, *The Emergence of Modern Turkey* (Oxford, Oxford University Press, 1961) 110–21; Shaw and Shaw, above n 45, at 2:76–2:82; R Kasaba, 'A Time and a Place for the Nonstate: Social Change in the Ottoman Empire during the "Long Nineteenth Century"' in JS Migdal, A Kohli and V Shue (eds), *State Power and Social Forces: Domination and Transformation in the Third World* (Cambridge, Cambridge University Press, 1994) 215; H İnalcık, 'Application of the Tanzimat and its Social Effects' (1973) 5 *Archivum Ottomanicum* 97, rpt in H İnalcık, *The Ottoman Empire: Conquest, Organization and Economy* (London, Variorum Reprints, 1978) XVI, 8.

[49] N Berkes, *The Development of Secularism in Turkey* (Montreal, McGill University Press, 1964; rpt New York, Routledge, 1998) 152.

conflicts of interest between those who gained from these changes and those who lost, and the distress generated by the fact that tax demands were imposed before state services were delivered or equality enforced, gave the common people new economic difficulties and led after mid-century to a new sense of injustice.[50]

In order for the Circle of Justice to be used to justify the changes of modernisation, the ideological stress had to shift away from the preservation of the social order toward the prosperity that would result from good administration. The Sultan, in the Gülhane rescript, protested that:

> ever since the day of our enthronement, the thought of the public welfare, of the improvement of the provinces and regions, and of relief to the people and the poor has not ceased to engage [our mind].[51]

Sultan Mahmud II in 1833 had already proclaimed himself 'a monarch whose sweetest joy is to know that they [the subjects] are happy' and one who was 'accessible to all'.[52] Now Abdülmejid proclaimed that the Gülhane rescript would be the beginning of:

> further beneficial and advantageous measures to make certain the execution of orders insuring the wellbeing of the people, rich and poor, whose happy state is a necessary precondition for the reinvigoration of religion and state and the prosperity of country and nation.[53]

In the second reform edict, the Imperial Rescript of 1856, the Sultan declared:

> It has always been my most earnest desire to insure the happiness of all classes of the subjects ... Thanks to the Almighty, [my] unceasing efforts have already been productive of numerous useful results. From day to day the happiness of the nation and the wealth of my dominions go on augmenting.[54]

These assurances generated such hope for improvement that in the 1850s and 1860s, when people did not see the results promised or did not see them quickly enough, they began to rebel on new grounds. A revolt in Vidin (modern Bulgaria) in 1850 was set off by those whose privileged status was threatened by the reforms, while one in Kisrawan (modern

[50] A Cevdet Paşa, *Tezakir-i Cevdet*, 4 vols (Ankara, Türk Tarih Kurumu Basımevi, 1953) 1:18–1:22, cited in Issawi, above n. 47, at 350; A Salzmann, 'Citizens in Search of a State: the Limits of Political Participation in the Late Ottoman Empire' in M Hanagan and C Tilly (eds), *Extending Citizenship, Reconfiguring States* (Lanham, Rowman and Littlefield, 1999) 56–7.

[51] Lütfi, above n 45, at 6:61; cf Hurewitz, above n 45, at 114.

[52] Quoted in H Temperley, *England and the Near East: the Crimea* (London, Longmans, Green, 1936; rpt Archon Books, 1964) 40.

[53] R Kaynar, *Mustafa Reşit Paşa ve Tanzimat* (Ankara, Türk Tarih Kurumu Basımevi, 1954) 183; quoted in Inalcık, 'Application of the Tanzimat', above n 48, at 4.

[54] Hurewitz, above n 45, at 150.

Lebanon) in 1858 was fuelled by peasants who demanded more and faster change.[55]

The overturning of the social pyramid and the injustices resulting from heedless application of central government dictates caused a new generation of modernisers to retreat from the thorough Westernisation and bureaucratic centralisation of the Tanzimat reformers. These new thinkers, the Young Ottomans, had no desire to undo the economic and technological advances of the previous decades, but they wanted to temper what they saw as the excessive autocracy of the bureaucracy through individual political participation and a more central role for Islam, and to bring reform to people outside the reach of Western thought patterns.[56] Shibli Shmayyil, a late nineteenth-century Syrian in Egypt, actually devised a version of the Circle of Justice appropriate for a modern economy:

> There can be no justice without freedom; no learning without justice; when knowledge is absent, there is no strength because strength is contingent on wealth, and the instruments of wealth (agriculture, commerce and industry) are dependent for success on education.[57]

The Circle of Justice provided a perfect critique of the dark side of modernisation—its rigid centralisation, onerous fiscal exactions, elimination of traditional tax exemptions, suppression of provincial autonomy and non-traditional promotion patterns. For the Young Ottomans, the answer to these disruptions lay in the rule of law, Islamic and constitutional, for which the Circle acted as a kind of shorthand.

Ali Suavi, for example, considered the *mazalim* court as a precursor of representative government, since it fulfilled the sultan's duty to protect his subjects from the tyranny of the bureaucracy and it made him aware of the need for popular representation.[58] Namık Kemal referred to the philosophical sources of the Circle of Justice, the works of Tusi, Kashifi, Davvani, and Kınalızade, from which he learned the term 'Circle

---

[55] H İnalcık, 'The Nature of Traditional Society: Turkey' in RE Ward and DA Rostow (eds), *Political Modernization in Japan and Turkey* (Princeton, Princeton University Press, 1964) 42–63; rpt in H İnalcık, *The Ottoman Empire: Conquest, Organization and Economy* (London, Variorum Reprints, 1978) xv, 60; *idem*, 'Application of the Tanzimat', above n 48, at 30–1; E Burke III, 'Rural Collective Action and the Emergence of Modern Lebanon: a Comparative Historical Perspective' in N Shehadi and DH Mills (eds), *Lebanon: a History of Conflict and Consensus* (London, Centre for Lebanese Studies and IB Tauris, 1988) 23.

[56] Ş Mardin, 'The Just and the Unjust' (Summer 1991) 120(3) *Daedalus* 121.

[57] S Shmayyil, *Shakwa wa-Amal Marfu'a ila Jalalat al-Sultan al-Mu'azzam 'Abd al-Hamid Khan* (Cairo, 20 March 1896) 4, quoted in CE Farah, 'Reformed Ottomanism and Social Change' in A Temimi (ed), *La vie sociale dans les province arabes à l'époque ottomane*, 3 vols in 2 (Zaghouan, CEROMDI, 1988) 3:141.

[58] Ş Mardin, *The Genesis of Young Ottoman Thought: a Study in the Modernization of Turkish Political Ideas* (Princeton, Princeton University Press, 1962; rpt Syracuse, Syracuse University Press, 2000) 376.

of Justice'; he then used this term in an 1868 newspaper article to refer to constitutionalism:

> For the government to stay within that Circle of Justice, there are two basic measures, of which the first is to announce to the world that it has the purpose of freeing the basic organisations of the administration ... The second is the plan for a council which ... is to take from the hands of the men of the government the power of laying down the law.[59]

Other nineteenth-century thinkers also found the Circle's concept of justice relevant to the new politics of the period. Şinasi, one of the leaders of the Young Ottoman movement, wrote in an ode to Mustafa Reşid Paşa:

> Your justice is a lantern to guard us from the blast of oppression ...
> Your law is an act of manumission for men.[60]

The law he revered was constitutional law, which 'informs the Sultan of his limits' and guards 'Life, property, and honour'. The exiled Egyptian prince Mustafa Fazil, like Namık Kemal, saw justice as protection of the citizens' fundamental rights by a representative body.[61] Searching for historical antecedents for representation in government, some Young Ottomans pointed to the Janissaries; ever since the Janissary rebellion of 1730, the Janissaries had been seen as 'expressing popular grievances', particularly unhappiness with Westernising reforms made at the expense of the common people. They were felt to be one of the few groups that would support popular resistance and act as a check on the sultan. The *'ulama'* were another such check, and the provincial notables as well were sometimes considered a barrier to sultanic tyranny.[62]

Thinkers in other parts of the Ottoman realm also used the Circle of Justice in analysing modern politics. The Egyptian social commentator Rifa'a al-Tahtawi, in his report on his trip to Paris, began a description of French government by quoting the Circle, observing that even without revelation from God:

> [French] intellect has decided that justice and equity are the causes for the civilisation of kingdoms, [and] the wellbeing of subjects ... There is no strength without

---

[59] N Kemal, 'Wa-shawirhum fi 'l-'amr', *Hürriyet*, 20 July 1868, 1; Mardin, above n 58, at 82, 99, 306.

[60] Quoted in Lewis, above n 48, at 134.

[61] Ş Mardin, 'The Mind of the Turkish Reformer, 1700–1900' (1960) 14 *Western Humanities Review* 429.

[62] Mardin, above n 58, at 133, 165; Lewis, above n 48, at 167; B Lewis, 'Some English Travellers in the East' (1968) 4 *Middle Eastern Studies* 303, 306; V Fontanier, *Voyage en Orient* (Paris, 1829) 1:322, quoted in Mardin, *Genesis*, 165 n 108; N Kemal, 'Usul-ü Meşveret Hakkında Mektuplar', *Hürriyet*, 14 September 1868, 6; Ş Mardin, 'Freedom in an Ottoman Perspective' in M Heper and A Evin (eds), *State, Democracy and the Military: Turkey in the 1980s* (Berlin, Walter de Gruyter, 1988) 25.

the support of men, whereas there are no men without money, no money without civilisation, and no civilisation without justice.[63]

He evaluated the clauses of the French constitutional charter of 1814 against the Circle's concept of justice, noting that the French observed justice through equality before the law:

> What they hold dear and call liberty is what we call equity and justice, for to rule according to liberty means to establish equality through judgments and laws, so that the ruler cannot wrong anybody.[64]

Khayr al-Din al-Tunisi, in his book of political advice, *Aqwam al-Masalik fi Ma'rifat Ahwal al-Mamalik* (*The Surest Path to Acquaintance with the Conditions of the Nations*), likewise discussed European government in terms of the Circle of Justice:

> The basic requirement is good government from which is born that security, hope and proficiency in work to be seen in the European kingdoms ... Europe has attained these ends and progress in the sciences and industries through *tanzimat* based on political justice ... It is God's custom in His world that justice, good management and an administrative system duly complied with be the causes of an increase in wealth, peoples and property ... And one of the wise maxims of Aristotle pictures
>
> the world as a garden whose fence is the state.
> The state is the legitimate authority through which the *umma* is given life.
> The *sunna* is the policy followed by the king.
> The king is the organiser who is supported by the army.
> The army is the bodyguard paid by the treasury.
> The treasury is the wealth accumulated by the subjects.
> The subjects are slaves protected by justice.
> Justice is custom, which serves as the foundation of the world.[65]

Struggling to institute Westernising reforms in Tunisia, he too saw the Circle of Justice as legitimising the changes he wanted to make. If he increased the

[63] Rifa'a Rafi' al-Tahtawi, *An Imam in Paris: Account of a Stay in France by an Egyptian Cleric (1826–1831)* (DL Newman (intro and trans), London, Saqi Books, 2004) 194–213; quotation on 194.

[64] *Ibid* 206; see also Rifa'a Rafi' al-Tahtawi, *Takhlis al-Ibriz ila Talkhis Bariz* (Beirut, 1973) 2:96–2.97, 102–4, 205–8, quoted in R Khuri, *Modern Arab Thought: Channels of the French Revolution to the Arab East* (I Abbas (trans), C Issawi (rev and ed), Princeton, Kingston Press, 1983) 103. Al-Tahtawi wrote a later work of political advice in which he restated his earlier point linking the Circle's concept of justice to Western notions of equality and freedom: *Manahij al-Albab al-Misriyya fi Mabahij al-Adab al-'Asriyya* (*The Paths of Egyptian Minds through the Joys of Modern Manners*), quoted in G Delanoue, *Moralistes et politiques musulmans dans l'Égypte du XIXe siècle, 1798–1882*, 2 vols (Cairo, Institut Français d'Archéologie Orientale, 1982) 2:433.

[65] Khayr al-Din al-Tunisi, *The Surest Path: The Political Treatise of a Nineteenth-Century Muslim Statesman* (LC Brown (trans), Cambridge, Center for Middle Eastern Studies of Harvard University, 1967) 74, 81, 97.

Tunisian government's efficiency, it would be better able to provide for the needs of the people and resist Western encroachment; he therefore reorganised taxes and encouraged economic growth, and he even installed a complaint box to ensure that people's protests were heard.[66] The box has been called 'a fitting symbol for a Weberian model of rational bureaucracy', but it could be seen as a modern version of *mazalim.*

The Tanzimat reformers had generally opposed constitutional and parliamentary rule because it would have brought into the central government the same provincial and non-Muslim elements that the state was trying to subordinate and control.[67] The Young Ottomans, in contrast, rejected the bureaucratic absolutism of the Tanzimat and pushed for constitutional rule. Whether liberal Westernisers, Islamists or Turkish nationalists, they all wanted the security of a constitutional regime, but they had wildly differing ideas as to what such a regime should consist of. The liberals drew up a draft for a constitution in Western style, but the conflictual process of producing an official version resulted in one that was not satisfactory to any of the participants.[68] As promulgated in 1876, the constitution dropped all reference to the Circle of Justice and all Islamic language; rhetorically it resembled the constitutions of the West.[69] Its actual provisions, however, created not a constitutional monarchy balanced by a parliament, nor even a sultanate in interdependence with elite and popular forces, but a monarchy with complete sovereignty through the caliphate and absolute control over the ministers, legislation and the parliament, which became in essence a consultative body. It also established Islam as the state religion and source of sovereignty, acknowledged both state law and Islamic law, and made both sets of laws into limits on popular rights and freedoms. Although the autocratic Sultan Abdülhamid II prorogued parliament in 1877 and refused to reopen it, he still could validly claim to be governing in accordance with the constitution in all other respects.[70]

The status of the constitution as a suspended and largely unread document, however, allowed people to believe that it enshrined the liberal ideas of its original drafters and that its restoration would remedy what became known as 'Hamidian despotism'. Demands for its reinstatement spurred the progressive Young Turk Revolution of 1908, but the restoration of the 1876 Constitution could not prevent conservatives from coming to power soon afterward. Only in 1921, after the war of independence, was a new constitution adopted that made the sovereignty of the people the basis of the state.[71]

---

[66] LC Brown, 'The Tunisian Path to Modernization' in M Milson (ed), *Society and Political Structure in the Arab World* (New York, Humanities Press, 1973) 205.

[67] Mardin, above n 58, at 19–20.

[68] Berkes, above n 49, at 213, 225–41.

[69] Ottoman Constitution, available at www.bilkent.edu.tr/~genckaya/documents1.html (22 February 2005).

[70] Berkes, above n 49, at 242–8, 250.

[71] *Ibid* 367–9, 446, 450.

THE IMPACT OF SOCIO-POLITICAL AND IDEOLOGICAL MODERNISATION

The movement of the 1876 Constitution away from the Circle of Justice reflected not only changes in political thought and power relations, but also social changes within Ottoman society, particularly among the elites. The economic reforms of the nineteenth century altered the whole social structure of the Middle East. The control of land was no longer an administrative responsibility in which men, often military men, were appointed by the ruler to collect the taxes of an area and see to its security on behalf of the state. Land became a commodity whose value lay in its ability to produce for the market. The transformation of land use and land-holding rights created a new upper class, large landowners (and later businessmen) producing for the world market, whose positions depended not on state appointment but on wealth. Members of this class had no need to adhere to the Circle of Justice, which was essentially an idea about how the state could maintain its power and prosperity, since their role was not governmental. Their function was not to protect the peasants but to profit from them.[72] This change in the social structure created new tensions between the ideology of the Circle and the institutions of society. The change actually occurred earlier and more gradually than it appeared in legal terms. Production for the market had already become widespread in the century before the new land codes of 1858, and in periods of governmental weakness or preoccupation, tax farmers and other landholders had gotten away with behaving like property owners who could do whatever they wanted with their land and labour force. The 1858 land laws legitimised and generalised what was in many cases already happening.

One way to deal with the new disjuncture between social institutions and political language was to alter the language. In parallel with the social changes of the late nineteenth century, direct quotations of or references to the Circle of Justice in Middle Eastern political discourse decreased and were replaced by political language borrowed from the West. The Circle of Justice had required rulers to give justice, and also to provide those infrastructural supports that would enable the peasants, artisans and merchants to produce a surplus for the treasury. Now the Western rhetoric of bureaucratic efficiency and order began to be used to describe the first part of this responsibility, while the language of progress and civilisation, which stressed the importance of science, development and the increase of wealth, expressed the second part in modern terms.[73]

---

[72] D Warriner, *Land Reform and Development in the Middle East: a Study of Egypt, Syria, and Iraq* (2nd edn, London, Oxford University Press, 1962) 62; RA Hinnebusch, *Authoritarian Power and State Formation in Ba'thist Syria: Army, Party, and Peasant* (Boulder, Westview Press, 1990) 24. For a similar interpretation reached through study of the new law codes introduced in Egypt about this time, see G Bechtor, '"To Hold the Hand of the Weak": the Emergence of Contractual Justice in the Egyptian Civil Law' (2001) 8 *Islamic Law and Society* 188.

[73] For examples, see 'Khedive Isma'il's Speech to the Egyptian Assembly of Delegates, January 1869' in RG Landen (ed), *The Emergence of the Modern Middle East: Selected Readings* (New York, Van Nostrand Reinhold Company, 1970) 68; and an *'alim*'s sermon

The disappearance of the traditional language of the Circle of Justice, however, did not mean that the idea itself disappeared, particularly on the popular level. Another response that intensified during this period was popular resistance and rebellion against the social and economic changes that were taking place. This resistance, though rarely verbalised, often reflected the Circle of Justice as an expression of the moral economy of the Middle Eastern peasant. Peasants and townsmen continued to petition their rulers to provide the means of life and to cease oppression. Popular unrest also began to increase all over the empire after about 1880, embodying people's demands for justice and relief from oppression. For example, in Syria and Lebanon, when peasants were unable to secure reductions in tax and conscription levels or increases in governmental services, they abandoned cultivation and migrated en masse to Europe, Africa and the Americas; leaving the land had long been the signal of a ruler's inability to protect his people. Similarly, resistance to increased Ottoman taxation in Libya was manifested by the wholesale destruction of olive groves. In Algeria, the French occupation, monetary exactions and rearrangement of tribal lands impelled tribesmen to resist by refusing to give up traditional farming methods and by supporting brigands as social bandits. In Egypt, urban resistance likewise began to increase around 1880; urban riots lasted longer and became more severe, because the means for meeting popular demands were not forthcoming.[74] Under British colonial rule, Egyptian peasants petitioned the British King, complaining of oppression and appealing to the king's 'glorious sense of justice'.[75]

In the twentieth century, colonialism and direct rule by Europeans overturned old forms of government and substituted structures based directly on Western models, structures that were largely continued by indigenous rulers in the postcolonial period. Political discourse then employed the Western languages of constitutionalism, parliamentarianism, democracy, socialism, rights and the rule of law. The new kinds of rulers—kings, presidents and dictators—wielded these political terms to impress their own people as well as powerful Western states, and it is usually only by reading between the lines that we can tell how much they continued to draw on traditional relationships such as those embodied in the Circle of Justice to legitimate their policies. Neither the ideologies nor, apparently, the actions of the liberal states of the early twentieth century embodied or

---

quoted in JL Gelvin, *Divided Loyalties: Nationalism and Mass Politics in Syria at the Close of Empire* (Berkeley, University of California Press, 1998) 190.

[74] LS Schilcher, 'Violence in Rural Syria in the 1880s and 1890s: State Centralization, Rural Integration, and the World Market' in F Kazemi and J Waterbury (eds), *Peasants and Politics in the Modern Middle East* (Miami, Florida International University Press, 1991) 51–74; L Anderson, 'Nineteenth-Century Reform in Ottoman Libya' (1984) 16 *International Journal of Middle East Studies* 333; A Sainte-Marie, 'La commune d'Azeffoun à la fin du XIXème siècle' (1974) 9 *Revue algérienne des sciences juridiques, économiques, et politiques* 446, 450; JRI Cole, *Colonialism and Revolution in the Middle East: Social and Cultural Origins of Egypt's `Urabi Movement* (Princeton, Princeton University Press, 1993) 209, 233.

[75] PRO: FO 141/380, 22 September 1904; my thanks to Ziad Fahmy for alerting me to this document.

expressed the concepts of the Circle of Justice and, perhaps not coincidentally, they had little popular legitimacy. In mid-twentieth century political rhetoric, however, the ideas of the Circle acquired a nationalist framework, creating what Annika Rabo has called 'the myth of the just welfare state, ... known and accepted literally as a political goal in much of the Middle East'.[76] The aspect of the Circle of Justice recommending that the ruler provide the organisation and infrastructure that would permit ordinary people to produce a surplus and pay taxes to support the state and the military was subsumed under the concepts of development and/or socialism. The speeches of leaders such as Nasser, Qaddafi and Muhammad Reza Shah were filled with expressions that resonated with the Circle's concepts of the interdependence of social classes and the responsibility of the state to provide justice, good government and a workable infrastructure, and their policies to some extent reflected those commitments.[77] The transition from a sultanate with a responsibility to provide justice and good administration, in order to create a prosperous and militarily strong state, to something like 'Islamic socialism' or state capitalism under an authoritarian populist president, was not a very large step.

In the late twentieth century, however, as the promises of these Western panaceas failed to materialise and externally-imposed economic restructuring forced governments to cut social programmes and infrastructural support, the political discourse of the state ceased to refer to the Circle of Justice. At that point, the concepts of the Circle became tools for popular and Islamist critiques of government, as they had under the Ottomans.[78] Clearly these concepts still express a widespread popular sense of the state's role and responsibilities, one that is deeply embedded in the culture of the Middle East. As long as that is the case, modern constitutions or polities not incorporating ideas and policies congruent with the Circle of Justice will probably have little stability or popular acceptance.

[76] A Rabo, *Change on the Euphrates: Villagers, Townsmen and Employees in Northeast Syria* (Stockholm, Akademitryck, Minab/Gotab, 1986) 124. It became a legal goal as well around mid-century; Bechtor, above n 72, 190–1.
[77] For example, see G Abdel-Nasser, 'Speech delivered at Damascus on February 21, 1961' in *Speeches and Press-Interviews* (Cairo, United Arab Republic Information Department, 1961) 21; G Abdel-Nasser, 'Speech delivered at Damascus on February 24, 1961' in *ibid* 53; J Bearman, *Qaddafi's Libya* (London, Zed Books, 1986) 128; Mohammed Reza Pahlavi, *Mission for my Country* (London, Hutchinson & Co, 1961) 31.
[78] For example, see AE Sonbol, 'Egypt' in ST Hunter (ed), *The Politics of Islamic Revivalism: Diversity and Unity* (Bloomington, Indiana University Press, 1988) 23–38; SA Morsy, 'Islamic Clinics in Egypt: the Cultural Elaboration of Biomedical Hegemony' (1988) 2 *Medical Anthropology Quarterly* 355; UF Abd-Allah, *The Islamic Struggle in Syria* (Berkeley, Mizan Press, 1983) 206; D Seddon, 'Riot and Rebellion in North Africa: Political Responses to Economic Crisis in Tunisia, Morocco and Sudan' in B Berberoğlu (ed), *Power and Stability in the Middle East* (London, Zed Books Ltd, 1989) 114–35; M Tessler, 'The Origins of Popular Support for Islamist Movements: a Political Economy Analysis' in JP Entelis (ed), *Islam, Democracy, and the State in North Africa* (Bloomington, Indiana University Press, 1997) 93–126; Geneive Abdo and Jonathan Lyons, *Answering Only to God: Faith and Freedom in Twenty-First-Century Iran* (New York, Henry Holt and Company, 2003) 230.

2

Islam and Constitutionalism since the Nineteenth Century: the Significance and Peculiarities of Iran

SAÏD AMIR ARJOMAND

A WATERSHED SEPARATES the two fundamentally different places of Islam in the constitutional order in classic, liberal and post-Second World War ideological constitution-making.[1] Before the watershed, the *shari'a* (Islamic law) appeared as a *limitation* to government and legislation. There was never a presumption that it should be the basis of the constitution itself. In this period Islam is considered a part of the larger issue of constitutional governance and not as the basis of the constitution. In the wave of ideological constitution-making after it, Islam increasingly appears as the *basis* of the constitution and the state rather than a *limitation* to them. The constitutional experience of Iran is the critical case for documenting and understanding this fundamental shift.

EARLY CONSTITUTIONALISM AS LIMITATION OF GOVERNMENT BY THE LAW

Contrary to widespread belief that Islam is a theocracy, the idea and normative principles of monarchy as elaborated in the literature on ethics and statecraft were fully integrated into Islam by the time of the development of the ethico-legal order based on the *shari'a* in the tenth century CE. From the twelfth century onward, the idea was firmly established that God had chosen two classes of mankind above the rest, the prophets to guide mankind to salvation, and the kings to preserve order as the prerequisite for the pursuit of salvation. I have called this a theory of the two powers, with

---

[1] For the justification of this distinction, see SA Arjomand, 'Constitutions and the Struggle for Political Order: a Study in the Modernization of Political Traditions' (1992) 33(4) *European Journal of Sociology* 38.

deliberately provocative intent.[2] The Safavid monarchs, who established Shi'ism in Iran at the beginning of the sixteenth century, claimed to be the descendants and lieutenants of the 12 Holy Imams, and this deviated somewhat from the dualist tradition. Their deviation was, however, corrected, and the theory of the two powers was reconciled with Shi'ism, the Shah being the Shadow of God on earth and the Shi'ite jurists (*mojtahed*s), the highest ranking of whom were considered the 'sources of imitation' (*maraje'-e taqlid*) for the laity, assuming the mantle of the prophets and the Holy Imams.[3] The theory, however, was more typically stated *without* any specific reference to Shi'ism.[4] The dual traditional constitutional order rested on justice of the ruler,[5] unwritten norms of statecraft (*siyāsa[t]*), and state or public law (*qānun*), all three serving as instruments of the maintenance of order under monarchy, and on the effectiveness of the increasingly formalised sacred law (*shari'a[t]*) thereby assured.

With the advent of constitutionalism from the West during the second half of the nineteenth century, the two traditional powers were challenged in the name of modernity, first by reforming bureaucrats. Let me make an analytical distinction between the impact of constitutionalism on Islam, and the impact of Islam on the transplanted constitutionalism in the late nineteenth and early twentieth century. The impact of constitutionalism on Islam manifested itself in the writings of a group of Islamic modernists among the reformist bureaucrats, notably Khayr al-Din Pasha in Tunisia and Namik Kemal in Turkey, who, writing in the 1860s and early 1870s, challenged the theory of the two powers in the name of Islam as well as modernity, arguing that representative, constitutional government captured the spirit of Islam. This argument was forcefully made by the Iranian diplomat, Yusof Khan Mostashar al-Dawla, in a short tract published in 1871, *Yak kalama (One Word)*. But whereas Khayr al-Din and Kemal had the satisfaction of participating in the drafting of the Tunisian and Ottoman constitutions respectively, the Shah not only denied Yusof Khan the same satisfaction but also suppressed his tract.

The nineteenth-century constitutionalism was not sustained by any popular movement, except in Egypt when a national uprising was suppressed by the

---

[2] SA Arjomand, 'Medieval Persianate Political Ethic' (2003) 1 *Studies on Persianate Societies* 7.

[3] The title '*Āyatollāh*' (sign of God) for the sources of imitation is not attested in the constitutional period (1906–11) and emerges in the following decades as they withdrew from Iranian politics. More recently, especially after the Islamic revolution of 1979, it has been extended to all clerics who have the rank of *mojtahed*.

[4] SA Arjomand, *The Shadow of God and the Hidden Imam: Religion, Political Organization and Societal Change in Shi'ite Iran from the Beginning to 1890* (Chicago, University of Chicago Press, 1984) 223–8, and 'Political Ethic and Public Law in the Early Qajar Period' in Robert M Gleave (ed), *Religion and Society in Qajar Iran* (London, Curzon, 2005) 24.

[5] For justice as the cornerstone of the medieval Persianate theories of kingship, see AKS Lambton, *Theory and Practice in Medieval Persian Government* (London, Variorum Reprints, 1980).

British occupation in 1882. The life of the Tunisian Constitution of 1861, the Ottoman Constitution of 1876 and the Egyptian Constitution of 1882 had therefore been very short. Iran's constitutional revolution of 1906 ushered in the second wave of constitutionalism in the Middle East, being soon followed by 'the second constitutional period' (*ikinci meşrutiyet*) (the Young Turks revolution of 1908) in the Ottoman empire. This second wave was socially much deeper, and it involved new actors, and because of them, brought up new controversies. These controversies manifest the gradual impact of Islam on transplanted constitutionalism. Its first bearers or carriers, to use an English term for Max Weber's '*träger*', were the Shi'ite *ulema* of Iran during the 1906–1911 Constitutional Revolution. The *ulema*, the official interpreters of the *shari'a*, had been invited to participate in the drafting of the Tunisian Constitution of 1861, but declined, arguing that it was a political matter and therefore did not concern them.[6] A distinctive feature of the Constitutional Revolution in Iran, by contrast, is the prominence of the leading Shi'ite *mojtahed*s in the popular protest movement that forced the Shah to grant Iran a constitution in 1905–06, and in the ensuing Constitutional Revolution, 1906–11.

Despite this prominence, however, references to Islam and the *shari'a* were incidental. The key ideas of the Iranian constitutionalist movement were rather the new notions of the rule of law and constitutional or 'conditional' (*mashruta*) government, thoroughly blended with the old notions of justice ('*adl, 'adālat*) and the removal of oppression (*zolm*), a traditional term that acquired the connotation of tyranny and was coupled with despotism (*estebdād*) as the typological opposite of constitutional government.[7] The leading *ulema* not only tended to draw their notion of justice from the traditional theory of kingship rather than the Islamic law, but also famously (mis)conceived the parliament as a House of Justice ('*adālat-khāna*).[8] As the revolution proceeded, however, the continued involvement of the Shi'ite

---

[6] Kh Chater, 'Le Constitutionalisme en Tunisie au 19e siècle' (1975) 40–43 *Revue tunisienne de sciences sociales* 253. The role of the Ottoman *ulema* in 1876 is more complicated. Young clerics (*softa*s) did demonstrate in favour of Midhat Pasha's draft constitution with shouts of 'Long Live Constitutional Government (*meşrutiyet*)', but shortly thereafter expressed their reservation about its secularising aspects in a letter to him. The high-ranking *ulema* had comprised 10 of the 28 members of the commission that drafted the Ottoman constitution, but their function was to rein in Midhat, Kemal and other liberal drafters. See R Devereux, *The First Ottoman Constitutional Period* (Baltimore, Johns Hopkins Press, 1963) 36–40, 47. They played no role in the Young Turks movement that forced the Sultan to restore it in July 1908, but led the movement against it a year later.

[7] For a contrasting, tripartite typology applied to the Ottoman empire, see N Berkes, *The Development of Secularism in Turkey* (Montreal, McGill University Press, 1964) 94–5, 147, 156–60.

[8] The flood of telegraphed petitions was only stemmed after repeated explanation by the *fokoli* deputies of the first Majles (the constitutionalists in Western attire with the *faux col*) that the parliament was not a judicial organ and the petitions had to wait until the judiciary was reorganised. See N Shohrabi, 'Revolution and State Culture: the Circle of Justice and Constitutionalism in 1906 Iran' in G Steinmetz (ed), *State/Culture State-Formation after the Cultural Turn* (Ithaca, Cornell University Press, 1999).

religious leaders assured the first broad public Middle Eastern discussion in the political arena of the relation between the *shari'a* and constitutional government. Over a period of some five years, this debate demonstrated that, with the traditional theory of the two powers as the starting point, once autocracy is replaced by constitutional government, the *shari'a* is bound to appear as a *limitation* to constitutional government and *not* the basis of it.[9] Let me supply some historical details to support this assertion.

The vocabulary of Ottoman constitutionalism was quickly received in Iran during the process of constitution-making. There could be little doubt where and how the notion of constitution was to be accommodated in the Iranian political-legal universe. More precisely, there was no confusion as to the kind of law for which it was to be a modern replacement. The Tunisian Constitution of 1861 was called the 'Law of the State' (*qānun al-dawla*), and the Ottoman Constitution of 1876, the Fundamental Law (*kānun-i esāsi*). The conception of political community by the early constitutionalists is also noteworthy. The Tunisian Constitution uses the traditional term, *ra'iyya* (subjects) of the ruler,[10] but the Ottoman Constitution, putting the modern abstract notion of the state in place of the ruler, also modernises the term for subjects of the Ottoman empire: *taba'a* (subjects of the state). It should be noted that the Iranian parliament (the Majles) was elected on the basis of a royal decree in October 1906, almost three months before the signing of the first constitutional law, and in the meantime, the constitution in preparation was usually referred to as the fundamental charter (*nezām-nāma*). The Ottoman term was received after a short but interesting terminological struggle. The refractory Mohammad 'Ali Shah ascended the throne in January 1907, a few days after his father had signed the charter on his death-bed on 30 December 1906. He reportedly resisted the Ottoman term 'Fundamental Law' and the accompanying notion of *mashruta* (conditional or limited) government, and was more inclined to use the French term *constitution* but was dissuaded from doing so when the French term was said to have secularist implications. The term *mashruta* was used for the constitutional government by the newly arriving deputies of Azerbaijan (bordering on the Ottoman empire) who demanded its confirmation in early February 1907. In a remarkable anticipation of the position the anti-constitutionalist *ulema* were to develop in the following two years, the

---

[9] See Arjomand, below n 17. Bin Diyāf, a Tunisian bureaucrat steeped in the traditional dualistic political theory, had a remarkable intuition of this logical place of the *shari'a* in the constitutional order. He makes the intuition that the *shari'a* is a limitation upon autocratic monarchy into the pivot of his constitutionalist reading of Islamic history, claiming that constitutional government or 'monarchy limited by law (*qānun*)' was indeed the normative form of government in Islam after the pristine Caliphate, and it was restored by the Ottomans in the sixteenth century. See Ahmad ibn Abi Diyāf, *Consult Them in the Matter: A Nineteenth-Century Islamic Argument for Constitutional Government* (LC Brown [trans], Fayetteville, University of Arkansas Press, 2005) esp 75.

[10] NJ Brown, *Constitutions in a Nonconstitutional World: Arab Basic Laws and the Prospects for Accountable Government* (Albany, SUNY Press, 2002) 17.

new king resisted that term also, and proposed '*shari'a*-based' (*mashru'a*), instead of *mashruta*. The Majles representatives almost acquiesced, but the Azerbaijani deputies persisted and eventually won. On 11 February 1907, the new monarch issued a decree confirming that Iran was now included among 'the constitutional states (*doval-e mashruta*) possessing a *constitution*'. The French term was not naturalised, however, but was immediately replaced by *qānun-e asāsi* (Fundamental Law).[11]

The modernised Ottoman term *taba'a* enters the Iranian constitutional law of 1907 in reference to the subjects of Iran and foreign states (Articles 24 and 58). The neologisms for 'citizen' are nowhere to be found in early constitutional documents. The Iranians, however, had a readily available term for nation: *mellat*, which was free of the connotation of ethnic minorities associated with its Ottoman equivalent, *millet*. For the Iranian constitution-makers in 1906 and 1907, the transfer of legislative power—the right to make public laws (*qavānin*)—from the monarch to the people or the nation was conceptually non-problematic, and it did *not* involve Islam because the latter was not an abstract ideology but an institutionally embedded order.

The Fundamental Law of December 1906 had confined itself to the institution of parliament and avoided the statement of any constitutional principles. When the constitution-makers turned to the statement of these principles in the Supplement to the Fundamental Law (SFL) in 1907, the main political and conceptual struggle was over monarchy and sovereignty. The SFL[12] does not go so far as to state explicitly the principle of 'national sovereignty', which was to be translated explicitly as the *hākemiyyat-e mellat* in the 1979 Constitution only to be belied by the superior principle of leadership (*rahbari*) in the form of the mandate of the religious jurist (*velāyat-e faqih*). The SFL does declare, however obliquely, that the three powers of government 'derive from the nation (*mellat*)' (Article 26), and that 'monarchy is a trust given by the nation (through divine grace) to the person of the king (*pādshāh*)' (Article 35). This phrase in parenthesis was awkwardly added by the new Shah in his own handwriting before signing the document.[13] Thus was constitutional monarchy defined in relation to the nation. Islam did not enter this conceptual struggle, and there was no hint that it might conflict with monarchy. On the contrary, Article 1 requires the king not only to profess Shi'ite Islam as the official religion of Iran but also to act as its 'promoter' (*moravvej*).[14]

---

[11] See SA Arjomand, 'Constitutional Revolution. (iii) The Constitution' in *Encyclopaedia Iranica* (London, Routledge and Kegan Paul, 1992) 6: 187–92.

[12] The bulk of the Supplementary Fundamental Law of October 1907 consists of *verbatim* or slightly modified translation of the articles of the Belgian Constitution of 1831, see Arjomand above n 11.

[13] It appears parenthetically in the official edition of the constitution in 1907/1325. The brackets are removed in later editions.

[14] A vestige of the establishment and propagation of Shi'ism in Iran by the Safavid kings (1501–1722).

Islam *did* enter the public debate surrounding the SFL—and quite dramatically. The clash of the *shari'a* and constitutionalism in this phase, however, had little to do with the allegedly monolithic and political essence of Islam. The constitution-makers of 1907 and their constituencies in fact recognised the fundamental and institutionally embedded dualism of temporal and religious laws in the Muslim world, including in Iran. Article 27, section 2 of the SFL recognised this dualism and made provisions for secular and religious courts, as did Articles 71 to 89 on judicial organisation. The problem was *not* of a fundamental conceptual order, but one of delimitation. One cannot have legal dualism without the possibility of conflict between the laws and their heterogeneous principles. The issue of conflict and overlapping jurisdiction between the *qānun* and *shari'a* was a feature of the old system of the two powers, and now had to be faced anew as constitutionalism had an impact on both components of the traditional system.[15]

The clerical ideologues of the Islamic revolution of 1979 have since found an important source of inspiration in Shaykh Fazl Allāh Nuri (d 1909), the high-ranking *mojtahed* who fell out with the constitutionalists after a year and led the Islamic traditionalist opposition to the Majles (Iranian parliament). They have also since dug up the writings of some of Nuri's followers as forerunners of a *shari'a* -based constitution. Historically, Nuri's opposition to the draft supplement to the Fundamental Law forced all parties in the constitutional debate to scrutinise the principles of order that underlay the Western constitutional models, while he himself launched an Islamic traditionalist movement that eventually rejected parliamentary government altogether. In the year before his death, Nuri advocated a traditional autocracy on the basis of the theory of the two powers. Nevertheless, his intermediate, 1907 idea of '*shari'a*-based or *shari'* constitutionalism' (*mashruta-ye mashru'a*) gained considerable currency because it accurately described the position of a large number of pro-Majles *ulema* as well. This is how the idea developed.

The Majles committee that had prepared the draft supplement to the Fundamental Law consisted of a handful of reformist bureaucrats and merchants; the *ulema* were not invited to join the committee, nor were they consulted. Nuri did not trust the Westernisers in the committee and

---

[15] There was considerable rhetorical confusion of the two notions, however. For example, the oath administered to the Majles deputies in March 1907 was a pledge of allegiance to 'the principles of constitutional monarchy and the rights of the nation' and the observance of the 'interests of the Iranian nation and state according to the laws of the Mohammadan *shari'a*' (*qavānin-e shar`-e mohammadi*). See *Mozākerāt-e Majles-s Shurā-ye Melli* (Tehran, Ruznā ma-ye Rasmi-ye Keshvar, 1946–47/1325) 1: 103. This confusion was, however, not peculiar to Iran. On the contrary, we find it in Near Eastern constitutional documents and debates throughout the nineteenth century. In the Rose Garden Charter of 1839, for instance, the Sultan pledges himself to execute faithfully 'the *shari'a* laws' embodied in it (Berkes, n 7 above, at 133; Ibn Abi Diyāf, n 9 above, at 87). Similarly, Ibn Abi Diyāf speaks of 'the laws of the *shari'a*' (*al-qawānin al-shar'iyya*) (eg, Diyāf, 80–2), as do others.

proposed, in an autographed circular dated 20 April 1907, the inclusion of an article requiring the approval of all legislation 'in every age' by a council of *mojtaheds* of the first rank and pious jurisconsults. The Majles was responsive, and set up a special committee of *ulema* to consider Nuri's proposal and to examine the draft supplement generally from the viewpoint of Islam. Nuri participated in the deliberations of this second committee. He also posted 60 of his seminarians at the gates of the Majles to importune the deputies and intimidate anyone who refused to support his proposal. One of the Azerbaijani deputies reported in a letter that the Tehran *ulema* and the provincial deputies were meeting daily to discuss laws and legal terminology in Shi'ite jurisprudence.

The clause that became Article 8 of the Supplement made all Iranian citizens equal before the law. The equality of Muslim and non-Muslim citizens was the clearest instance of the incompatibility of constitutional law and the *shari'a*. It set off Nuri's popular agitation in defence of Islam, and split the *ulema*. Nuri and his followers vehemently objected to this article and mobilised broad clerical opposition to it. They also objected that compulsory education as proposed by what became Article 19 of the Supplement was against the *shari'a*, especially with regard to the inclusion of girls. The leading constitutionalist *mojtahed*, Sayyed 'Abd Allāh Behbahāni, and other constitutionalist clerics, too, opposed the equality of Muslims and non-Muslim minorities, pointing out that the latter should also pay the poll tax (*jizya*). However, the religious minorities counter-mobilised in support of the article, and the Armenians threatened armed resistance if it was not passed. Behbahāni is said to have withdrawn his objection after a credible threat on his life.[16] This allowed the passage of the article which was an important victory for the constitutionalists, and the only instance of the failure of the Islamic traditionalists to obtain any concession. The legal implications of this article were far-reaching. By declaring all citizens equal before the law, it established public law, the state law, as the law of the land, and overrode the typical legal particularism of the *shari'a* concerning the legal autonomy of the Muslim and non-Muslim religious minorities.

Meanwhile, the *ulema* committee completed its work on 29 May 1907, adopting Nuri's proposal and a number of other amendments. The constitutionalists who were willing to speak out against the Islamic amendments were very few. Although the constitutionalist *mojtaheds* Tabātabā'i and Behbahāni opposed Nuri's proposal, some of their followers in the Majles moved over to Nuri's side. The energetic Azerbaijani deputy, Sayyed Hasan Taqizāda, and his fellow democrats were alarmed by these amendments, but dared not admit the possibility of conflict between Majles legislation and the *shari'a*. Nor would they dispute the *ulema*'s exclusive jurisdiction for determining the norms of the *shari'a*. Taqizāda opposed Nuri's proposed

---

[16] A Hairi, *Shi'ism and Constitutionalism in Iran* (Leiden, EJ Brill, 1977) 232–3.

article, arguing sophistically that it would restrict the general right of all *ulema* to a particular committee. Another Azerbaijani deputy put forward the more cogent argument that the religious jurists determined the general norms of the sacred law, but 'deciding the subject matters' (*tashkhis-e mauzu'āt*)—that is, cases to which they were applicable—was with the laity. Another speaker added that, if the amendment were accepted, there should be a qualification that the *ulema* have no right to interfere with customary laws (*ahkām-e 'orfiyya*). Nuri knew that many constitutionalists did not like his proposal but few would dare reject it openly. He was proved right: on 14 June 1907, the Majles passed his proposed article, as amended by the committee of *ulema*, with an overwhelming majority (58 in favour, 3 against with 28 abstentions). Four months later, it became Article 2 of the Supplementary Fundamental Law.[17]

Outside the Majles, the democrats and other radicals demanded Nuri's banishment, and organised gatherings to intimidate him. A week after the passage of his article, Shaykh Fazl Allāh left Tehran to take refuge (*bast*) in the shrine of 'Abd al-'Azim, where he remained until mid-September. During these months, he launched a massive campaign against the imitative constitution-making of the Westernisers in Iran and the Shi'ite holy cities in Iraq. In this publicistic campaign, he formulated the *ulema*'s hitherto incoherent objections to parliamentarianism into a consistent Islamic traditionalist ideology, and succeeded in mobilising a considerable segment of the Iranian population that had not yet been drawn into constitutional politics.[18]

Nuri's journal and other publications in this period formulated a specifically Islamic variant of constitutionalism which rested on the newly approved Article 2 but extended beyond it. In one open letter issued from the shrine, he demanded that the word *mashruta* at the beginning of the Fundamental Law be followed by *mashru'a* and 'the Mohammadan law' (*qānun-e mohammadi*). Even though this demand was not met, the position defined by Nuri as *mashruta-ye mashru`a* (*shari'a*-based or *shar'i* constitutionalism) was fully recognised by the Majles so that Nuri would end his protest at the shrine of 'Abd al-'Azim. On 11 September 1907, the Majles affirmed that the scope of its legislation was limited to 'the customary laws' (*qavānin 'orfiyya*), and that the determination of the immutable norms of the *shari'a* would be the exclusive prerogative of 'the just *mojtaheds*'.[19]

---

[17] SA Arjomand, 'Islam and the Making of the Iranian Constitution of 1906–7' in H Chehabi and S Hashmi (eds), *Islam and Constitutionalism* (Harvard University Press, forthcoming).

[18] SA Arjomand, 'The 'Ulama's Traditionalist Opposition to Parliamentarianism: 1907–1909'(1981) 17(2) *Middle Eastern Studies* 174.

[19] See Gh-H Zargarinezhād, *Rasā'el-e mashrutiyyat. Hezhdah resāla va lāyeha darbāra-ye mashrutiyyat* (Tehran, Kavir, 1998/1377) 23, 27–8. The same is confirmed in an accompanying declaration signed by Nuri, the two constitutionalist *mojtaheds* and two other clerics, using instead the term 'customary matters' (*omur 'orfiyya*).

By incorporating Nuri's proposal, the SFL purported to solve the problem of mutual delimitation of the *qānun* and the *shari'a* and thus to bring the constitution into full congruence with Shi'ite Islam. Its Article 2 referred to the monarch as the 'Shāhanshāh of Islam' and declared: 'At no time must any legal enactments of the National Consultative Assembly ... be at variance with the sacred principles of Islam'. Furthermore, a committee of no less than five religious jurists (*mojtaheds*) was given the power to 'reject, repudiate, wholly or in part, any proposal which is at variance with the sacred laws of Islam. In such matters the decision of this committee of *ulema* shall be followed and obeyed, and this article shall continue unchanged until the appearance of His Holiness the Proof of the Age [ie, the twelfth, Hidden Imam]'.[20]

Nuri became the chief religious dignitary of the restored autocracy, which began with the bombardment of the Majles in June of 1908 and lasted until the constitutionalists recaptured Tehran at the end of July 1909 and hanged him summarily. During this period of restored autocracy, Nuri published a pamphlet forcefully denying that constitutionalism, as he had once believed, was a means of protecting Islam. On the contrary, he now saw it as a ploy to destroy Islam and spread irreligion. He also denied the right of the constitutionalist *mojtaheds* to interfere with the Shah's right to govern the kingdom.[21] In a different tract, Nuri justified the restored autocracy on the basis of the traditional theory of the two powers.[22]

Meanwhile, the centre of constitutionalist activity had shifted to Iraq. The constitutionalist *mojtaheds* of Najaf, Ākhund Mollā Mohammad Kāzem Khurāsāni and Mollā 'Abd Allāh Māzandarāni, who had consistently supported the Majles and countered Nuri's *fatva* on the illegitimacy of constitutional government with theirs on its incumbency, redoubled their efforts as the weakness of Mohammad 'Ali Shah's autocracy became evident. On 24 January 1909, they issued a *fatva* declaring the payment of taxes before the restoration of the Majles unlawful. A few days later, they endorsed a pamphlet explaining that 'opposition to the principles of constitutionalism is tantamount to waging war against the [hidden] Imam of the Age'. Both that pamphlet and a longer refutation of Nuri, which was published by another Shi'ite cleric in the following year, however, accommodate the substance of the idea of '*shar'i* constitutionalism' as regards the restriction of parliamentary legislation to customary affairs, and the separation of state and *shari'a* courts in judicial organisation.[23]

---

[20] The rationale, peculiar to Shi'ite Islam, is that the Shi'ite *ulema* collectively hold the 'the general vicegerency' (*niyābat-e 'āmma*) of the Hidden Imam.

[21] SFA Nuri 'Book of Admonition to the Heedless and Guidance for the Ignorant' (trans H Dabashi) in SA Arjomand (ed) *Authority and Political Culture in Shi'ism* (Albany, State University of New York Press) 354–70

[22] Zargarinezhād, above n 19, at 163.

[23] *Ibid* 453, 472–9, 518.

The most elaborate and influential justification of constitutionalism in terms of Shiʻite jurisprudence on constitutionalism was also written in Iraq in the same period, and similarly followed Nuri in insisting on the observance of the *shariʻa* as a limitation on parliamentary legislation. *Tanbih al-umma wa tanzih al-milla* was written in Persian despite its Arabic title by Mirzā Mohammad Hosayn Gharavi Nāʼini (d 1936) and published in Baghdad in 1909; and has acquired a new life in Arabic translation after the American invasion of Iraq in 2003. Nāʼini was a close consultant of Khorāsāni and had probably composed some of the joint declarations of the three constitutionalist *mojtahed*s of Najaf. He was suspicious of the Western-inspired secularist constitutionalists and Babi heretics in Tehran, and was careful to impose all the same limitations on parliamentary legislation as other constitutionalist *mojtahed*s. He thus accommodated the substance of the idea of *sharʻi* constitutionalism as regards the restriction of parliamentary legislation to customary affairs, and explicitly restricted equality before the law to man-made or positive laws (*qavānin mawduʻa*) on the assumption that they cannot override the *shariʻa*.[24]

Although he borrowed the key concept of despotism (*estebdād*) from the Arab modernist, ʻAbd al-Rahmān al-Kawākibi, Nāʼini's constitutional theory is distinctively Shiʻite, and thus has peculiarities which, unlike what we have considered so far, cannot readily be generalised to Sunni Islam. On the other hand, they provide interesting contrasts to Khomeini's clericalist theory that was to provide the theocratic basis of the 1979 Constitution of the Islamic Republic of Iran. Nāʼini takes for granted the dichotomy of despotic and constitutional governments, which al-Kawākibi had derived from Montesquieu and Alfieri, and weds it to his own typology of the two forms of government as proprietary or patrimonial (*tamallokiyya*) and custodial (*velayātiyya*). The first is said to be contrary to the spirit of Islam, and the second in conformity with it. The choice of the term *velāyatiyya* is very interesting in retrospect as it contrasts sharply with the idea of the *velāyat-e faqih* (authority of the jurist), which was, incidentally, rejected by Nāʼini's mentor, Khorāsāni, even in the restricted traditional sense which some nineteenth-century jurists had espoused. What has even greater contemporary resonance in Iran and Iraq is that Nāʼini also transmitted the Enlightenment idea that religion was a source of despotism, and in fact used it to make sense of the division of the Shiʻite *ulema* into the pro- and anti-constitutionalist camps, referring to the latter camp (Nuri's) as 'the branch of religious despotism'.[25]

Nāʼini takes constitutional government to belong to the custodial type, while implicitly relegating traditional monarchy to the despotic type. This

[24] Hairi, above n 16, at 225.
[25] *Ibid* 179.

makes obsolete the traditional theory of dual power, which had been explicitly reconciled with the Shi'ite theory of Imamate a century earlier, and had very recently been reiterated by Nuri during the restoration of autocracy. Nā'ini thus puts forward a new reconciliation of constitutional government and the Shi'ite theory of the Imamate which represents the maximal impact of constitutionalism on Shi'ite Islam. According to this new Shi'ite constitutional theory, it is necessary to change a despotic regime to a constitutional one because the former consists of three sets of usurpation or oppression: (1) it is a usurpation of the authority of God and an injustice to Him; (2) it is usurpation of the Hidden Imam's authority and oppression of the Imam; and (3) it involves oppression of the people. By contrast, constitutional government is only the oppression of the Hidden Imam because his authority is usurped. Thus, a constitutional regime reduces the three sets of oppressions to one and is therefore preferable to despotism as the lesser evil. With one condition, this qualified legitimacy of constitutional government can become categorical: if the constitutional ruler in his exercise of custodial authority 'gains the approval of the *ulema* [as deputies of the Hidden Imam], then there will remain no usurpation and no oppression of the Imam'.[26] This puts Nā'ini squarely in the camp of '*shar'i* constitutionalism'.

Let me return to the Iranian Constitution of 1906–07. Article 2 of the SFL represented a compromise between the Western-inspired constitutionalists who introduced modern constitutional law by drawing heavily on the Belgian Constitution of 1831 and the *ulema*'s demand for safeguarding the *shari'a*. As such, it reconciled two heterogeneous principles of order. The term *mashruta mashru'a* (*shar'i* constitutionalism) may not be entirely inappropriate for describing this compromise. It would be more accurate and less contentious, however, to describe this synthesis, which reflects the impact of Islam on constitutionalism, as double (or even treble) *mashruti-yyat* (limitation of government): the compromise quite simply amounted to the imposition of limitations not only on the executive power but also on the legislative power and on the bill of rights. The impact of Islam was thus a negative or rather a limiting one. It resulted in the imposition of limitations on the bill of rights in the constitutional text itself, and in the creation of the committee of five religious jurists as the institutional mechanism for securing the continuous limitation of ordinary laws by the *shari'a*. This result is due to the fact that, in the constitutional debates of 1906–07, Islam was discussed as part of the larger issue of constitutional governance and *not* as the basis of the constitution. The idea of Islam as *the* basis of constitution did not occur because it depended on the abstraction of Islam from embedded institutions which in turn allowed the construction of an ahistorical

---

[26] Mohammad Hossein Nā'ini, *Tanbih al-umma wa tanzih al-milla* (M. Tāleqāni (ed), Tehran, Sherkat-e Enteshar, 1955/1334) 46–8; English translation in Hairi, above n 16, at 193–4.

and ideological 'Islamic state', a development that was first to appear in the process of constitution-making in Pakistan.

Implementing Article 2 of the SFL proved difficult, however. The committee of five *mojtaheds* was never formed because the great majority of Shi'ite jurists selected by the Second Majles (1909–11) in several rounds considered it beneath their dignity to accept. Nevertheless, two politically ambitious clerics in the Majles, Sayyed Hasan Modarress and Hājj Mirzā Yahyā, the Imām Jom'ah of Khoi, did perform the supervisory role of insuring consistency of legislation with the *shari'a* in a fashion, without formally instituting a committee.[27] When the clash of the respective jurisdictions of the secular and religious courts became evident in the drafting of the first two laws of judicial organisation in 1911, Modaress in fact vetoed, albeit informally, one of them that was on judicial procedure, considering it inconsistent with the *shari'a* mainly because it expanded the jurisdiction of the secular at the expense of the *shar'i* courts.[28]

The non-implementation of Article 2 of the SFL and the Shi'ite peculiarity of clerical authority of the *ulema* as the deputies of the Hidden Imam that shaped it as well as Nā'ini's constitutional theory, should not obscure their significance as a logical solution to the problem of limitation of legislation by the Shari'a in the first, non-ideological era of constitutionalism in the Middle East. Although it was arrived at in a long process of popular constitutional struggle, it can be considered the most logical outcome of the pledge in the Ottoman Rose Garden Charter of 1839 that the Tanzimat laws would be in accordance with the *shari'a*[29] and of the Ottoman imperial order of 7 October 1876, that 'a commission be organized of *ulema* capable of applying and reconciling these new laws with the provisions of the Şeriat, and of civil officials worthy of confidence and capable of determining which of the laws in force in ... other civilized states would be beneficial ... and acceptable to the Şeriat'.[30] The drafting commission was thus instructed to adopt European constitutional laws consistent with the *shari'a*, and its clerical members were to bring the existing laws into conformity with the *shari'a*. From the beginning to the end of this process of constitution-making, the *shari'a* thus appears as a limitation on the constitution, implying the necessity of judicial review of legislation by the *ulema* for conformity to the *shari'a* as was eventually required by Article 2 of the Iranian SFL.

---

[27] SA Arjomand, 'Religion and Constitutionalism in Western History and in Modern Iran and Pakistan' in SA Arjomand (ed), *The Political Dimensions of Religion* (Albany, SUNY Press, 1993) 69–99.

[28] B 'Aqeli, *Dāvar va 'Adliyya* (Tehran, ʾElmi, 1990/1369) 321–34. 'Aqeli reproduces the memoirs of Mohsen Sadr on these pages.

[29] Berkes, above n 15, at 145.

[30] Devereux, above n 6, at 47.

TRANSFORMATION OF MIDDLE EASTERN PUBLIC LAW:
CODIFICATION IN THE OTTOMAN EMPIRE, EGYPT AND IRAN

While Iran was stagnating under the decrepit patrimonial monarchy of
the Qājār dynasty, a remarkable legal development began in the Ottoman
empire. Sultan Mahmud had revived the fifteenth to sixteenth-century
Ottoman legislation through *qānun*s, but this time, the state as the
impersonal legislative agency took the place of the ruler in law-making.[31]
Whereas the old *qānun*s were public laws of each ruler and remained
in force only through the confirmation of their successor, the new ones
were enacted by the Ottoman state and remained valid after the death of
the ruler. The organ of the state in charge of the new legislation was the
Council for Judicial Enactments *(Divān-i ahkām-i 'adliyya)*, which was set
up by Mahmud in 1826 and became the legislative organ of the Tanzimat,
and formed the new hierarchy of state courts after 1868 and became the
Ministry of Justice. It introduced a new age of codification into the legal
history of the Muslim Middle East. Codification became the chief dynamic
factor in legal development and acted as the engine of legal rationalisation
in the ensuing century. In fact, it can be argued that codifications of the
twentieth century—notably, the Iranian codes of the 1920s and 1930s, the
Egyptian Civil Code in 1948, adopted by Iraq, Syria and other Arab countries in the 1950s, and the Yemeni Civil Code of 1979—although formally
passed as Acts of Parliament, were works of jurists and fully displayed
the logic of codification rather than the usual inflection of parliamentary
legislation by current political interests.

The first code to be promulgated by Sultan Mahmud was the public law of administrative misconduct and corruption, which had been
entirely outside the *shari'a* and subject to the ruler's court of wrongdoings
(mazālim) since the Middle Ages. Then came two penal codes of 1840 and
1851. The penal provisions of the classical *kānun*s, following Mehmet the
Conqueror's, contradicted the penal provisions code of the *shari'a (hudud)*,
providing for substitute monetary payments *(bedel-i siyāset)*.[32] Curiously,
the first two Ottoman penal codes diverged from the classical *kānun*s, and
increasingly reintroduced the *shar'i* penal provisions. Between the two was
promulgated this first purely secular Ottoman code, the Commercial Code
of 1850, which was based on the French code of 1807.[33] A similar plan for
the adoption of the French law was, however, thwarted by Cevdet Pasha
who successfully argued for a code based on the Hanafi jurisprudence on
'transactions' *(mu'āmalāt)* which 'would be a book of the laws of the Ş
eriat for the Muslims and would be applied as *kānun* among the non-

---

[31] Berkes, above n 15, at 133.
[32] J Schacht ,'Šari`a und Qānān in modernen Ägypten' (1932) 20 *Der Islam* 212.
[33] Berkes, above n 15, at 98–9, 160–2.
[34] Cited in *ibid* 168.

Muslims'.[34] This seemingly innocuous statement hides two radical legal transformations: the translation of the *shari'a* from what Weber called a 'jurists' law' to the positive law of the state, and the termination of the legal autonomy of the millets and of the four-*madhhab* (school) legal pluralism of the Ottoman empire. But the *ulema* were not fooled and strenuously opposed this codification, which, despite its consistency with Islam, would put them out of business as religious jurists. Cevdet Pasha managed to publish 16 books (singular *mecelle*) of civil law between 1869 and 1876, but the *ulema* managed to stop the codification before it reached the inner core of the *shari'a*, namely the so-called personal status law—the family, marriage and inheritance—and prevailed upon the autocratic Sultan 'Abdul-Hamid to dissolve the codification committee in 1888.[35] Meanwhile, however, the code of civil procedure enacted in 1880, *pace* the Sultan and his pan-Islamic ideology, was based on French law and contradicted many of the provisions of the *Mecelle*.[36] It was only during the second constitutional period that the codification of those areas of the *shari'a* was resumed, with its methodology expanded beyond the jurisprudence of the Hanafi school to include European secular law as well as Jewish and Christian religious laws. The result was the Ottoman Family Law of 1917.[37] Although the Ottoman Family Law of 1917 remained in force in some of the Arab provinces after the disintegration of the empire, in Turkey itself it was replaced, in February 1926, by a new Civil Code based on the Swiss Civil Code of 1912. When introducing the transplanted code to the National Assembly, Atatürk's new Minister of Justice contemptuously alluded to the old method of codification of the Islamic jurisprudence as a part of the 'fluctuations since the Tanzimat', and claimed that with the new Civil Code, 'the Turkish nation ... will close the doors of an old civilization, and enter into a contemporary civilization of ... progress'.[38]

Nevertheless, the *Mecelle*—or to give their full title, the *Books of Judicial Enactments* (*ahkām 'adliyya*)—set the pattern for all future codifications of the *shari'a*. Muhammad Qadri Pasha published a similar civil code in Egypt in the last years of the nineteenth century, which was taken to have demonstrated the 'translatability of the Islamaic jurisprudence into legislation' (*qābiliyat al-fiqh al-islāmi li'l-taqnin*), and its methodology of selection among the opinions of the jurists of the four schools was taught in the school for the training of judges established by Sa'd Zaghlul in 1907.[39] The

[35] *Ibid* 168–9.
[36] M Khadduri and HJ Liebsney (eds), *Law in the Middle East* (Washington, DC, Middle East Institute, 1955) 307–8.
[37] Berkes, above n 15, at 417.
[38] *Ibid* 470.
[39] Boitveau, 'Contemporary Reinterpretations of Islamic Law: The Case of Egypt' in C Mallat (ed) *Islam and Public Law: classical and Contemporary Studies* (London, Graham & Trotman, 1993) 265–6.

methodology was the same as that of the Ottoman *Mecelle*, except that it was not restricted to the opinions of the Hanafi schools but was expanded to include all the four orthodox schools. The Egyptian family law of 1929 (Règlement des Mehkemehs No. 25) followed this method. It was followed in 1931 by the Règlement des Mehkemehs No. 78, which greatly restricted the *shar'i* rules of process and evidence, while giving primary importance to documentary and circumstantial evidence.[40] It is interesting that these were both law-decrees enacted between parliamentary sessions, but their essential character as codifications would have been little affected if they had been enacted by the parliament.

Iran had had its share of pre-modern codes in the classical age of *qānun*,[41] but public law stagnated, indeed regressed to discretionary rules of state-craft, whereas Shi'ite jurisprudence developed continuously and in fact generated a vigorous movement of formal rationalism, the Usuli movement, in the latter part of the eighteenth and throughout the nineteenth century. The Constitutional Revolution abruptly and radically shifted the locus of legal dynamism from religious jurisprudence to public law, ushering in the era of codification, which transformed much of the practical legal core of the *shari'a* into positive law of the Iranian state, while ignoring mostly the parts which were already obsolete, notably its penal provisions.

After a series of haphazard measures by the early constitutional governments setting up a number of courts in Tehran, the Law of Judiciary Organisation, approved provisionally on 21 July 1911/21 Rajab 1329, laid the foundation of a modern judiciary more systematically. A hierarchy of state courts were to be created, with appeal courts in provincial capitals and a court of cassation in Tehran, alongside a number of arbitration *(solhiyya)* courts, while recognising the non-hierarchical religious courts in accordance with the provisions of the constitution. The *shar'i* courts were to consist of a *mojtahed* to be known as its judge *(hākem)*,[42] and his two deputies, who were close to reaching that rank, and their verdicts were to be enforced by the state (Book 2, Articles 2, 3). This was in line with the recognition of the independence granted to *shar'i* courts in the civil code of the same year (1911) according to which the appellate courts had no jurisdiction over the verdicts of the *shar'i* courts, and the latter was the final arbiter of which of the two court systems was appropriate for a case in dispute[43] (Articles 146 and 149). Furthermore, an interesting attempt was made in the July

---

[40] Schacht, above n 32, at 231–3.

[41] The fifteenth-century Iranian *qānun* was the *qānun-nāmcha* of Uzun Hasan Āqquyunlu (d 1479?), which was enforced by the Safavid Shah Tahmasp (d 1576) until the latter proclaimed his own code.

[42] His rank as *mojtahed* had to be certified by at least two 'sources of imitation' (Article 4).

[43] A Banani, *The Modernization of Iran, 1921–1941* (Stanford, Stanford University Press, 1961) 77–8.

1911 law to involve the Shi'ite hierocracy in the arbitration courts, which
were to include a religious jurist (*faqih*), and the lower courts, which were
to include a cleric familiar with religious jurisprudence (Book 1, Articles
20, 37; Book 2, Articles 35, 37). Article 83 of the SFL had vaguely made
the appointment of the Attorney General by royal decree conditional upon
its approval by 'the hierocratic judge' (*hākem-e shar'*) without identifying
the latter. Article 153 of Book 2 of the 1911 Law followed this by requiring 'the permission of the designated (*mo'ayyan*) hierocratic judge' for the
appointment of the Prosecutor General and the Public Prosecutors of the
courts of appeal, but again failed to say how such designation was to be
made and by whom.[44]

The implementation of this law did not go far, and its limited effect
beyond Tehran is very doubtful. This, at any rate, was the justification given
for the dissolution of the judiciary in February 1927 when Reza Shah's most
energetic lieutenant,[45] 'Ali-Akbar Dāvar, took over the Ministry of Justice
to set up a uniform modernised national judiciary. When the new judiciary
was inaugurated in April 1927, a significant number of clerics (at least
six) were among the first appointed judiciary cadre of some 40 judges and
prosecutors.[46] By the latter part of 1929, the judiciary cadre had expanded
into about 260, including seven clerics in the highest court, the Court
of Cassation, of whom three were *mojtaheds*.[47] The clerical jurists were
equally prominent in the all-important commission for drafting new codes,
which was headed by Dāvar himself,[48] and vigorously produced the bulk
of Iran's modern laws, including the Civil Code, which was to be passed by
the Majles in 1928/1307 (Book 1) and in 1935/1314 (Books 2 and 3).[49] In
addition to only two regular hierocratic judges mentioned in 'Āqeli's list, a
new kind of *hākem-e shar'* appears as integrated into the hierarchy of state
courts in four instances, one *hākem-e shar'* for the lower court of Rasht,
one for an arbitration court and two for the appeal courts of the provinces
of Isfahan and Fars.[50]

De facto, the locus of the prolific modern law-making of the late
1920s and 1930s was the Ministry of Justice, as it essentially consisted

[44] And to my knowledge, none was ever made.
[45] Rezā Khan had carried out the coup of February 1921 as a colonel in the Cossack Brigade
to establish himself as Iran's most powerful man. In 1925, a Act of Parliament transferred
monarchy to his family as the new Pahlavi dynasty, and he was accordingly crowned as Rezā
Shah.
[46] 'Āqeli, above n 28, at 161–73.
[47] *Ibid* 167, 173–4.
[48] It included four clerical jurists. *Ibid* 172.
[49] The final version of the Civil Code, which remains in force with minor modifications
after the Islamic revolution of 1979, was passed by the Majles in 789 articles on 16 September
1939, with 378 articles being added on 23 June 1940. See Banani, above n 43, at 74.
[50] 'Āqeli's list (above n 28, at 179, 182–3) may well be incomplete, and there may have
been more such judges integrated to the new system of state courts in the early years, but such
appointments discontinued before long.

of codification, with legislation amounting to the rubber-stamping of the codes by the Majles. The prominence of the clerical jurists in this law-making and at the highest echelon of judges can therefore be interpreted as their performing the function of assuring reasonable conformity to the *shari'a* assigned to the five *mojtaheds* by the defunct Article 2 of the SFL, especially as some of them (for instance, Shaykh Asadollāh Mamaqāni[51]) had been active constitutionalists earlier.

Be that as it may, the *shar'i* courts were left in limbo alongside the mod-ernised judicial hierarchy of state courts. Partial appellate jurisdiction over *shar'i* courts had been given to the secular courts in 1922 and 1926. Iran's penal code of 1925/1304 had paid lip service to the theoretical dualism of the traditional judiciary system by specifying that it dealt with punishments from the viewpoint of the maintenance of public order while 'crimes that are discovered and presented according to Islamic standards will be dealt with according to the *hudud* and the *ta'zirāt* (discretionary punishments) of the *shari'a*'[52] (Article 1). Dāvar's Civil Code, by contrast, no longer alluded to the old theoretical dualism. Although it began with a statement of principles which were a verbatim translation from the French Civil Code, it included much of the Shi'ite personal status and contract law in substance,[53] as determined by Dāvar and the clerical jurists of the commission in accor-dance with the same method of translation of religious jurisprudence to legislation practised by the Ottoman and Egyptian jurists, now expanded to allow selective borrowing from European laws as well. In 1929 the Majles passed a law explicitly prohibiting the *shar'i* rules of procedure as they were incompatible with the rationalised judicial procedures transplanted from the West. In the same year, a dress code for the judges was decreed, and the clerical members of the judiciary were required to discard their clerical garb. Most of them complied and became civilians, though a few resigned and one obtained a special dispensation from Dāvar to continue wearing his turban and cloak.[54] The final blow came with the law of the *shar'i* courts in 1931/1310, which restricted their jurisdiction as special courts narrowly to disputes over marriage and divorce,[55] and to the appointment of trustees and guardians (under the supervision of the Attorney General). Furthermore, cases could only be referred to them by secular courts with the authorisation of the Attorney General, and their verdicts had to be sent

[51] He discarded his clerical garb and later served as Minister of Justice in the Sā'ed Government in 1944.

[52] The second part of this article remained a dead letter until it was removed altogether by an amendment in 1973/1352. See H Mehrpur, *Didgāhhā-ye Jadīd dar Masā'el-e Hoqouqī* (Tehran, Enteshārāt-Ettelā'āt, 1993/1372) 32–6.

[53] Banani, above n 43, at 71–2; 'Āqeli, above n 28, at 188.

[54] *Ibid* 164, 191.

[55] Dāvar had already announced in his inaugural reform speech in February 1927 that the jurisdiction of the *shar'i* courts would be restricted mainly to marriage and divorce. (*Ibid* 144.)

back to the referring secular court and be pronounced by it. This law can be taken to mark the end of the *shariʻi* courts in Iran. Though they were never formally abolished, there is no mention of them in the reorganisation of the Ministry of Justice in 1936 or in any subsequent legislation.[56]

Dāvar also pressed the Ministry of Science to amalgamate the two existing schools of law and political science into a Superior School of Law and Political Science to train judges and lawyers for the new secular judiciary.[57] Although its small faculty of a dozen Iranian, French and Italian professors included at least two clerical jurists for teaching Shiʻite jurisprudence systematically,[58] the Law School became the organ of secular legal education and produced judges and lawyers who were overwhelmingly laymen.[59]

The Egyptian process of codification a decade and a half later was a close parallel of Dāvar's, except obviously for translating the Sunni rather than Shiʻite jurisprudence into positive laws of a nation-state. Its final result, the Egyptian Civil Code of 1948, also embodied the more sophisticated jurisprudence of ʻAbd al-Razzāq al-Sanhuri, and served as the model for a number of Arab countries, including the Civil Code of Iraq in 1953.[60] The Egyptian Civil Code, however, diverged from the Iranian one in one notable respect. Whereas Dāvar, when introducing his legal reforms, had explicitly forbidden any residual resort to Shiʻite jurisprudence where there was a gap in the statutes,[61] Sanhuri included a provision for residual resort to Islamic jurisprudence in the absence of a statutory provision, or an applicable custom, in Article 1 of the Egyptian Civil Code. [62]

---

[56] Banani, above n 43, at 78–9. The 1911 Law of Judiciary Organisation refers to the *sharʻi* courts as *(mahāzer-e sharʻiyya)*. Traditionally, an important function of these courts had been the registration of marriage, divorce and property deeds. With the withering of their jurisdiction, this function appears to have been assimilated to that of the offices of the public notaries in the civil law systems, and many of the courts *(mahāzer)* in the hands of the *mojtahed*s or their clerks seem to have been converted to Offices of Public Notaries integrated into the new Ministry of Justice on the basis of an experimental law of registration of documents in 1929. The new public notaries were almost exclusively clerics (there was only one laymen among the 33 listed for Tehran by ʻĀqeli (above n 28, at 186). With the passing of the permanent Law of Registration of Deeds and Property in March 1932/Esfand 1300, however, these clerics too were forced to discard their garb or find alternative employment (Banani, above n 43, at 72–3).

[57] ʻĀqeli, above n 28, at 186–7.

[58] *Ibid* 187; Banani, above n 43, at 75.

[59] The offices of the public notaries remained almost entirely in clerical hands, but they had no judicial function and were merely in charge of the official registration of real estate and commercial transactions, marriage and divorce. Later, however, Reza Shah forced the notary publics to discard their clerical garb if they wished to retain their licences.

[60] ʻA Al-ʻAzmeh, *Al-ʻAlmaniyya min manzur mukhtalif* (Beirut, Markaz darasat al-wahda al-ʻarabiyya, 1998) 211–14.

[61] ʻĀqeli, above n 28, at 144.

[62] C Chehata, 'Islamic Law' (1971) 2 *International Encyclopedia of Comparative Law* 142. Giving precedence to custom over Islamic jurisprudence, however, reverses the traditional order.

It is worth noting that Afghanistan under monarchy followed the above-discussed method of codification based on Islamic jurisprudence, and its Constitution of 1964 (Article 69) allowed residual resort to Hanafi jurisprudence in the absence of statutory law. The corresponding article of the 2004 Constitution of the Islamic Republic of Afghanistan confirms this (Article 130), while the following Article (131) recognises similar residual use of Shi'ite jurisprudence. Strange as it may seem, the position of the Shi'ite jurisprudence in the theocratic Islamic Republic of Iran is no different.[63]

REVOLUTION, ISLAMIC IDEOLOGICAL CONSTITUTION-MAKING AND CONSTITUTIONAL REVIEW IN IRAN

Constitutional trends in the Muslim world and the rest of the world have moved in opposite directions in the past three decades. The Islamic revolution of 1979 in Iran happened at the end of the era of ideological constitutions outside of the Middle East—an era that had begun with the Mexican Constitution of 1917 and the Soviet Constitution of 1918. The neologism of 'Islamic government' (*hokumat-e eslami*) had been the key slogan of Khomeini's revolutionary movement,[64] and he ordered its translation into constitutional law after the overthrow of monarchy. Islam was simply put in the place of the dominant ideology in the constitutional documents in the Preamble to the Fundamental Law of 1979. The *shari'a* thus came back with a vengeance and swallowed the modernised state and its constitution. An Appendix consisting of a number of Traditions (*hadith*s) pertaining to its most important articles demonstrates that the 1979 Constitution of the Islamic Republic of Iran is partially derived from the *shari'a*; and its Article 4 declares all laws found inconsistent with the *shari'a* null and void, including the constitution itself. The critical function of nullification of all proposed and existing laws found inconsistent with the *shari'a* is given to the six clerical jurists of the Council of Guardians.

The late coming of the age of ideology in the Middle East ushered in a new phase of the impact of Islam on constitutionalism, which was radically different from the first and far more destructive. The first bearers of the Islamic ideology were not the *ulema* but lay intellectuals, although the *ulema* were eventually to join under the pressure of competitive mass

---

[63] See the last section below.
[64] As far as I know, the source of the neologism is Mawdudi's *hākimiyya[t]*, via the Arabic translation. Khomeini's modified rendition allows him to conflate the common meaning of *hokumat* as government with a possible technical meaning as the authority of the above-mentioned hierocratic judge (*hākem-e shar'*) in his *Kitab al-bay'*. See SA Arjomand, 'Authority in Shi'ism and Constitutional Developments in the Islamic Republic of Iran' in W Ende and R Brunner (eds), *The Twelver Shia in Modern Times: Religious Culture and Political History* (Leiden, Brill, 2000) 301–32.

politics. Once more, the Iranian *ulema* were the first in the Islamic world to succeed in revolutionary mobilisation under Khomeini. They were quick studies in picking up the Islamic political ideology and giving it a sharp clericalist twist. The result has been a novel wave of ideological constitution-making in the Muslim world, just as the age of ideology came to a close in the rest of the globe with the collapse of communism in 1989. In this wave of ideological constitution-making, the *shari'a* appears as the *basis* of the constitution and the state rather than a *limitation* to them.

There had been ideological constitutions in the Middle East earlier, but the general significance of the 1979 Constitution of the Islamic Republic of Iran is that it was the first one based on the Islamic ideology, following the first successful Islamic revolution. Its peculiarity, however, consisted in the institution of a novel Shi'ite interpretation of clerical authority as *velayat-e faqih*. This peculiarity is wearing off.

Let us examine the place of the *shari'a* in the Constitution of the Islamic Republic of Iran. Not only is its most important constitutional principle, the *velayat-e faqih* as Leadership Principle, based on the *shari'a* as interpreted by Khomeini, but the judiciary has been fully Islamicised by abolishing the hierarchy of appellate courts and collapsing the functions of the judge and the prosecutor into that of the Kadi. Even the atavistic punishments of the *shari'a*, which were never implemented in Safavid or Qajar Iran or earlier, are now fully enforced in a state whose primary function is allegedly the execution of the *shari'a*, as in Gibb's model. Rosen notes that 'the strict application of Islamic law by fundamentalist regimes has consistently failed in modern times. [These] governments have failed to turn Islamic law into an arm of the state'.[65] I think this assertion is borne out in the case of Iran if we look at this Islamic constitutional state closely with the following twin questions in mind: What are the contradictions between the *shari'a*, on the one hand, and other constitutional principles and ordinary laws of the Islamic Republic of Iran? And what are the mechanisms for resolving these contradictions? We can then decide whether the experience of the Islamic Republic of Iran suggests the possibility of resolving the contradiction between legislation and Islamic jurisprudence, or, as Rosen maintains, whether it cannot.

Regarding the first question, there is a three-way contradiction among three principles of legitimate authority—namely, the constitutional authority of the legislature, the new *shari'a*-based constitutional authority of the supreme jurist (*vali-ye faqih*), and the old *shari'a*-based authority of the highest rank of *mojtaheds* (the *marāje'-e taqlid* or 'sources of emulation'). The mechanism devised by the constitution-makers of 1979 for overcoming the first set of contradictions was the inclusion of six clerical jurists

---

[65] L Rosen, *The Justice of Islam: Comparative Perspectives on Islamic Law and Society* (Oxford, University Press, 2000) 64.

in the Council of Guardians to veto any item of legislation passed by the Majles which was inconsistent with the *shari'a*. The Council thus incorporated the 1907 idea of a committee of *mojtaheds* into the model of a *Conseil constitutionnel* adopted in Bazargan's draft constitution from the 1958 Constitution of the French Fifth Republic. Khomeini himself intervened in the constitutional crisis that resulted from the clashes between the Majles and the Council of Guardians, and his solution, which was duly incorporated into the constitutional amendments of 1989, consisted in the reception of the long-rejected Sunni principle of *maslahat* or public interest into Shi'ism, and the establishment of the Maslahat Council. The Council was originally to arbitrate between the Council of Guardians and the Majles, but has since taken on the task of expanding legislation beyond matters specifically vetoed by the jurists of the Council of Guardians, and of setting up the general policies of the state as the advisory arm of the Leader (Supreme Jurist). The solution proposed by the former Head of the Judiciary, Ayatollah Sayyed Mohammad Yazdi, addressing the second set of contradictions, was to force the recognition of the Supreme Jurist as the sole *marja'*. It failed, as did the attempt to restrict the number of *marja'* to seven through semi-official designation by the Association of the Modarresin (Professors) of Qom.[66]

The current Head of the Judiciary, Ayatollah Sayyed Mahmud Hashemi Shahrudi, has strengthened the Legal Office (*edara-ye hoquqi*) of the Judiciary and instituted a Research Centre in Jurisprudence (*markaz-e tahqiqāt-e feqhi*) to answer enquiries from the courts and provincial branches of the Ministry of Justice. The Centre draws on the ruling (*fatva*s) of the seven designated 'sources of imitation', including the Leader, Ayatollah Sayyed 'Ali Khamane'i, but does so alongside the rulings of other living *marāji'*, as well as those of the late Ayatollahs Khomeini and Kho'i and the classics in Shi'ite jurisprudence. This Research Centre, like the Legal Office of the Ministry of Justice, follows Article 167 of the Constitution, consistently upholding the priority of ordinary laws over Shi'ite jurisprudence. The resort to the latter is thus residual. Furthermore, it is usually inconclusive, as the *fatva*s presented to supplement ordinary laws are often contradictory, and categorical instructions seem to be provided only when a pertinent positive law is found additionally.[67] Indeed, the latter seems to make the *fatva*s redundant. For example, four out of five *fatva*s produced in response to the question of whether women can be judges according to the *shari'a* give a negative answer but are overruled by the Legal Office of the

---

[66] See Arjomand, above n 64.
[67] Markaz-e Tahqiqāt-e Feqhi-ye Qovva-ye Qadāiyya, *Majmu'a-ye Nazariyyāt-e Moshvarati-ye Feqhi dar Omur-e Kayfari* (Qom, 2002/1381), and Markaz-e Tahqiqāt-e Feqhi-ye Qovva-ye Qadāiyya, *Majmu'a-ye Nazariyyāt-e Moshvarati-ye Feqhi dar Omur-e Qadā'i* (Qom, 2002/1381).

Judiciary which cites an ordinary law of 1374 (1995–96) on the appointment of women as judges.[68]

As for the areas of law where the *shari'a* is relevant, problems do arise residually in procedural and civil law, but are much more intractable in penal law because of the laws of retribution (*qesās*) and blood-money and compensation for injuries (*diyāt*) passed in 1981/1369,[69] and the law of discretionary punishments (*ta'zirāt*) passed in 1996/1375, which are now referred to as the Islamic Penal Code (*qānun-e mojāzāt-e eslāmi*). The Penal Code provides inadequate guidelines to the determination of compensations for many parts of the body in cases of injury and malpractice, and is not self-sufficient and refers the judges to Shi'te jurisprudence for procedural rules for the *hudud* (including the so-called rights of God (*hoquq Allāh*) and rights of men (*hoquq al-nās*)). The inadequacy of the law of discretionary punishments is even more problematic for the courts,[70] as sometimes only the upper limits of punishment are specified and the judge can even pardon the culprit. The *Ta'zirāt* Law of 1996 itself was a response to the chaos created by the exercise of this *shar'i* discretionary authority by the Islamicised courts, but did not eliminate its indeterminacies and ambiguities, nor the consequent pressure on the branch of the Supreme Court issuing opinions on 'procedural unity' (*vahdat-e raviyya*) or the Legal Office of the Ministry of Justice.[71] An interesting question here is the extent to which Shi'ite jurisprudence can in fact fill the gap in the rational-legal framework of the constitutional state. Only a minority of the jurists cited in the recent publications of the Centre for Research in Jurisprudence—Khamene'i is, predictably, one of them—consciously try to do this by taking a statist position. By contrast, it is striking how rigidly bound are all the jurists, including the above-mentioned minority and Ayatollah Abdol-Karim Musavi Ardabili, for long a leading member of Iran's ruling elite who is known as a leading advocate of 'innovative jurisprudence' (*fiqh-e puyā*), by the *hadith* and the traditional rules of jurisprudence. To give one important example, both Musavi Ardabili and Ayatollah Ruhollāh Sāfi Golpāygāni, a long-time member of the Council of Guardians who could also be assumed sympathetic in adopting jurisprudence to its new function within the Islamic state, ignore the requirements of rational judicial administration through the state by confirming that a judge who is a *mojtahed* can pardon a *hadd* punishment, but one who is not, cannot.[72]

---

[68] Markaz-e Tahqiqāt-e Feqhi-ye Qovva-ye Qadāiyya, *Majmu'a-ya Ārā-ye Feqhi-ye Qadā'i dar Omur-e Hoquqi* (Qom, 2002/1381) 209–11.

[69] It was approved 'experimentally' for five years in 1982, but has remained in force.

[70] Markaz, *Majmu'a-ye Nazariyyāt-e Moshvarati-ye Feqhi dar Omur-e Kayfari*, above n 67, at 243–5.

[71] B Keshāvarz, *Majmu'a-ye Mohshā-ye Qānun-e Ta'zirāt-e Mosavvab-e 1375* (Tehran, Ganj-e Dānesh, 1996/1375).

[72] Markaz, *Majmu'a-ya Ārā-ye Feqhi-ye Qadā'i dar Omur-e Kayfari*, above n 67, at 108–9. The disregard of the entire system of judicial authority based on the *velayat-e faqih*

The same inflexibility is apparent in the *fatvas* concerning the 'knowledge of the judge' as a supplement to the *shar'i* proof (*bayyanāt*), and the possibility of appeal—issues of great importance in view of the enormous discretionary power of the judge who also acts as the prosecutor and whose verdict is final. The resort to Shi'ite jurisprudence appears to boost the knowledge of the judge, though the *fatvas* produced are far from unanimous. In astonishing disregard of procedural rationality, some jurists affirm the well-known personalism of Islamic law[73] by considering the knowledge of the judge before his appointment legitimate grounds for a decision! Others, ignoring the haphazard appeal system the judiciary had been forced to introduce for verdicts considered patently wrong by the judiciary itself, affirm the traditional Islamic position that there is no appeal against the Kadi's verdict. Last but not least, except for one statist jurist, they do not require the judge to give (written) reasons for his decision.[74] The last point is important in a system where judges have such broad discretionary power. It precludes the development of a jurisprudence based on court opinions as a force for rationalisation and increasing the predictability of law.

The effectiveness of the current measures to reconcile ordinary laws and the *shari'a* is hard to determine at this stage. At any rate, residual resort to Shi'ite jurisprudence through the supervision and advisory services of the judiciary is a secondary mechanism for insuring the consistency between the *shari'a* and the constitutional state. The primary institution for performing this function is the Council of Guardians, which has a much longer record that we must now examine. It can be stated categorically that the Council of Guardians has made no contribution to institution-building in the Islamic Republic of Iran. I would argue that the main reason for this failure is the absence of a written jurisprudence remotely comparable to the jurisprudence of other constitutional courts (or the Supreme Court in the United States), and the increasing politicisation of judicial review, which preceded the politicisation of the judiciary and the use of courts as an instrument of political repression. An incidental feature of its French model, supervision of elections, suggested the Council of Guardians as an instrument of political control to Iran's ruling elite after the death of Khomeini and the end of his charismatic leadership. It interpreted its function of supervising elections as the power to reject the qualification of candidates for all elected offices, including Presidency, without giving its reasons, as is also the case when it vetoes legislation. This resulted in a serious overload of the functions of the

---

by Ayatollah Sayyed 'Ali Sistāni, who inherited most of the large global following of the late Grand Ayatollah Kho'i, is less surprising. In response to the question concerning the right of a judge appointed by the supreme jurist as the *vali-ye amr*, Sistāni simply reaffirms that judgeship is the exclusive right of the fully-qualified *mojtahed* who requires no one else's permission (Markaz, above n 67, at 29).

[73] C Geertz, *Local Knowledge* (New York, Basic Books, 1983).
[74] Markaz, *Majmu'a-ya Ārā-ye Feqhi-ye Qadā'i dar Omur-e Kayfari*, above n 67, at 7–16.

Council of Guardians and overwhelmed its functions of judicial review and determination of conformity of legislation with Islamic standards. In fact, it is quite clear that since 2000, the effect of the Council of Guardians on institution-building has been negative—consisting in the paralysis of legislation and near-destruction of the Majles as an institution. This has been done by its blanket extension of inconsistency with the *shari'a* to such items of legislation as the annual government budget![75]

The Council of Guardians has not shown any concern with removing abundant internal contradictions of the Constitution of the Islamic Republic of Iran. One obvious contradiction is between the *shari'a* and the principle of equality of all citizens before ordinary state laws. This contradiction is the basis for the vast majority of complaints by members of religious minorities to the presidential Commission for the Implementation of the Constitution.[76] Nor is this contradiction resolved through the secondary mechanism of Shi'ite jurisprudence. In a question concerning inheritance, the jurists consulted advised that the Baha'i heirs of a deceased Baha'i could inherit from him as infidels only if no Muslim could be found in any category of presumptive heirs.[77] It goes without saying that removing contradictions between Iranian law and international law is even further removed from the increasingly politicised concerns of the Council of Guardians. What I have in mind here is the fact that the gruesome *shar'i* punishments are in obvious contradiction to the international human rights instruments which outlaw cruel and inhumane punishments. In January 2002, the Council of Guardians vetoed as contrary to the *shari'a* bills that were found at variance with the governmental orders of the Leader, the orders of the late Imam, and even the regulations of the Supreme Council for Cultural Revolution;[78] and in January 2003, it rejected a Majles bill against torture on the grounds that it contravened the internal regulations (*ā'in-nāma*) of state prisons! In August 2003, the Council of Guardians then vetoed the ratification by the Majlis of the UN Convention against Torture and Other Cruel, Inhuman, or Degrading Treatment or Punishment.

IRAN IN COMPARISON WITH AFGHANISTAN

To put the discussion of the compatibility of Islam and constitutionalism in perspective, it is instructive to contrast the constitutional experience of Afghanistan with that of Iran. The small constitutionalist movement among

---

[75] SA Arjomand, 'Democratization and the Constitutional Politics of Iran since 1997' (2001) 136 *Polish Sociological Review* 349.

[76] Interview with the Commission's Chairman, 2001.

[77] Markaz *Majmu'a-ye Nazariyyāt-e Moshvarati-ye Feqhi dar Omur-e Qadā'i*, above n 67, at 109–11.

[78] *Ettelā'āt*, 1/11/02.

the urban Afghan intelligentsia in the first decade of the twentieth century was stimulated by the constitutional revolutions in Russia, 1905, Iran, 1906 and the Ottoman Empire, 1908, but was abruptly ended in 1909 with the execution of eight of their leaders and imprisonment of another 35 after the discovery that the group had decided to arm itself. The king's brother and regent, Sardār Nasrallāh Khan commented: 'Education produces constitutionalism, and constitutionalism is opposed to the power of the ruler as sanctioned by the *shari'at*'.[79] Nevertheless, the king allowed the publication of the modernist newspaper, *Serāj al-akhbār*, which advocated constitutionalism as part of the introduction of modern civilization to Afghanistan and became the mouthpiece of the Afghan intellectuals, who called themselves the Young Afghans, following the Young Ottomans and Young Turks, and included the king's second son, Amānallāh. After the assassination of his father in 1919, apparently with his complicity, Amānallāh Khan ascended the throne of Afghanistan. Calling himself the 'revolutionary king' (*pādshāh-e inqilābi*), he appointed constitutionalists to government posts and promulgated the first constitution (*nizām-nāma-ye asāsi*) on 9 April 1923.

Article 16 of the Constitution declared 'all the subjects of Afghanistan have equal rights and duties before the state regarding the *shari'at* and the state law'.[80] With regard to the reconciliation of the *shari'a* and state or public law (*qānun*), it acknowledged the duality of the legal system by stating that 'all cases and lawsuits in the courts of justice will be resolved on the basis of the ordinances of the *shari'at* and the civil and penal state laws' (Article 21). It should be noted that criminal laws were being codified since 1921, and the severe Penal Code of 1924–25 offered a synthesis of the *shari'a* provisions and the tribal customary law, the *Pushtunwali*.[81] Furthermore, Article 72 stated that 'in the process of legislation, the actual living conditions of the people, the requirements of the time and particularly the ordinances of the *shari'at* will be given serious consideration'.

Hidden by the theoretical recognition of the *shari'a* and state law as the two pillars of the legal order is the radical secularisation entailed by the translation of Islamic jurisprudence into positive statute laws. The *shari'a* is no longer what Max Weber called a 'jurists' law', left to the interpretation of the *ulema*, and the state is given jurisdiction over all cases and courts.[82]

---

[79] Cited in MH Kakar, 'Constitutional History of Afghanistan' in *Encyclopaedia Iranica* (London, Routledge and Kegan Paul 1992) 6: 159.

[80] I have consulted the English translation of the constitutions published in one volume in Kabul in 1996 under the title of *The Constitutions of Afghanistan*. The Persian texts of these constitutions had been published in Kabul by Sarvar Dānish a year earlier (in 1995/1374) under the title of *Qavānin-e asāsi-ye Afghānistān*. As the English translations are not always accurate, I have translated the cited articles from the official Dari (Persian) texts myself.

[81] V Gregorian, *The Emergence of Modern Afghanistan. Politics of Reform and Modernization, 1880–1946* (Stanford, Stanford University Press, 1969) 248–51.

[82] As the Preamble to the Penal Code of 1924–25 put it, crimes committed against an individual or the state 'come under the jurisdiction of the state, so do religious and political crimes' (cited in Gregorian, above n 81, at 248).

In practice, the government encroachment over the autonomy of the local Mullahs in regulating family problems became evident with the officials' attempts to improve the position of women in accordance with the adminis- trative code of 1923. Some Mullahs attacked the new code and the opening of schools for girls as contrary to the *shariʿa*, and their cause was taken up by the Mangal tribe which rebelled in the Khost region in 1924. The Khost rebellion lasted over nine months into January 1925, and the king was forced to revoke important sections of the new code and limit the school- ing of girls to those under 12.[83] More significantly from our point of view, he was forced to Islamicise the constitution, amending Article 2, which had declared Islam the official religion, also making official 'the sublime Hanafi rite' (concerning the norms of the *shariʿa*), and adding that 'Hindus and Jews must pay the poll tax and wear distinctive clothing'. Article 24 prohib- iting torture was modified to except the punishments of the *shariʿa*.[84]

Yet worse was to come. Amānallāh Khan's reforms, especially the removal of the veil, education of women, adoption of Western clothing and the changing of the weekly holiday from Friday to Thursday, provoked a strong traditionalist reaction throughout the country. In October 1928, the Shinwari tribe rebelled and soon captured Jalalabad, and a Tajik bandit known as Bacha-i Saqqā (water-carrier's boy) rose against 'the infidel Amir,' vowing to 'serve the cause of God ... and helping the cause of the *ulema* and the *shariʿat* and the Holy Prophet.'[85] Neither Amānallāh's hasty rescinding of most of his reforms and other concessions to the ulema in early January 1929,[86] nor his abdication in favor of his brother were to any avail, and the bandit captured Kabul and held the throne until October 1929, when he was defeated by Sardār Mohammad Nādir Khan, who became the new king of Afghanistan and assumed the title of Shah.

Nādir Shah's Constitution of 1931 retained the principle of equality: 'all the subjects of Afghanistan have equal rights and duties before the state regarding the *shariʿat* and the state law' (Article 13), and the dual formula was repeated elsewhere.[87] Nādir Shah's Constitution, however, omitted all mention of women as a concession to the *ulema*, and was much more emphatic that the previous one in its recognition of the *shariʿa*. The king was required 'to rule the country according to the tenets of the *shariʿat* of the Holy Prophet (peace be upon Him), the sacred Hanafi rite and the

[83] *Ibid* 254–5.
[84] Three other Articles were also amended. The amendments were passed by a Loya Jirgah convened in Paghman and signed by the king on 28 January 1925 (Dalv 8, 1303).
[85] Gregorian, above n 81, at 276.
[86] These included the granting of automatic right of residence in Afghanistan to the *ulema* of Deoband, and the inclusion of religious luminaries in a new council of 50 notables. (*Ibid* 264–5).
[87] The dual formula appears in Article 19, and a similar one in Articles 11 and 16, which prohibit the search of persons and private domicile without 'ordinances of the *shariʿat* and enacted codes'.

constitution of the state' (Article 5). Although both secular (*'adliyya*) and religious courts were mentioned and the latter were required to base their decisions on Hanafi jurisprudence (Article 88), the former was also said to deal with 'general cases pertaining to the *shari'at*' *(Article 87)*. Article 65 required that the enactments of 'the National Consultative Assembly should not clash with the ordinances of the holy religion of Islam and the policy of the state'.

Although the constitution did not invest any organ or person with the power of judicial review of laws for conformity with the *shari'a* or the constitution, as a part of his *rapprochement* with the *ulema* and the tribal chiefs, Nādir Shah decided to submit all laws and regulations to a certain Jam'iyyat al-'Ulamā' (society of the *ulema*) to ascertain their conformity with the *shari'a*. He also rescinded Amānallāh's secularist measures and made the *shari'a* the basis of civil and criminal laws. Nevertheless, the king remained the highest court of appeal according to the Muslim tradition that requires the ruler to be accessible to all his subjects and charges him with the removal of 'injustices' (*mazālim*). It is interesting to note that to fulfil this charge, Nādir placed a complaint box at the Ministry of Defence.[88] In practice, the co-existence of the religious and semi-secular state courts resulted in a disorganised and contradictory legal system for decades to come.[89]

The Afghan Constitution of 1964 is much more interesting. It was the product of the meeting of liberal constitutionalism and Islamic modernism that proposed to interpret the principles of Islam without undue restriction from the rigidities of medieval Islamic jurisprudence, and succeeded in finding the finest formula for the reconciliation of Islam and constitutionalism in the Middle East to that date or since. Its Article 64 stated: 'No laws can be in contradiction (*munāqiz*) to the principles of the sacred religion of Islam and the other values contained in this Constitution'. As had been the case with the 1931 Constitution, the article was addressed to the legislature, and again no organ was given the power of judicial review. But in contrast to the early 1930s, a secular body, the National Centre for Legislation in the Ministry of Justice, was in charge of the determination of the constitutionality of the existing laws and proposed legislation and their conformity with the principles of Islam.[90] Article 69 further stated that all laws of Afghanistan were the enactments of the parliament, and the Hanafi jurisprudence was valid only by default in the absence of statute law. It is interesting to note that the constitutionalists and Islamic modernists

---

[88] Gregorian, above n 81, at 299. An interesting earlier parallel is the setting up of the 'boxes of justice' by the Shah of Iran in 1864. See I Schneider, 'Religious and State Jurisdiction during Nāsir al-Din Shāh's Reign' in Robert M Gleave (ed), *Religion and Society in Qajar Iran* (London, Curzon, 2005) 87.

[89] L Duprée, *Afghanistan* (Princeton, Princeton University Press, 1980) 468.

[90] *Ibid* 580.

completely carried the day in the debates of the constituent Loya Jirga, airing their frustration with the inadequacies of the judicial system and religious courts, and in the end only a few clerical members voted against Article 69. Furthermore, Article 102, which similarly allowed the court to resort to Hanafi jurisprudence only residually and in the absence of a pertinent statute, was passed almost unanimously as the Mullahs sensed the general hostility of their lay colleagues and dared not oppose it.[91]

Although the January 2004 Constitution of the Islamic Republic of Afghanistan has been hailed as a model for Islamic democracy, 'pervasively Islamic and thoroughly democratic',[92] it represents, in my opinion, a definite regress from the subtle formulations of the Constitution of 1964 in this regard. In a memorandum submitted to the Constitutional Commission of Afghanistan through the United Nations Assistance Mission for Afghanistan, I had praised the subtlety of the formulation, while emphasising that the projected constitutional court was indispensable for sensitive and balanced judicial review in the light of the Islamic and constitutional values, and suggested that the 1964 wording might be updated in a 'new constitutionalist' direction by making explicit that the constitutional principles include internationally recognised human rights.[93] I was very pleased to see the formulation of Article 64 of the 1964 Constitution reappear (Article 3) in the draft constitution published by the Commission on 3 November 2003, even without my suggested addition. I was equally disappointed, however, when the wording of the draft was changed without any discussion in the Loya Jirga. The Constitution of January 2004, omits the reference to constitutional values[94] and contains the following inferior formulation: 'Article 3: In Afghanistan no law can be contrary (*mukhālif*) to the tenets and ordinances of the sacred religion of Islam'. What is more distressing is that the worthy idea of creating a constitutional court had been dropped by the Commission, and the constitution gives power of judicial review not only to the Supreme Court but also to the ordinary courts, which means that every small town Mullah can strike down any law as contrary to the *shariʿa* without the slightest consideration for other constitutional values and rights.[95]

---

[91] *Ibid* 573, 580–3.

[92] N Feldman, 'A New Democracy, Enshrined in Faith', *New York Times* (Op-Ed), 13 November 2003.

[93] SA Arjomand, 'The Role of Religion and the Hanafi and Jaʿfari Jurisprudence in the New Constitution of Afghanistan' in *Afghanistan: Towards a New Constitution* (New York University, Center for International Cooperation, 2003) 20–1.

[94] The formula survives in Article 35, section 1, which requires the manifestos and byelaws of political parties 'not to be in contradiction to the ordinances of the sacred religion of Islam and the texts and the values contained in this Constitution'. In the main Article 3, however, the words of the official text were changed, most probably at the printing house after the deputies of the constituent Loya Jirga had gone home. (Interviews with Lakhdar Brahimi and Barnett Rubin)

[95] The great majority of Afghan judges are Mullahs, many of them were apparently associated with the Taliban. Only a third of judges and prosecutors are educated to university standards, and although a large number of positions in the courts are vacant, the very low salaries are unlikely to attract scarce educated manpower. See United Nations Development

Chief Justice Shinwāri of the Supreme Court (2001–06) was known for his fundamentalist views, and had appointed several more judges than the nine mandated by the constitution. So far, there has been no need to resort to this power of judicial review, as 'judges routinely make decisions without reference to written law'.[96]

Let me mention other Islamic provisions of the 2004 Constitution for the sake of completion. Shi'ite jurisprudence, for the first time in Afghan history, is granted official recognition not only by being given the same residual validity as the Hanafi jurisprudence but also categorical validity concerning the personal status law of the Shi'a (Article 131), which seems to cover some 15 per cent of the Afghan population who are Twelvers, as well as the Isma'ili minority of perhaps 1 to 2 per cent of the population.[97] Article 45, which problematically mandates the basing of the educational system on 'the ordinances of the sacred religion of Islam, the national culture and scientific principles', also requires the religious instructions at school to take into consideration 'the existing Islamic rites in Afghanistan'.

CONCLUSION

Concluding with the lessons to be drawn from the Iranian experience, the question of the viability of Islamic jurisprudence in the civil-law based modern Middle Eastern states may be answered negatively. The quarter-century experience of the Islamic Republic of Iran does not suggest the possibility of removing the contradictions between legislation and Islamic jurisprudence. A *shari'a*-based Islamic state cannot be a modern constitutional state without serious contradictions. There is no way to modernise the traditional system of the two powers by exempting one of them as sacrosanct. Let me therefore conclude by suggesting that this realisation is behind the current

Program (UNDP), *National Human Development Report: Security with a Human Face* (Kabul, 2005) 147. Pursuant to the Bonn Agreement, an Afghan Judicial Commission was set up in May 2002 to reform the judiciary but so far remains dormant (C Johnson, W Maley, A Tier and A Wardak, *Afghanistan's Political and Constitutional Development* (London, Overseas Development Institute, 2003) 27). For a general survey of the deplorable condition of the Afghan judiciary, including unavailability of printed books of statutes, the extreme scarcity of lawyers and the rather ineffective aid for judicial reform offered by Italy, see United States Institute for Peace (USIP), *Establishing the Rule of Law in Afghanistan: Special Report* (Washington, DC, March 2004).

[96] *Ibid* 5.

[97] The same Article 131 also mentions 'courts for Shi'ite people' and charges them with reconciling the Shi'ite personal status law with statute laws. The presumption may be that the latter incorporate the Hanafi law. My recommendation to the Afghan Constitutional Commission, drawing the lesson from the unhappy petrification of Muslim personal status law in India as a result of a similar constitutional concession to the Muslim minority, had been to *avoid* such a concession that would freeze personal status law for the Shi'a, while making possible progressive or at any rate new legislation for the majority Hanafi Sunnis. The better alternative was to make special provisions in conformity with Shi'ite law in the family law statutes of Afghanistan for the Shi'ite citizens. See Arjomand, above n 93, at 22.

reformist attack in Iran on clerical authority as the heir to both kings and prophets. In Iraq, Āyatollāh ʿAli Sistāni has upheld the position of *sharʿi* constitutionalism as elaborated by Na'ini in the same Najaf in 1909 as a starting point; they would do well to remember[98] that the nineteenth-century idea of the *shariʿa* as a limitation to the constitution, though more historically rooted and vastly less problematic than the ideological insistence of a *shariʿa*-based constitution for the Islamic state, as was demanded by Moqtadā al-Sadr, does not seem viable even in the Islamic Republic of Iran and is in any event a far cry from the 'new constitutionalism' of the twenty-first century.

[98] And the same goes for Noah Feldman who, in an excessive display of legal *naïveté*, not only takes the sovereignty of God as the connotation of the very word 'Islam' but also finds the same divine sovereignty implicit in the American Declaration of Independence! See N Feldman, *After Jihad. America and the Struggle for Islamic Democracy* (New York, Farrar, Straus and Giroux, 2003) 57.

3

Bargaining and Imposing Constitutions

Private and Public Interests in the Iranian, Afghani and Iraqi Constitutional Experiments

NATHAN J BROWN

I
N THE MIDDLE East, most constitutions have been written by existing
regimes attempting to reform themselves, settle internal differences or
send ideological messages.[1] Yet on a few occasions, constitutions have
been written in dramatically different circumstances—after revolution in
Iran and after invasions and forced regime changes in Afghanistan and Iraq.
In these three cases (and arguably in an earlier one, the constitutional revolution in Iran at the dawn of the twentieth century), writing a constitution
was an act of political reconstruction of a polity that had suffered extreme
crisis or collapse.

While very unusual in a regional context, constitutional avenues of
political reconstruction have been common outside the Middle East. Many
different countries have attempted to write constitutions in the midst—or
the wake—of similar crises, beginning with the United States, France and
Poland at the end of the eighteenth century. When scholars or political
activists devote energies and invest hopes in processes of constitution drafting, it is almost always such efforts that they have in mind. (Or rather,
it is efforts like the American—which has survived to this day—and the
French—which, though rapidly replaced, did bequeath much language as
well as models of republican institutions to subsequent generations—that
are recalled. The Polish effort, taking place in a country that subsequently
disappeared from the political map for over a century, should offer a cau-
tionary note to constitutional enthusiasts but is almost never considered).

---

[1] See NJ Brown, 'Regimes Reinventing Themselves: Constitutionalism in the Arab World'
(2003) 18 *International Sociology 33–52*; and *Constitutions in a Non-Constitutional World:
Arab Basic Laws and Prospects for Accountable Government* (Albany, SUNY Press, 2001).

It is odd that constitutions written during times of tumultuous political change and severe crisis should be seen as expressions of far-sighted institutional design. But a strong strain of liberal political thought has embraced and even glorified these efforts, exploring how constitutions should be written and what they should say—based on the assumption that the drafters of such documents were not only trying to stave off political collapse, secure partisan goals and reconcile opposing interests, but also constitute political systems to serve the interests of unborn generations.

When some Middle Eastern polities began to experiment with written constitutions in the nineteenth century, there were various elements of regional political traditions that could be used to guide these efforts. There was a tremendously rich tradition of Islamic jurisprudential discourse, though its translation into terms relevant to constitutional design was hardly a simple task. And there was a broader political tradition of political thought that stressed the duties of rulers to serve as trustees or stewards for the interests of the community.[2]

The problem for constitutional architects in the Middle East, however, is that neither the liberal nor local traditions grasp the difficult nature of the process: both provide a rich vocabulary for expressing the common interest of a society and for rational design, but neither give a basis for understanding the clash of interests and passions that actually arise. In this chapter I will briefly explore the idealised images that might guide constitution writing, show how the actual experience differs in some fundamental ways from such idealised images, and finally speculate on how constitutions that depart from such ideals can still attain a measure of legitimacy.

LIBERAL AND LOCAL TRADITIONS

Liberal constitutionalists have placed tremendous faith in a human ability to regulate power through law and reason. For them, constitutional politics is constitutive not merely in the sense that it results in drafting fundamental legal documents but also in that it makes other politics possible. More civic-minded and less self-interested, constitutional politics should involve reasoned deliberation over the nature of the political community and the rules that should govern normal politics.

Many liberal views of constitutional politics rest on a broader vision of the proper nature of politics, one grounded in what John Rawls has described as public reason, in which citizens deliberate in a framework 'that expresses

---

[2] In the nineteenth century there were some intellectuals who attempted to develop strong arguments for constitutionalism based on the tradition of Islamic legal and political thought. See eg, Ahmad Bin Diyaf, *Consult Them in the Matter: a Nineteenth-Century Islamic Argument for Constitutional Government* (LC Brown (trans), Fayetteville, University of Arkansas Press, 2005).

political values that others, as free and equal citizens might also reasonably be expected reasonably to endorse'.[3] For many, Rawls' requirement that the endorsement 'reasonably be expected' rather than explicitly given grants the powers of citizens to theorists, and much effort has therefore been devoted to understanding how such an endorsement might actually (and not merely theoretically) take place. Cass Sunstein writes: 'I contend that a constitution should promote *deliberative democracy*, an idea that is meant to combine political accountability with a high degree of reflectiveness and a general commitment to reason-giving'.[4] If reason, rationality and deliberation are the hallmarks of constitutional politics, then passion, self-interest and bargaining would seem to represent contamination at best and mortal dangers at worst.

Liberal constitutionalist theory-especially in its Rawlsian variety-may seem like a rarefied and alien intellectual tradition in the Middle East. Yet if local political traditions are considered, they give no firmer ground for the role of partisan interest and political passions in constitution writing. Elsewhere in this collection, Linda Darling argues for the continued relevance of the 'Circle of Justice' dating back to the ancient Near East and operating up to the present. One striking aspect of this intellectual tradition is that it insists that various elements of a society have very different contributions and roles, and all must operate in harmony for a society to prosper. A ruler or political regime has the duty of providing the order necessary that underlies a web of mutual interdependence. There is little room for party, class or ethnic politics in such a vision.

Nor do Islamic political traditions provide any sounder basis for a politics of partisan interest. Historically, those approaches that were more realistic or deferential (or perhaps pessimistic) still insisted that the ruler provide a minimal level of order, not so much that his subjects could pursue their private pursuits but so that they could live their lives in accordance with divine guidance. More ambitious approaches—which Said Arjomand shows are often very modern in origin even as they masquerade as timeless-insist that the entire political order be based on such divine guidance. The alternative to Islamic government, for many radical Islamists, is a political system that simply serves the interests of particular individuals (according to Sayyid Qutb) or even anti-Muslim political forces (Khomeini).[5] The tussle of normal politics—bargaining for the interests of a particular individual, party, or ethnic group—again lies outside these images of politics. And it is quite instructive that when one attempt to implement a particularly

[3] J Rawls, *The Law of Peoples* (Cambridge, Harvard University Press, 1999) 140.
[4] CR Sunstein, *Designing Democracy: What Constitutions Do* (New York, Oxford University Press, 2001) 6–7.
[5] Sayyid Qutb, *Milestones* (Cedar Rapids, Mother Mosque Foundation, 1981); Imam Khomeini, *Islam and Revolution* (Hamid Algar (trans and annotated, Berkeley, Mizan Press, 1981).

demanding form of Islamic politics began to founder—the construction and operation of an 'Islamic republic' in Iran—it was forced to take recourse (as Arjomand notes in passing) in the idea of *maslaha* (public interest) in order to explain its inability to determine all its actions by the Islamic *shari'a*. In other words, even when bowing to political realities, the Islamic republic resisted any acknowledgement that a proper political order could be based on anything other than the good of the society as an organic whole.

The various forms and combinations of nationalism and socialism, while often a nemesis of Islamist approaches, shared with them a refusal to recognise the legitimacy of partisan interests. Nationalists rejected any divisions of the national community on economic or partisan grounds. Socialism prevailed in some countries, but those varieties based on any conception of class struggle were generally rejected as dividing the community. Even when some class-based rhetoric seeped into official discourse (especially in a few states like Egypt and Syria in the 1960s), the denunciation of 'feudalists' and 'capitalists' was generally based on their perceived failures to serve any interest but their own (or perhaps those of imperialism); socialism was a way to harness the resources of society for the good of the whole. No dictatorship of the proletariat was contemplated; instead, phrases like 'the working forces of the nation' were deployed to minimise class differences and accentuate common societal goals.

Thus, those confronted with the task of writing constitutions can find no real vocabulary for particular interests or bargaining. The interest of the society as a whole might be viewed from many different angles—liberal, Islamic, nationalist or socialist—but the reality of clashes of interest can find no purchase in such approaches. Society is properly an orderly and organic whole; there is no place for disorder or political passions.

And indeed, in considering the constitutional texts that have generally been written in the Middle East, there is generally no reason to cast about for a language that confronts conflict and difference: the texts that have been written have generally been written—whether by deeply entrenched regimes or new ones—as expressions of the will of rulers confident that they represented the will of the entire community. Such texts draw happily on nationalist, liberal, socialist and religious language apparently unvexed by the failure of these traditions to allow them to address conflict and partisan interest. On rare occasion, a discordant note has broken through, such as the constitutional acknowledgement—in Ba'thist Iraq of all places-that the society was binational (Arab and Kurdish), generally an all but explicit acknowledgment of bitter debate. But even in these rare cases, difference is apparent but not addressed. The Iraqi constitutional provision recognising Kurdish national identity was hardly implemented in a way that satisfied Kurdish concerns—indeed, it did not prevent the Iraqi government from suppressing Kurdish national expressions in the harshest possible ways.

THEORY AND PRACTICE IN IRAN, AFGHANISTAN AND IRAQ

Yet the truly constitutive constitutions written in the region—those that are not simply designed to rearrange the existing order—show a very different and far more tumultuous history. Contests among particular groups, ethnic politics and jockeying for position and power play a far greater role than abstract deliberations about the appropriate goals for the community. Even when general societal principles are debated—and they are—contests take a form of short-term maneouvering that make them difficult to distinguish from the other confused tactical political manipulations occurring.

In Iran in 1979, the constitution was written just as a very diverse revolutionary coalition was coming to power and (in the process) coming apart. The initial drafting begun by members of the revolutionary coalition was dominated by more liberal forces who sought to update Iran's 1906–07 basic laws and move them in a republican direction. The constitutional architecture more closely resembled France's Fifth Republic than any previous system of government in the Islamic world.[6] Very little institutional basis was given to any form of Islamic republic, though the Islamic elements of the earlier constitution, described more fully in Arjomand's chapter, were retained. Nevertheless, when presented with the draft, Khomeini indicated his assent. Presumably his attitude was informed by a realistic understanding of the role of such documents in the history not only of Iran but also its neighbours: constitutions were expressions of power relations but not constitutive of them; the most fateful decisions concerning the Iranian political order were no more to be made in a constitutional text than they were in the design of the flag.

Yet constitutionalist leaders in Iran viewed constitutions as emanating from the popular will and therefore insisted that the draft, however laudable, be submitted to a constituent assembly. While leaders from the *ulema* resisted this idea, a compromise was finally agreed in which a smaller body would be elected to edit the draft. That process resulted in radical changes, however. The body elected was dominated by members of the *ulema* enthusiastic about practical application of the *shari'a* and institutional expression of Khomeini's conception of *wilayat al-faqih*.[7]

In Afghanistan in 2002, the process of drafting a new constitution began outside the country—this time in Bonn, where a large number of

[6] See SA Arjomand, 'Authority in Shi'ism and Constitutional Developments in the Islamic Republic of Iran' in W Ende and R Brunner (eds), *The Twelver Shia in Modern Times: Religious Culture and Political History* (Leiden, Brill, 2001).
[7] This account is based primarily on Arjomand, above n 6; Shaul Bakhash, *The Reign of the Ayatollahs* (New York, Basic Books, 1984); Said Arjomand, *The Turban for the Crown* (New York, Oxford University Press, 1988); and Asghar Schirazi, *The Constitution of Iran: Politics and the State in the Islamic Republic* (London, IB Tauris, 1997). The interpretation here follows Arjomand's in spirit most closely.

Afghan political leaders gathered in a grand national assembly. The Bonn conference established general constitutional principles, but the drafting itself was left to a constitutional commission that operated largely out of public view. While it held a large number of workshops to discuss constitutional issues, various drafts and documents were not publicly vetted. In January 2004, the final draft was approved by a national assembly meeting in Kabul. The process is expertly discussed by Barnett Rubin in chapter 7; for the purposes of this chapter, it is sufficient to note that the process was international, inclusive but also fairly opaque.

The Iraqi constitutional process had a far more torturous and contested history than the Iranian and the Afghan. Unlike the Afghan, it began within the country, but only after a foreign invasion. In 2003, an American-led force toppled the Iraqi government and quickly established a Coalition Provisional Authority (CPA) to rule in its stead. After an awkward silence of some months concerning the occupation's purpose and duration, the CPA announced in the summer of 2003 that it would move to transfer full legal authority to an Iraqi government as soon as a constitution could be put into operation. The Iraqi Governing Council (IGC)—a body of Iraqi leaders appointed by the CPA but recognised by a United Nations Security Council Resolution—was assigned the task of producing an appropriate procedure. But the IGC proved too nervous, divided, weak and slow to move decisively on the matter. The CPA's desire for an abbreviated process (especially as a series of insurgencies took root), Iraq's inchoate political environment and the belief that Islamists would do well in elections, led the CPA to press the IGC into signing an agreement on 15 November 2003 that provided for an expedited transitional process. Under that agreement, the IGC would write a 'transitional administrative law' (TAL) to govern the country while a constitution was written. The IGC and CPA would then dissolve and Iraq would be governed by an assembly that was initially to be selected in vaguely defined caucuses rather than direct elections. That assembly would oversee elections, however, for a body that would write a permanent constitution.[8]

Yet the CPA's desire to avoid quick elections sparked deep suspicions that it sought to dominate the entire process and early drafts of the TAL did little to allay such suspicions. Under intense pressure, the caucus system was scrapped and the final draft of the TAL provided for a popularly-elected assembly that would write the country's permanent constitution. The TAL left many matters related to the interim government overseeing the process unclear. But it did provide for a popularly-elected assembly that would write a constitution. It also established an ambitious timetable: the permanent constitution was to be drafted by 15 August 2005.

[8] 'Timeline to a Sovereign, Democratic, and Secure Iraq', www.iraqcoalition.org/government/ AgreementNov15.pdf (accessed 3 June 2007).

An assembly elected in January 2005 decided to assign the initial drafting to a committee of 55 parliamentarians. But since Iraq's Sunni Arab population had largely boycotted the elections, they had few representatives on the committee. Early drafting efforts therefore consisted largely of efforts by secular Kurdish separatist parties to reach an accommodation with religious Shi'i parties. Under intense external pressure, the parliament agreed to appoint some Sunni Arabs to the committee. Yet as the deadline neared—and with the Americans pressing heavily for the committee to meet the deadline-the bargaining process returned to one in which Shi'i and Kurdish leaders dominated in a series of informal meetings. When a final draft was produced, it turned out to be late, full of ambiguities and of dubious legality. (Actually, its legality in terms of the TAL was worse than dubious: the way the constitution was written and approved blatantly contradicted the TAL's meagre requirements: the constitution was never approved by the parliament, for instance, and anonymous officials made a series of changes even after the draft had been proclaimed as final.) While the constitution was approved in a referendum in October 2005, it did not represent an Iraqi national consensus so much as it was a simple bargain between Kurdish and religious Shi'i leaders-as Andrew Arato makes clear in chapter 8.[9]

The Iranian, Afghan and Iraqi constitutional processes share three elements in common. First, they were all ad hoc, improvised and revised in response to the shifting pressures of a chaotic political environment. The most clearly articulated procedure, in Iraq, was also the one most obviously violated. In all three cases, the process was negotiated and renegotiated, sometimes up to the final moments before the document was finalised.

Secondly, not only were the processes confused, so were most of the actors. In all cases, the major actors generally had some idea of where they wanted to lead the country but no firm ideas on how to get there. General strategic concerns were married to unstable, shifting and often misguided tactics.

Thirdly, even though the situation and many of the actors were confused, the stakes were very high: in one case (Iraq), the very existence of the state was at issue with one significant set of parties (the Kurds) viewing national unity as an undesirable outcome which they would accept only in return for significant concessions. In the two other cases (Iran and Afghanistan) the

[9] For analyses of the drafting process, see A Arato, 'From Interim to Permanent Constitution in Iraq', www.law.nyu.edu/kingsburyb/fall05/globalization/Arato_Interim_Iraq.pdf (accessed 3 June 2007); International Crisis Group, 'Unmaking Iraq: a Constitutional Process Gone Awry' http://www.crisisgroup.org/library/documents/middle_east__north_africa/iraq_iran_gulf/b19_unmaking_iraq_a_constitutional_process_gone_awry.pdf, (accessed 3 June 2007); Jonathan Morrow, 'Iraq's Constitutional Process II: an Opportunity Lost', United States Institute of Peace Special Report, www.usip.org/pubs/specialreports/sr155.pdf (accessed 3 June 2007); and NJ Brown, 'Iraq's Constitutional Conundrum', Carnegie Endowment for International Peace, www.carnegieendowment.org/files/brown8_314.pdf (accessed 3 June 2007).

country's borders were the only fixed element in political reconstruction: everything else was contested.

Yet the constitutional process was not simply confused; it showed little focus on questions of long-term public interest: participants were consumed with short-term manoeuvering and particular interests. This was most obviously the case in two respects.

First, ethnicity played a significant role in all three efforts at political reconstruction. In Iran, regionalist and non-Persian ethnic groups saw the revolution as an opportunity to pursue the regional and ethnic autonomy that had been denied them under the pre-revolutionary regime; in some cases, such issues were connected with religious disputes as well. The new constitution denied them much protection, however, and the post-revolutionary regime revealed itself to be every bit as centralising in its inclination as its predecessor. In Afghanistan, the constitution was written in a context in which decentralisation was a fact if not an ideology; ethnic and religious divisions were also relevant as previously subordinate groups sought some constitutional protection. Constitution drafting offered an opportunity for regional and other leaders to bargain directly with each other and with the central government about distributing power and government positions. In Iraq, Kurdish leaders bargained hard over the degree of autonomy to be granted to their regional government, the status of their own militias, the fate of Kirkuk (a city of mixed population in an oil-rich area), and the mechanisms for adoption of the permanent constitution. The outcome in all of these issues was detailed, confusing and sometimes tortured compromise language that deferred disputes just as much as it settled them.

A second indication of the short-term and partisan nature of the bargaining is displayed in the distribution of authority among several offices. In two of the three cases, offices were designed with particular individuals in mind, and in the third case the distribution of authority still reflected the short-term interest of particular parties. In Iran, supporters of Khomeini wrote him by name into the constitution, taking advantage of revolutionary passions to enshrine their leader in a position of immense political authority. In Afghanistan, the supporters of the president, Hamid Karzai, were more bashful but still ensured that the presidency was a significant office; they succeeded in eliminating the position of prime minister in last-minute manoeuvering over the final text. Only Iraq escaped the design of institutions around personalities, but even there, short-term interests significantly shaped the authorities granted specific institutions. The TAL created a three-member presidency council (with the assumption that it would have a Shi'i, a Sunni and a Kurdish member) required to act unanimously because of Kurdish fears of being subordinated. And it also insulated security issues and the relations with the United States from Iraqi institutions. The permanent constitution reversed these decisions, but, in a last-minute concession to the interim president, maintained the presidency council for the first parliamentary term, allowing it to continue to exercise its veto over legislation for the first parliamentary term.

This does not mean that there was no consideration given to general public interests. But when public interest appeared, it did so in a manner that was far from any idealised image of rational deliberation. Instead, such debates tended to take two forms: passionate but symbolic arguments about fundamental issues; and hard-headed bargaining about specific formulas that ultimately reflected not so much consensus as eagerness to reach a deal. This was most notably the case with Islam.

On the one hand, all the countries involved witnessed very wide-ranging debates about the appropriate relationship between Islam and the constitutional order. For some, Islam's legal aspects trumped all human attempts to write laws and should be given supreme status; for others, Islam should form the basis of the ordinary legal order; and for still others, Islam should be viewed primarily as a matter of faith rather than of law. A large number of other positions were developed. Yet, with the exception of Iran, very little of this debate moved past the symbolic level to focus on concrete political institutions.

Even in Iran in 1979, it was unclear how the various constitutional provisions for implementing an Islamic polity would actually operate. In Iran there was much less bargaining and the final draft showed that far greater attention had been paid to devising structures that would realise the vision of an Islamic government. But even in Iran, the Islamic elements were contested and co-existed with a large number of republican elements. As the drafting progressed, Islamist forces increasingly gained the upper hand and the result was a process that reflected less the bargained outcomes and more the imposed will of religious forces. But the decline in bargaining did not result in a defeat of ambiguity: it remained unclear how many of the structures devised would operate in practice. The Iranian constitutional system proclaimed a series of principles ranging from the democratic to the theocratic. It called for institutions that had never existed before (such as a theocratic leader with vaguely defined but potentially sweeping oversight powers) and transformed others (such as a council to ensure conformity of laws with the Islamic *shari'a* and the constitution). Nobody could be certain how these institutions would work, and they did indeed work in unexpected ways. Even more remarkable was the real way that religious authority, held by Khomeini himself until his death, did not even operate within the boundaries of the constitutional system-as leader, Khomeini certainly did not exercise many of his latent authorities but also moved outside of them to contain the tensions they created. It was not until the end of his life that an effort was made to resolve the institutional tensions and textual ambiguities.[10]

---

[10] See Arjomand, above n 6 and Schirazi, above n 7.

In the other two countries, very heated debates attracted international attention but rarely moved past the level of general formulas and slogans; neither in Afghanistan nor Iraq was serious sustained attention to institutional design given in the debates over Islam. Thus, when the constitutional texts were written, therefore, drafters managed to develop formulas that very different parties could all find acceptable. The texts did not so much resolve or even clarify debates as obscure and defer them.

The Afghan Constitution omitted all mention of the Islamic *shari'a* by name but in its third article barred laws that violated Islamic beliefs or provisions (*ahkam*, a word that might also be translated as rulings and is difficult to interpret as other than a reference to Islamic law). In this way every party, even those most suspicious of religious clauses (perhaps most notably the international overseers of the constitutional process), could congratulate themselves as having forestalled a religious state; more religiously-inclined figures could accept a text that appeared to restrain the positive legal order by divine injunctions as interpreted by generations of jurists. Little of the analysis and debate over institutional matters (that is, over who would interpret and apply this constitutional language) seeped outside the circles of technical experts.

The Iraqi Constitution offered the most tortured phrasing, showing every sign of having been drafted by a committee responding to contentious parties. Article 2 proclaims:

> First: Islam is the official religion of the State and it is a fundamental source of legislation:
> A. No law may be legislated that contradicts the fixed elements of the rulings [*ahkam*] of Islam.
> B. No law may be legislated that contradicts the principles of democracy.
> C. No law may be legislated that contradicts the basic rights and freedoms provided for in this Constitution.
> Second: This Constitution guarantees the protection of the Islamic identity of the majority of the Iraqi people and guarantees all religious rights to all individuals, such as Christians, Yazidis, and Mandean Sabeans to freedom of creed and religious practices.[11]

The outcome is thus not a collective decision on the role for Islam in the political community but a series of phrases that veer back and forth between a secular and religious regime without any attention to the institutions that might sort out the various promises made by the document. Only one practical matter received any attention at all—the Supreme Federal Court, which was designated as having responsibility for interpreting the

[11] I have translated Article 2 based on the text of the Iraqi Constitution published by the Iraq Foundation, available at www.iraqfoundation.org/projects/constitution/arabicconstitution_unsept1505.doc (accessed 3 June 2007).

constitution. The Court itself was already a strange hybrid (combining an American name with many of the duties of a German-style specialised constitutional court) before it was dragged into the disputes over religion. But those who took strong positions on such issues did realise the Court could be a critical structure for giving meaning to the vague provisions they had hammered out. In a sense, the constitution's drafters acknowledged that they had deferred debates but having done so they then began to debate whether religious authorities could serve as judges on the court. And once again, they struck an awkward bargain: the final draft allowed but did not require experts in Islamic jurisprudence to serve on the Court; all other details were referred to ordinary legislation. And because such a solution would occasion a new round of bargaining over the Court law, the drafters required that the parliament pass the necessary legislation by a supermajority (essentially giving major political actors a veto over any Court law they did not like).

ATTAINING LEGITIMACY IN AN EVERYDAY POLITICAL WORLD

Politics in practice always falls short of normative or theoretical ideals. But in the case of constitutional politics, the intrusion of everyday politics is particularly troubling. Constitutional politics is supposed to establish the rules by which everyday politics operates, not be its creature. As was claimed at the outset, the normative and theoretical approaches that might inform constitutional politics in the region give no conceptual framework for sifting out good from bad bargains. What makes for a legitimate constitution in the confused conditions that prevailed in Iran, Afghanistan and Iraq? We might define a legitimate constitution as one which most political actors will accept or embrace over a prolonged period. It is difficult to assess legitimacy in all cases empirically, since the fate of the Afghani remains unclear and the Iraqi failure is so striking on many dimensions that it is not clear how much can be related to the constitutional process. The Iranian experiment has succeeded in terms of its lifespan—it has governed Iran for over a quarter century-though many of its internal contradictions have greatly complicated political life during that period.

Yet we can speculate from the drafting process what sorts of arrangements and bargains are more likely to be sustained over time. Here we can learn most from the contrasts among the three cases. The first lesson is the importance of inclusiveness. A bargaining process that includes all major actors will be far more difficult and protracted but if successful, it is likely to be viewed as one that serves the interests of all those represented. In this respect, the Afghan Constitution and the Iraqi Constitution might be seen as having positive aspects, though the Iraqi process was so rushed that the various parties might find that they have papered over differences rather than addressed them. And in both cases, there were significant problems with the selection of those actors who were involved in drafting the text. Important elements of the society remained aloof from the process. The Iranian Constitution did have some broad participation but the position of politicised clerics was so powerful that none of the other actors felt that they had a stake in the resulting product.

A second principle is publicity. Not all bargaining must take place in public, but it is not enough for broader public discussions to be limited to mere ratification; this only accords the constituents of the various bargainers the ability to accept or reject an agreement. More recent practice in many settings has been to conduct a series of local 'town meetings' to discuss constitutional issues, though it is striking how in many settings (including Iraq and Afghanistan) such discussions seemed to have little influence over those writing the text. Indeed, only the Iranian Constitution was composed in anything resembling a public process. The full contents of the Afghan and the interim Iraqi Constitutions were not released until after the documents were signed. The permanent Iraqi Constitution was modified in a process that might be charitably termed opaque right up to the time it was presented for a referendum. (Oddly, the justification for the last-minute tinkering was inclusiveness: as part of a desperate attempt to bring dissident Sunni actors into the process, they received some fairly meagre last-minute concessions.) Barring a full, boisterous and contentious discussion of all constitutional issues, it is not likely that leaders will have a good sense of where their constituencies or even their interlocutors stand. In Iran, however, publicity did have the effect of revealing to religious forces how strong they were and thus undermined inclusiveness.

The final principle is that international involvement, while often enormously helpful in sponsoring and supporting a process, can easily undermine the document's legitimacy if it becomes intrusive or even substantive. In two of the three cases, there was significant foreign participation in the constitution drafting process. In Afghanistan, the United States and the United Nations both were actively involved; in Iraq, the United States played a major role, supplemented in some less significant ways by other international actors (including Britain and the United Nations). In both countries, the international participants saw part of their role as facilitating bargaining among the parties (and indeed a significant part of that effort was simply identifying which parties should be bargaining). But there were some sharp differences between the two cases. In Iraq, American involvement was far greater but did not focus solely on facilitation. Perhaps more significantly, the United States did not simply stand outside the bargaining process in Iraq; it was very much an interested and active party seeking to shape the outcome on a host of issues—Islam, women's rights, security arrangements and transition timeline. On some of these issues, American domestic political actors played a significant role (such as in the provisions for religious freedom). Such extensive and intensive involvement cannot avoid undermining the legitimacy of the outcome. The TAL reflected the interests and preferences of the United States as much as it did those of any of the Iraqi parties, and the central bargains thus became difficult to sustain in the absence of a central American role. In the permanent constitution, the American influence over the content of the constitution receded considerably and in the final phases of drafting, the Americans focused on an inclusive process, often to the exclusion of their interest in substantive issues. But the final product was still derided by its opponents as an American imposition.

In Afghanistan, there was a far greater multilateral and facilitating role but it came in ways that made the document seem less an imposed product. In Iran, the purely domestic nature of the process was one of its primary claims to legitimacy.

None of these countries wrote its constitution on a blank slate. All three efforts took place largely as a reaction against a past in which constitutions had been an ineffective tool against (and indeed were sometimes even an expression of) authoritarianism; the determination to write a constitution that reflected long-term interests of the society as a whole, rather than the short-term interests of particular parties, was understandable. But assuming a single national interest does not create one. In one case (Iran) alternative visions were suppressed. In the other two cases, it is too soon to tell if more particular interests will find protection (though in Iraq it is difficult to avoid deep pessimism), but their involvement in the process—however unjustified by liberal or local political thought—is vital to the new constitutions' legitimacy.

It is thus not surprising that the collective practical wisdom of the set of individual experts and institutions has a sharply different tone from most writings of a normative, philosophical or scholarly bent. In this case, the practitioners have stumbled over an uncomfortable reality that many more academic writers often downplay or overlook: constitutions are very much products of the same kinds of political manoeuverings, partisan bargains, personal rivalries, shortsighted reasoning and ethnic jealousies that make up everyday politics. It is not merely the case that these aspects cannot be wholly removed; it turns out that they are essential elements of a successful constitutional process.

But here we come to the fundamental difficulty of constitution writing in such difficult contexts. Constitutions are more likely to be legitimate if the processes by which they are written are inclusive, transparent and domestically driven (at least in terms of content). The conditions that facilitate their legitimation make them difficult (and in some cases—including, quite possibly Iraq—even impossible) to write. Including every party distributes vetoes so generously that one is likely to wind up with a text that is either vacuous or not written at all. Publicity often actually maximises the difficulties. Despite the oft-cited argument that publicity privileges public-spirited argument, in practice, the opposite phenomenon has been noted by observers of democracies since the form of government was invented over two millennia ago. A political leader speaking in public often succeeds in achieving broad support to the extent that he or she can appeal to passion and short-term interest. A party or ethnic leader is far more likely to be inclined to argue that his or her group's interests were secured than ask for those interests to be sacrificed for the greater good of the society as a whole. And international involvement is often necessary to begin and guide the process. Neither Iraqis nor Afghanis would likely have written a constitution when they did without international actors taking a leading role in initiating the process.

This is not to say that constitutions should never be written. They can indeed be instruments of political reconstruction. But any successful effort must engage rather than sidestep those aspects of constitution writing that make the process so difficult.

4

The Respective Roles of Human Rights and Islam: an Unresolved Conundrum for Middle Eastern Constitutions

ANN ELIZABETH MAYER

INTRODUCTION

THIS ARTICLE REVIEWS selected constitutional developments in the Muslim Middle East in comparative perspective to assess patterns in how constitution-drafters have weighted the respective concerns of human rights and Islam over the last decades. It proposes that over the last decades, during a period when pressures to conform to international human rights law were mounting and when demands that constitutions uphold the primacy of Islamic law were also escalating, a tendency grew to treat these two factors as if they were an oppositional pair. The impression has spread that provisions securing the constitutional role of human rights tend to undermine the role of Islam and vice versa. One observes that in periods of regime change, disputes about the respective weight to be accorded to these factors are likely to be particularly intense. Due to space limitations, only a few dimensions of the tensions in this area can be covered—how provisions on Islam relate to human rights provisions concerning women's equality and religious freedom. The focus will largely be on constitutions in countries where policies on human rights and Islam have undergone dramatic reorientations and on a few models that have heretofore received relatively little attention. How these provisions typically wind up being interpreted in practice lies outside the scope of this study, but, fortunately, this topic has been covered in other scholarship.[1]

---

[1] See C Lombardi, *State Law as Islamic Law in Modern Egypt: The Incorporation of the Shari'a into Egyptian Constitutional Law* (Brill, Islamic Law and Society Series, 2006); N Brown and C Lombardi, 'Do Constitutions Requiring Adherence to Shari'a Threaten Human Rights? How Egypt's Constitutional Court Reconciles Islamic Law with the Liberal Rule of Law' (2006) 21 *American University International Law Review* 379.

AN ERA OF AGGRAVATED TENSIONS BETWEEN HUMAN
RIGHTS AND ISLAMIC LAW

Positions at odds with human rights recently articulated by various governments and ideologues can convey the impression that human rights are necessarily perceived as principles clashing with Muslims' culture. Extrapolating from this, one might surmise that in Muslim milieus, international human rights instruments have always been considered Western artifacts and have been viewed as inherently alien or objectionable on the grounds of their incompatibility with the Islamic religion.

In reality, Muslim complaints that human rights were too Western were rarely voiced at the outset of the UN human rights system. If one examines the historical record, one sees that in the period from the 1940s to the 1960s, many representatives of Muslim countries not only accepted human rights universality but also played influential and constructive roles in fashioning UN human rights instruments.[2] It was common to speak of human rights and Islam as if they self-evidently embraced similar ideals. Of course, such opinions tended to correlate with progressive, reformist interpretations of the Islamic sources.

Muslims who are more tradition-bound have continued to rely on medieval juristic readings of Islamic sources, sometimes in neo-traditional formulations that express recent political preoccupations. As social and economic transformations have unsettled old hierarchies and traditions, their resistance to liberal ideas and associated legal change has hardened. Initially, international human rights law did not attract much attention on the part of Muslims committed to retaining aspects of medieval Islamic jurisprudence. However, as international law grew in influence, they found it necessary to challenge it. Arguments were often put forward to the effect that encroaching international law was part of the inroads of Western cultural imperialism. For example, calls for banning discrimination against women could be seen both as a product of Western cultural imperialism and as a result of the influence of the Universal Declaration and other UN human rights instruments. Thus, when advocates of Islamisation urged upholding Islamic principles and resistance to Westernising influences, this could easily extend to condemnation of international human rights principles. Over the last decades, as proponents of Islamisation have increased their political influence, contestation has intensified between partisans of international human rights law and those Muslims who insist that divine law ranks higher and must be obeyed even where this entails flouting international standards, standards that they insist on identifying with an alien West even as their societies are evolving in ways that bring them closer to Western models. Such

---

[2] See the valuable discussion in SE Waltz, 'Universal Human Rights: the Contribution of Muslim States' (2004) 26 *Human Rights Quarterly* 799.

contestation now encumbers the process of constitution-drafting, and stalemates over how to rank the respective claims of human rights and Islamic law are often manifested in constitutional provisions.

The inclusion of human rights provisions in contemporary Middle Eastern constitutions reflects global forces that are compelling governments in the Middle East to make at least token gestures in their constitutions indicating that they respect human rights.[3] Increasingly, even governments with philosophies that are antithetical to constitutionalism and that are in practice deeply hostile to human rights succumb to pressures for endorsing human rights in their constitutions. Although this does not mean that the regimes involved are ready to ensure respect for human rights in practice, concessions made to demands for laws upholding human rights can start a dynamic that leads to progress in the human rights domain regardless of the original intentions of the governments involved.[4] Thus, even if offered initially as tokens, human rights provisions possess transformational potential.

Middle Eastern constitution-drafters confront a combination of external pressures and domestic demands that provides an incentive for signalling their commitment to international human rights law. Powerful Western countries criticise Middle Eastern governments for their human rights deficiencies. In UN forums, regimes face harsh public scrutiny when they submit their reports on their compliance with international standards, and this scrutiny extends to their constitutional rights provisions. Domestic human rights NGOs agitating for enhanced constitutional rights protections have proliferated throughout the Middle East. The Internet and email enable local human rights advocates to form networks with influential international human rights groups, magnifying the impact of their critiques.

At the same time that circumstances compel constitution-drafters to take human rights into account, the upsurge in political Islam since the 1970s has meant demands for both governments and constitutions to be formulated according to Islamic models. The Islamic tradition comprises a vast collection of medieval concepts and rules which, like medieval rules in other traditions, tend to restrict rights. In an era of Islamisation, medieval rules of Islamic law which have otherwise largely been left in abeyance, can be selectively resuscitated and reinterpreted to suit agendas of regimes and political factions aiming to restrict rights.

---

[3] Julian Go has noted the trend of producing constitutions upholding fundamental human rights. J Go, 'A Globalizing Constitutionalism? Views from the Postcolony 1945–2000' (2003) 18 *International Sociology* 83.

[4] Using a classification from a recent study, one could propose that, depending on their character, such changes could be classified as middle stages in the penetration of international human rights into domestic systems, stages where states make some tactical concessions or even accord human rights law prescriptive status. Only in the final stage do states actually change their behaviour to conform to international human rights law. See T Risse, SC Ropp and K Sikkink (eds), *The Power of Human Rights: International Norms and Domestic Change* (Cambridge, Cambridge University Press, 1999).

Besieged by complaints about their bad human rights performance, Middle Eastern governments have occasionally banded together in group efforts to deploy Islam to rationalise their resistance to international human rights, speaking as if their shared religious values stood between them and full acceptance of international standards. Among the most important efforts in this connection was the 1990 Cairo Declaration on Human Rights in Islam, an initiative of the Organization of Islamic Conference (OIC) that was strongly promoted by Iran and Saudi Arabia. Not surprisingly, in the guise of offering rights attuned to Islamic values, this declaration devised a hierarchy that subordinated human rights to vague, unspecified Islamic criteria, thereby stripping human rights of any force. Moreover, rights like equality for women and freedom of religion were eliminated.[5]

The 1994 Arab Charter on Human Rights proposed by the League of Arab States appeared more secular in character but constituted a related initiative, reducing the scope of rights protections and reflecting elements of the medieval Islamic tradition. As one might have expected, its deficiencies included a lack of firm guarantees for women's equality or for religious freedom. This charter was widely scorned by human rights NGOs, leading to an attempt by the Permanent Arab Commission on Human Rights in 2003 to produce a more acceptable version. This second version of the charter likewise fell short of meeting international standards, and the International Commission of Jurists (ICJ) was prompted to publish a negative assessment.[6]

The common deployment of Islam as the pretext for denying Muslims the protections of international human rights law has been strongly condemned by one of the most prominent human rights advocates in the Middle East, Iranian Nobel Laureate Shirin Ebadi. A lawyer who speaks as a believing Muslim, Ebadi takes a position that is currently endorsed by many other progressive Muslims, insisting that Islam, correctly understood, does not clash with human rights and democracy and that those who argue that it does so clash are motivated by their own political interests rather than by fidelity to genuine Islamic requirements.[7] That is, from the standpoint of Muslims like herself who see a congruence between human rights and Islamic beliefs, human rights and Islam should not be treated as an oppositional pair. Seen from their perspective, it would be possible to have

---

[5] The Cairo Declaration is available on many websites, one being www1.umn.edu/humanrts/instree/cairodeclaration.html For an assessment of this declaration in context, see generally AE Mayer 'Universal versus Islamic Human Rights: a Clash of Cultures or a Clash with a Construct?' (1994) 15 *Michigan Journal of International Law* 307.

[6] Position Paper of the International Commission of Jurists, *The Process of 'Modernising' the Arab Charter on Human Rights: a Disquieting Regression* (20 December 2003), available at www.icj.org/news.php3?id_article=3269&lang=en&print=true

[7] See eg, a recently published interview, A Pal, 'Shirin Ebadi', *The Progressive*, September 2004, available at www.progressive.org/sept04/intv0904.html

constitutional provisions affirming Islamic values—values embodying enlightened religious views—without this necessarily entailing any diminution in the scope of human rights that might be afforded elsewhere in the same constitution.

Among supporters of human rights in the Arab world, the proposition that human rights must be circumscribed by superimposed Islamic criteria is unacceptable. For example, the First International Conference of the Arab Human Rights Movement, which reflected the views of Arab human rights NGOs, produced the 1999 Casablanca Declaration, which emphatically rejected the watered-down substitutes for international human rights law that had been offered by Middle Eastern governments. The declaration included a ringing affirmation of support for international human rights law and its universality, stating that:

> (T)he only source of reference in this respect is international human rights law and the United Nations instruments and declarations. The Conference also emphasized the universality of human rights.[8]

Those who want constitutions to make unequivocal endorsements of human rights as set forth in international law see these as ways of buttressing rights and shielding them from being eviscerated by governmental deployment of overriding Islamic criteria. However, if they become engaged in drafting constitutions, they may be obliged to make certain tactical concessions and to accept provisions that show deference to Islam. They may hope that such calls for deference to Islam will be only pro forma, leaving human rights intact.

For those determined to ensure that traditional rules of Islamic law are respected, constitutional endorsements of international human rights law pose an unwelcome threat. However, in a sign that they are reluctant to expose their agendas of resorting to Islamic law to eviscerate rights, they may opt for evasive or equivocal constitutional formulations that obscure rather than advertise their intentions to strip rights of any real substance.

That is, rights provisions for Middle Eastern Constitutions are being devised at time of broad regional tensions between advocates of human rights universality and proponents of the notion that Islamic criteria must outrank all other legal standards. These factions are contending at a juncture when both sides appreciate the prudence of paying at least nominal tribute to the values espoused by their opponents. In these circumstances, it is not surprising that constitutions should exhibit many unresolved tensions regarding how to weigh the competing claims of human rights and Islam.

---

[8] Casablanca Declaration, available at www.al-bab.com/arab/docs/international/hr1999.htm

INDIGENISING CONSTITUTIONAL RIGHTS ACCORDING TO ISLAMIC
STANDARDS OR OPENING THEM TO INTERNATIONAL STANDARDS?

The Iranian case shows what happens when after a revolutionary upheaval
the government-sponsored version of Islam is accorded supremacy and
human rights are subordinated to it. Under the Shah's rule, Iran was one
of many Muslim countries that actively participated in developing the UN
human rights system. Tehran hosted the important 1968 International
Conference on Human Rights, resulting in the Teheran Proclamation,
which affirmed that the Universal Declaration of Human Rights (UDHR)
'states a common understanding of the peoples of the world concerning
the inalienable and inviolable rights of all members of the human family
and constitutes an obligation for the members of the international community'. After the Islamic Revolution, Iran's new clerical ruling elite reversed
course and produced in 1979 a purportedly 'Islamic' constitution after
rejecting pleas by some Iranian groups for including the rights set forth in
the UDHR.[9] Article 20 asserts that Iranians enjoy human rights subject to
Islamic criteria, perfectly encapsulating the new trend of turning inward
toward the Islamic tradition. In practice, the government policy of relying
on Islam as interpreted by Shi'ite clerics to curtail rights has correlated with
human rights violations on a massive scale.[10] Placing its official Islam above
human rights, Iran has discriminated against women, constrained freedom
of expression and association, crushed democratic freedoms, persecuted the
regime's critics, justified a style of criminal justice that involves cruel and
inhuman punishments, eliminated freedom of religion, executed supposed
apostates from Islam and persecuted religious minorities.

An illustration of the consequences of constitutional provisions upholding the supremacy of Islamic law at the expense of human rights came after
Iran's Parliament voted to ratify the Women's Convention. This vote was
overridden on 12 August 2003, by the Council of Guardians. According
to Article 94 of Iran's Constitution, the Council can block proposed legislation that it deems to be in conflict with Islam or with the constitution.
In the case of the Women's Convention, which calls for eliminating all
forms of discrimination against women, the Council ruled that ratification
would violate both Islamic law and the constitution. Thus, an attempt by
the elected representatives of the Iranian people to incorporate women's
international human rights in Iranian law was thwarted by constitutional
provisions prioritising upholding Islamic law. In the aftermath, Mahboobeh
Abbasgholizadeh, a prominent feminist and women's rights activist, pre-
dicted that women's rights could only be achieved if the constitution were

[9] S Bakhash, *The Reign of the Ayatollahs* (New York, Basic Books, 1984) 77–8.
[10] See R Afshari, *Human Rights in Iran: the Abuse of Cultural Relativism* (Philadelphia,
University of Pennsylvania Press, 2001).

altered.[11] Not surprisingly, Iranians hungry for progress in the human rights domain have clamoured for replacing Iran's 1979 Islamic Constitution by one that offers human rights unclouded by overriding Islamic conditions.

In reaction against the policies of Iran's clerical hardliners, there has been a mounting groundswell of popular support for devising a secular constitution and for upholding rights as stipulated in the UDHR. That is, clerical abuse of the Islamic elements in Iran's Constitution has provoked a backlash that means that, when and if they are given the chance to choose, Iranians will in all likelihood endorse including international human rights standards in any new constitution. As the Iranian example shows, although the idea of Islamic constitutionalism may have potent appeal in the abstract, in practice Muslims may chafe under a constitution where Islamic criteria override human rights.

The Moroccan case embodies a strikingly different trend, providing an illustration of how an endorsement of international human rights law in a constitution, without provisions requiring deference to Islamic law, may correlate with trends favourable for human rights. Such a move signals that, at least at the time of the constitution-drafting, there is some support for opening the domestic system to the influence of international standards which, in the Middle Eastern context, are inevitably far more protective of rights than are the local standards.

When King Hassan II changed the wording of the Preamble to the Moroccan Constitution in 1992, the results illustrated the potential significance of referring to international human rights law. The rewording was actually a harbinger of a peaceful revolution that would vastly expand Moroccans' rights and freedoms. After the change the Preamble provided, among other things, that Morocco reaffirmed its attachment to human rights 'as they are universally recognised'.[12] This affirmation of Morocco's attachment to 'universally recognised' human rights, which was not qualified by any affirmation of a commitment to adhere to Islamic principles, suggested that Morocco was reorienting its human rights policies.[13] For the optimists, it hinted that Morocco might back away from its former practice of appealing to Islamic particularism as an excuse for its non-compliance with women's international human rights, a practice that feminists had condemned.

The following period witnessed a remarkable turnaround in Morocco's human rights policies. Attempting a difficult transition from a repressive

---

[11] Nazila Fathi, 'Iranian Women Defy Authority to Protest Sex Discrimination', *New York Times*, 13 June 2005, A8.

[12] Moroccan Constitution, available at www.oefre.unibe.ch/law/icl/mo00000_.html

[13] I offered an assessment of this change as it was occurring in AE Mayer, 'Moroccans: citizens or subjects?' (1993) 26 *New York University Journal of International Law and Politics* 63.

monarchical system to something along the lines of a Spanish-style constitutional monarchy, Morocco, which has long afforded more religious freedom than is common in Arab countries, has moved into the forefront of Arab countries pursuing measures designed to advance human rights and democracy.

In 2003 dramatic reforms advancing women's rights in the family were undertaken under the auspices of King Muhammad VI, who came to the throne in 1999. The King pressed the reforms in the face of a vigorous Islamist opposition that insisted that enhanced rights for women clashed with Islamic law and whose large popular following potentially menaced the survival of the Moroccan monarchy. Not coincidentally, the king in a 1999 speech had already publicly asserted that there was no contradiction between Islam and human rights, expressly rejecting the notion that human rights clashed with a real or supposed cultural specificity.[14] That is, the king, a descendant of the Prophet and within Morocco the official arbiter of what Islam requires, sided with progressive Muslims who interpret their religion as encompassing human rights, thereby reminding the world that human rights and Islam—so often treated as inherently opposed—could be blended and harmonised.

The contrasting developments in Iran and Morocco suggest that using the constitution to establish a self-contained 'Islamic' system of rights correlates with policies undermining human rights. They also give grounds for concluding that, in the proper circumstances, adopting a constitutional reference to international human rights law may correlate with a transition to policies of strengthening human rights and freeing them of Islamic restrictions.

MIDDLE EASTERN SECULAR SOCIALIST CONSTITUTIONAL MODELS AND HOW THE EROSION OF SECULARISM AFFECTED RIGHTS PROVISIONS

To gain some perspective on how unstable and how mutable constitutional provisions assigning roles to human rights and Islam have been, it is useful to review the fate of constitutions in Somalia and Yemen, two countries with turbulent histories that have been battlegrounds for secular and Islamist ideologies. In the 1960s and 1970s, both governments were shaped by Marxism, only to be destabilised when powerful Islamist currents altered the political landscape. In the era when Marxist ideologies flourished, some Middle Eastern constitutions relegated Islam to a marginal role and invoked international human rights with little or no deference being shown to Islamic tradition. These secular experiments provoked a

---

[14] 'Mohammed VI renouvelle son engagement en faveur des droits de l'homme', *Agence France Presse*, 10 December 1999, available in LEXIS, Allwld File.

backlash, and later political shifts led to constitutional models where the balance tilted sharply in favour of Islamisation.

With Marxist ideals triumphant, Somalia and the southern part of Yemen adopted constitutions that were imbued with socialist ideals. The constitutions of both countries were produced in the wake of successful anti-colonial struggles that led to achieving independence from their former European masters. Somalis had been divided by the boundary separating British Somaliland and Italian-dominated Somalia. The two achieved independence and united in 1960 to form one Somalia, only to see Somaliland much later go its separate way in 1991 after the country disintegrated. In southern Yemen, in 1967 the beleaguered British withdrew from their protectorate and their colony in Aden, leading to independence for what would later be called the People's Democratic Republic of Yemen (PDRY). Until 1990, when the PDRY united with the Yemen Arab Republic, its conservative northern neighbour, the two had a tense and conflict-ridden relationship.

As the Turkish precedent shows, after a triumph in a struggle for independence, there can be a moment when the potency of nationalist ideology trumps Islamic traditions and enables a secular system to take root. However, even in circumstances highly favourable to secularism, both Somalia and the PDRY felt the need to placate Islamic loyalties by establishing Islam as the state religion. Islam was made the state religion in Article 3 of the Somali Constitutions of 1960[15] and 1979[16] and in Article 47 of the 1978 PDRY Constitution.[17] However, in context, this kind of nominal establishment did not correlate with general state policies of following Islamic law.

While upholding the conventional idea that in a Muslim country Islam must be established as the state religion, these constitutions (with variations in wording) treated the UDHR as a model. Article 7 of the 1960 Somali Constitution stated: 'The laws of the Somali Republic shall comply, insofar as applicable with the principles of the UDHR'. In the 1979 Constitution, this provision was moved to Article 19 and slightly reworded to read: 'The Somali Democratic Republic shall recognise the Universal Declaration of Human Rights and generally accepted rules of international law'. Article 10.a of the 1978 Constitution of the PDRY provided that the state would work 'in accordance with the principles of the United Nations, the Universal Declaration of Human Rights and the generally recognised rules of international law'.

---

[15] 'Constitution of the Somali Republic' in A Blaustein and GH Flanz (eds), *Constitutions of the Countries of the World* (Dobbs Ferry, Oceana Publications, 1961).

[16] 'Constitution of the Somali Democratic Republic' in A Blaustein and GH Flanz (eds), *Constitutions of the Countries of the World* (Dobbs Ferry, Oceana Publications, 1981).

[17] 'Constitution of the People's Democratic Republic of Yemen' in A Blaustein and GH Flanz (eds), *Constitutions of the Countries of the World* (Dobbs Ferry, Oceana Publications, 1986).

It is interesting to examine how Marxist regimes that felt obliged to make Islam the state religion chose to deal with the problem of devising provisions governing religious freedom. Of course, in Muslim countries dominated by Marxist leaders, there was a delicate problem; as proponents of a secular ideology with only thin support, the leaders would be exposed to charges of apostasy and/or atheism. Despite being hostile to religion, a Marxist ruling clique would therefore want to have protections for freedom of belief or conscience placed in the constitution to accommodate secular beliefs, while remaining wary of antagonising the populace at large by including provisions that could prompt charges that the government was condoning apostasy from Islam or that it was endorsing atheism.

The PDRY 1978 Constitution deals with the delicate issue of the role of Islam in an unusual way. Normally, provisions enshrining Islam are placed among the first articles of a constitution. In the PDRY case, the provision is set in an inconspicuous place in Article 47. That article provides:

> Islam is the state religion.
> The freedom of faith in other religions is guaranteed.
> The state shall protect the freedom of religious faith and of beliefs in accordance with the observed customs provided it accords with the principles of the Constitution.

It is worth noting that the provision that Islam is the state religion appears not as a separate article but in the context of the treatment of basic rights and duties of the citizens. The ramifications of the principle establishing Islam are thereby limited, especially since it is juxtaposed with affirmations of freedom of belief in other religions and freedom of religious faith and belief. However, to avoid clashing with Islamic law, there is no affirmation of freedom of religion in a manner that would guarantee the right to change religion.

Not only did Article 47 offer these affirmations, but it set forth a hierarchy of norms in which constitutional principles seemed to outrank religious ones. This article qualifies freedom of religious belief by saying that this protection accords with 'observed customs', customs that ordinarily would comprise limitations on such freedom imposed by Islamic law. But then, the 'observed customs' appear to be overridden by the final provision, which says that the state protects this freedom in accordance 'with the principles of the Constitution'. Although this article, like many crucial constitutional articles purporting to sort out the relationship of Islam to other constitutional principles, is less clear than readers would wish, it ultimately suggests that, where religious freedom is concerned, the constitution supersedes conflicting customs and Islamic traditions. This contrasts with Article 20 in the Iranian Constitution, which explicitly makes Islamic law supreme regarding rights issues.

In the 1978 PDRY Constitution, the human rights provisions are unusually extensive by Middle Eastern standards. Especially significant are the unequivocal and repeated endorsements of women's equality in rights and affirmations of the state's commitment to take steps to support women's equality. Affirmations of women's equality carry the implication that Islamic law is being displaced from the area of personal status law, the area where it is most deeply rooted. Article 27 provides that 'the law shall regulate the family relations on the basis of equality between man and woman in their rights and duties'. Article 35 provides: 'All citizens are equal in their rights and duties irrespective of their sex, origin, religion, language, standard of education or social status. All persons are equal before the law'. Article 36 provides:

> The state shall ensure equal rights for men and women in all fields of life, the political, economic and social, and shall provide the necessary conditions for the realisation of that equality.

These express and unequivocal guarantees constitute rare exceptions to the general pattern of obscurity in provisions on women's rights in Middle Eastern constitutions, which are normally designed to allow for discrimination against women while using formulations that seek to cloak this aim.

In a similar vein, the 1960 Somali Constitution in Article 3 guaranteed equal rights and duties before the law, specifically providing that this was without distinction as to sex. However, where freedom of religion was concerned, the Somali provision was more cautious. Article 29 asserted:

> Every person shall have the right to freedom of conscience and freely to profess his own religion and to worship it subject to limitations which may be prescribed by law for the public health or order. However, it shall not be permissible to spread or propagandise any religion other than the religion of Islam.

The peculiar terminology and the failure to provide squarely for 'freedom of religion' suggests that, despite the earlier reference to the UDHR, this article did not aim to provide the safeguards of international law. The vague qualifications on freedom of conscience and free profession of religion and worship seem secular and might be ascribed to the Marxist rulers' wish to have principles that could be invoked to curb religion. However, barring attempts to make conversions to religions other than Islam shows leaders making concessions to *shari'a* rules. This determination to ban future missionary efforts may have been prompted by memories of Christian attempts to win Somali converts during the era of European colonisation.

Changes in the 1979 Somali Constitution evinced a new willingness to abandon the previous compromise language and to provide not only unqualified freedom of belief in any religion but also freedom of conscience more generally. Article 31 stated: 'Every person shall be entitled to profess any religion or creed'. Article 6 continued the principle established in the 1960 Constitution of providing for equality in rights and duties regardless of sex. That is, as in the case of the PDRY Constitution, by 1979 Somali socialist ideology trumped Islamic law in crucial rights provisions notwithstanding the pro forma establishment of Islam as the state religion, and the result was an expanded scope of rights.

How the consequences of Islamisation for Iran's Islamic constitution have generated a pro-secular backlash has been noted, but excesses in the other direction have likewise provoked popular anger. In an era when support for Islamisation was mounting, the secular Somali Constitution of Siad Barre's harsh Marxist regime generated a backlash, as events showed after his overthrow in 1991.

What had formerly been British Somaliland sought to win recognition as an independent state and composed a draft constitution that was approved by referendum in 2001. This constitution included an unusual feature—a specific attack on the previous constitution. In the Preamble, which begins with an invocation of Allah, one reads a complaint about the unsuitability of secular constitutionalism, complaining that Somalis had 'experienced the dire consequences of the application of a constitution not grounded on the nation's beliefs, culture and aspirations, as was the case for a period of thirty years'. That is, anger over past infusions of Marxist ideology engendered demands for a new constitution that would affirm Somali cultural specificity. As part of this anti-secular reaction, the proposed constitution of Somaliland,[18] in Article 5, effectively made the state into a vehicle for implementing Islamic law and promoting Islam, including also an express prohibition of proselytising for other faiths:

5.1 Islam is the religion of the nation, and the promotion of any religion in the territory of Somaliland, other than Islam, is prohibited.
5.2 The laws of the nation shall be grounded on, and shall not be valid if they are contrary to, Islamic Sharia.
5.3 The state shall promote religious tenets (religious affairs), and shall fulfil Sharia principles and discourage immoral acts and reprehensible behaviour.[19]

However, this embrace of Islamisation did not mean that Somaliland was following the route of Iran, where Islamisation had correlated with blocking the influence of international law on constitutional rights provisions. Despite the call for laws to be based on and conform to Islamic law, this draft constitution at the same time specifically promised to abide by the UDHR, providing in Article 10.2 that Somaliland 'recognises and shall act

[18] The country has so far struggled unsuccessfully to win international recognition as a state or to obtain UN membership.
[19] The Revised Constitution of the Republic of Somaliland, available at www.somalilandforum. com/somaliland/constitution/revised_constitution.htm

in conformity with the United Nations Charter and with international law, and shall respect the Universal Declaration of Human Rights'.

In what is a potentially important development, Article 21.2 states:

> The articles which relate to fundamental rights and freedoms shall be interpreted in a manner consistent with the international conventions on human rights and international laws referred to in this Constitution.

By mandating reference to UN instruments in interpreting rights, the constitution of Somaliland indirectly precludes recourse to Islamic law to curtail the scope of rights. How this is to be reconciled with what seems to be the state's conflicting duty to fulfil *shari'a* principles is left open to speculation.

In terms of specific rights provisions, Article 8 seems to adhere to international standards on women's rights, affirming the equal rights and obligations of all citizens, with a ban on according any precedence on the basis of categories that include gender. In contrast, Article 33 fails to offer a straightforward affirmation of the right to freedom of religion. Instead, with an express reference to *shari'a* rules barring Muslims from abjuring their faith, it stated:

> Every person shall have the right to freedom of belief, and shall not be compelled to adopt another belief. Islamic *Shari'a* does not accept that a Muslim person can renounce his beliefs.

Thus, the constitution of Somaliland provides a distinctive model of drafters struggling inconclusively with the problem of balancing international human rights law and Islamic law. Unless Islam is reconceived along progressive lines, it is not possible to reconcile the Article 5.2 provisions that laws should be based on *shari'a* and that they should be invalidated if clashing with *shari'a*, on the one hand, with the commitments to following international human rights law in Articles 10.2 and 21.2, on the other. The support in Article 33 for the ban on abjuring Islam cannot be reconciled with provisions elsewhere supporting international human rights standards. The fact that the drafters preferred to place naked self-contradictions in the text reveals the extent to which they felt simultaneously pulled in opposing directions by calls for Islamisation and calls for respecting the UDHR.

The evolution of the constitutions drafted for the rival Yemens and for the unitary state that was created by their eventual reunification in 1990 also merits review. As in Somalia, political turbulence afflicted the Yemens, and frequent upheavals meant that the constitutional roles assigned to human rights and Islam underwent repeated modifications.

The contrast between the Marxist PDRY constitution and the constitution of the Yemen Arabic Republic (YAR), promulgated after a bloody civil war concluded in 1970, could not be more striking. Unlike the PDRY, the northern part of the country had not been colonised by Europeans but had been traumatised by a civil war in which Egypt and Saudi Arabia had supported rival factions. Underlining its Islamic orientation, the YAR Constitution begins with four Qur'anic verses and includes in its preambular language yet another Qur'anic verse. The Preamble treats Islam as a central component of Yemen's identity, asserting that Yemenis will have 'no life to live ... except through our true Islamic religion ... and through following its divine guidance, achieving its precepts, abiding by its directions and strictures, and by remaining within its bounds'.[20] Article 1 establishes Yemen as an 'Arab Islamic state', and Article 2 makes Islam the state religion.

There is only the barest hint of concern for human rights; the end of the Preamble refers to 'solidarity with all nations who believe in human rights' and calls for creating 'a Yemeni popular democracy on the basis of equality in rights and obligations between citizens'. These suggest that the Yemeni system may have some affinity for human rights and democracy. However, as is typical in constitutions where the Islamic elements predominate, the specific provisions for rights turn out to be feeble. There is no provision for freedom of religion or belief. The treatment of women's rights makes a striking contrast to the unqualified endorsements of women's equality in the PDRY Constitution. Article 34 provides:

> Women are the sisters of men. They have their mandatory rights and obligations as stipulated in the *Shari'ah* and in accordance with the law.

This is a classic example of a provision that might look innocuous to many readers but that actually aims to preclude women from challenging discriminatory Islamic rules, indirectly ratifying the disabilities peculiar to women under Islamic law. For example, in Islamic law, a sister is entitled to only one-half the share of inheritance that her brother takes, so what may seem a benign affirmation of the sibling relationship under Islamic law in fact opens the door to subjecting women to harshly discriminatory treatment. The harmful impact that providing separately for the rights of women—as opposed to men—being governed by *shari'a* law can have is shown by the consequences of adopting an analogous provision in Article 21 of the 1979 Iranian Constitution, which correlated with stripping women of the expanded rights that they had won under the progressive reforms in family law enacted under the last Shah.

However, there is also an indication that this was a contested provision; almost hidden at the end of the section on 'Public Rights and Obligations' one finds Article 43, which bars the state from imposing 'distinction in

---

[20] 'Constitution of the Yemen Arab Republic' in A Blaustein and GH Flanz (eds), *Constitutions of the Countries of the World* (Dobbs Ferry, Oceana Publications, 1971).

human rights' based on several categories, including sex. If taken at face value, this could mean that women's rights 'in accordance with the law' in Article 34 might comprise the Article 43 ban on distinctions based on sex, a ban that dovetails with relevant principles of international law barring discrimination. As often happens, the YAR Constitution provides no mechanism for reconciling what appear to be clashing provisions on the respective roles of human rights and Islam.

The draft constitution of 1990, issued at the time of the unification of the two Yemens, represented a tentative blend of incompatible constitutional traditions from the conservative north and Marxist south. For example, the Article 3 provision that *shari'a* law is 'the main source of legislation' accords a central role to Islamic jurisprudence, which would predictably lead to curtailing human rights.[21] This stipulation was difficult to reconcile with the former PDRY provision that the state would work in accordance with the UDHR, which was included in Article 5 of the 1990 draft. That all the PDRY provisions providing firm safeguards for women's rights were eliminated from the 1990 draft constitution suggested which way trends were heading, but Article 27 did bar discrimination based on several categories, including sex. No provision for freedom of religion was included.

This tentative draft was soon replaced in 1994 by the final constitution of the reunified country, which again contained conflicting provisions on human rights and Islam. Article 6 provided that the state 'shall abide' by the UN Charter, the UDHR and the universally recognised rules of international law. In contrast, other provisions were modelled on those in the 1970 YAR Constitution, including Articles 1 and 2, calling the new country an Arab Islamic state and making Islam the state religion. The position of Islamic law was greatly enhanced by Article 3, which, with no effort to explain how this would fit with the commitment to abide by the UDHR, made the ambitious claim that *shari'a* would be 'the source of all legislation'.[22]

The family is, according to Article 26, 'based on religion, morality, and love of the homeland', implying that Islamic law will apply to personal status matters. Roughly approximating Article 19 of the 1970 YAR Constitution, Article 31 provides that: 'Women are akin to men having rights and obligations as demanded by the *Shari'ah* and stipulated by law', which permits using *shari'a* criteria to curb women's rights. Thus, when in Article 40 one encounters: 'All citizens shall have equal rights and obligations', one understands that this guarantee of equal rights will not likely be interpreted to nullify discriminatory rules of Islamic law applying to women. In a related move that shows that Article 47 of the old 1978 PDRY

[21] 'Draft Constitution of the Yemen Arab Republic' in A Blaustein and GH Flanz (eds), *Constitutions of the Countries of the World* (Dobbs Ferry, Oceana Publications, 1990).
[22] 'Constitution of the Yemen Arab Republic' in A Blaustein and GH Flanz (eds), *Constitutions of the Countries of the World* (Dobbs Ferry, Oceana Publications, 1995).

Constitution has been repudiated, no protection whatsoever is afforded for freedom of religion or freedom of conscience.

The curbs on rights that have resulted from enhancing the role of Islam in the 1994 Yemeni Constitution cannot be reconciled with UDHR principles. However, despite their tilting the balance in favour of upholding Islamic law, the drafters apparently felt that the PDRY provision on the UDHR could not be set aside, resulting in yet another constitution comprising incompatible provisions affecting human rights.

SORTING OUT THE ROLES OF HUMAN RIGHTS AND ISLAM IN THE AFGHAN CONSTITUTION AND THE IRAQI TRANSITIONAL LAW AND CONSTITUTION

The recent histories of Afghanistan and Iraq cannot be recapitulated here, but they are obviously both countries where recent political upheavals have been traumatic and where tensions between proponents and opponents of Islamisation have been particularly acute. In the last decades Afghanistan has boomeranged from a regime committed to Marxism, which governed oppressively but gave women equality, to the Taliban regime, which espoused a reactionary Islamism that required a gender apartheid system and crushed all freedom of religion. Iraq was governed for decades by a brutal Sunni military clique that pursued elements of a secular Baathist agenda, which enhanced women's participation in society. At the same time, the Shi'i majority suffered from harsh repression, and its religious leaders were targeted for persecution and assassination. Against this background of political turbulence, both countries have had to devise new constitutions after American invasion and occupation.

In the light of the previously-considered comparisons of various constitutions crafted at political turning points, one is prepared for the fact that settling on the provisions on human rights and Islam was a central problem in the work leading up to the January 2004 Constitution of the Islamic Republic of Afghanistan and the March 2004 Iraqi Transitional Administrative Law. The tortuous formulations of the relevant constitutional provisions reflect the same inconclusive struggles to define how the state's embrace of Islam would relate to human rights protections that one saw in other Middle Eastern constitutions, an indication that the American presence in Afghanistan and Iraq was not a determinative factor.

The Afghan Preamble starts out with lines that effectively treat Islam and the UDHR as pillars of the new system, stating in the first line that the constitution is written: 'With firm faith in God Almighty and relying on His lawful mercy, and Believing in the Sacred religion of Islam'.[23] Four lines below, one

---

[23] Afghanistan Constitution, available at www.oefre.unibe.ch/law/icl/af00000_.html

reads: 'Observing the United Nations Charter and respecting the Universal Declaration'. In section 8 of the Preamble human rights are stipulated as being among the goals of Afghan society—without any Islamic qualifications being added. Article 7.1 reinforces the commitment to the UDHR, providing that the state shall abide by the UN charter, international treaties, international conventions that Afghanistan has signed, and the UDHR.

At the same time, the Afghan Constitution in Article 3 advises that no law shall contravene the beliefs and provisions (*ahkām*) of the sacred religion of Islam. This provision establishes Islam as the criterion of legality. Requiring laws to satisfy Islamic criteria can have negative consequences for women's rights, because it opens the door to referring to conservative interpretations that would block laws designed to advance women's rights. True, the constitution in Article 22 bars any kind of discrimination and privilege between the citizens of Afghanistan and provides also that citizens, whether men or women, have equal rights and duties before the law. However, in the absence of constitutional provisions offering more specific and unequivocal protections against gender-based discrimination, the ability of the constitution to support women's equality is uncertain. Afghan conservatives could claim that Article 22 means that women are to be given equality in rights only to the extent permitted by traditional readings of the Islamic sources, which might allow them to have some equality in the public domain (such as voting or access to jobs) but in the private sphere would assign them subordinate roles where they would be expected to dedicate themselves to their family duties.

More than one commentator has complained about the failure to offer Afghan women specific constitutional guarantees ensuring that they would never again be treated like chattels, as they had been under the Taliban. One critic has it that:

> Where they appear, the gender-neutral terms of the Constitution on their face technically grant equal rights to both men and women; however, much more is needed in order to make equality of the two sexes a reality for Afghan women. With a checkered women's rights history and the years of almost unmentionable horror experienced by women during the Taliban regime, the Constitution should acknowledge the abuses women have suffered in its establishment of equal rights to education, employment, and freedom from other discrimination. Without acknowledging the human rights abuses against women, the Constitution does not send a strong enough message about the importance of women's rights.[24]

Although Article 2, which makes Islam the state religion, also provides that followers of other religions are free to exercise their faith and perform their

---

[24] B Roshan, 'The More Things Change, the More They Stay the Same: the Plight of Afghan Women Two Years after the Overthrow of the Taliban' (2004) 19 *Berkeley Women's Law Journal* 285.

religious rites within the limits of the provisions of law, this is far from amounting to an unconditional guarantee of freedom of religion. In sum, the inadequate protection for religious freedom and the paucity of guarantees for women's rights indicate that in drafting the constitution Islamic criteria were being referred to *sub rosa* to curtail rights, notwithstanding the textual commitment to abide by the UDHR.

References to both human rights and Islam appeared in the 2004 Iraqi Transitional Administrative Law (TAL) which was merely an interim document. Its Preamble asserted that the Iraqi people were 'affirming today their respect for international law, especially having been amongst the founders of the United Nations, working to reclaim their legitimate place among nations'.[25] In contrast to the Afghan Constitution, the TAL in Article 12 specifically barred discrimination 'on the basis of gender'.

Islam's privileged status was affirmed, but in a format where it was bundled with other provisions that muddied the implications. Article 7A provided:

> Islam is the official religion of the State and is to be considered a source of legislation. No law that contradicts the universally agreed tenets of Islam, the principles of democracy, or the rights cited in Chapter Two of this Law may be enacted during the transitional period. This Law respects the Islamic identity of the majority of the Iraqi people and guarantees the full religious rights of all individuals to freedom of religious belief and practice.

As in the case of the old PDRY constitution, the same article that established Islam also provided for freedom of religious belief. Islam was only 'a source' of legislation, leaving room for other sources of law potentially having equal status. In proposing Islam's 'universally agreed tenets' as a basic criterion of legality, Article 7A used a vague category that left the significance conjectural. Furthermore, adding the requirements that laws should *also* not conflict with democracy and rights revealed that persons opposed to Islamic curbs on rights had had some input.

The struggle to draft a final constitution proved extremely arduous, and without the enormous pressures exerted by the United States, the process might have ended in a stalemate. However, in August 2005, a text was finally prepared.[26]

One might have expected the text to follow the outlines of the recent TAL, but the treatment of international human rights law and Islam was significantly altered. The 2005 Preamble failed to replicate the TAL's preambular affirmation of Iraqis' commitment to respect international law, although

---

[25] Law of Administration for the State of Iraq for the Transitional Period, available at www. cpa-iraq.org/government/TAL.html
[26] See the *Washington Post*'s English translation, available at www.washingtonpost.com/ wp-dyn/content/article/2005/10/12/AR2005101201450.html

Article 8 did say that Iraq would respect its international obligations—a somewhat vaguer formulation. As in the TAL, where human rights and Islamic law were concerned, the 2005 Constitution resorted to listing potentially conflicting criteria. In Article 2, it made Islam a main source of legislation and provided that no law could violate the established rules of Islam, leaving open how to classify what rules were meant. It simultaneously provided that no law could violate the principles of democracy or the rights and basic freedoms outlined in the constitution. Of course, what would determine the impact of Article 2 would be who interpreted the rules of Islam. Article 90 gave the Supreme Federal Court the task of interpreting the constitution, and Article 89 provided that it would comprise a number of judges and experts in Islamic law, deferring any decision on how many would serve and how they were to be selected. If powerful Shi'ite conservatives managed to dominate the new system, the contradictions would be resolved as they had been in Iran, with Islamic law overriding the guarantees of democracy and rights.

Article 44 stated that individuals were entitled to the rights in international human rights agreements endorsed by Iraq, but with a notable qualification, limiting this entitlement to situations where the rights did not conflict with principles in the constitution. Recalling that Iran's ruling clerics had invoked Islam and the constitution to block plans to ratify the Women's Convention, one appreciates that this article could set the stage for invoking the Islamic provisions in the constitution to override otherwise applicable rules of international human rights law. In a puzzling development, this provision was excised from the constitution in September 2005, while Article 2 provisions that could have similar implications for human rights were retained.

Article 14 of the Iraqi Constitution provided for equality before the law without discrimination because of religion, sect or belief. Probably as a result of American pressure, Article 40 guaranteed freedom of belief, and Article 2 guaranteed 'full religious rights of all individuals to freedom of religious belief and practice' (mentioning Christians, Yazidis and Sabeans), which was in addition to the Article 41 provision saying that the state guaranteed freedom of worship. However, given the Article 2 provisions on Islam, religious freedoms might be customised to fit Islamic criteria.

Some provisions affecting women's rights, likewise subject to being restricted by Islamic criteria, were contradictory on their face. Article 14 said that Iraqis were equal before the law without discrimination because of gender, and Article 20 gave male and female citizens political rights, including the right to vote and run for office. At the same time, Article 39 made a vague provision allowing Iraqis to have personal status matters governed by the religious law of their choice, which opened the way for men to demand the application of discriminatory rules of Islamic law that could potentially demote women to second-class citizens.

Overall, the 2005 Iraqi Constitution was more likely to satisfy the factions calling for upholding Islamic law than those campaigning to have strong constitutional protections for human rights.

CONCLUSION

As this selective review of provisions in several constitutions of Middle Eastern countries since 1960 demonstrates, drafters have struggled inconclusively with one of the most fundamental questions that they have had to confront: how to formulate constitutional principles on the respective roles of human rights and Islam. As the ambiguous and ambivalent compromise formulations in the recent Afghan and Iraqi Constitutions indicate, the battles over the respective roles of human rights and Islam are still not close to resolution.

Advocates of human rights and supporters of Islamisation have pursued sharply conflicting agendas. They have done so at a juncture when people in Muslim countries typically want constitutions to affirm human rights as well as to enshrine Islam in some form—this at the same time when debates continue regarding whether or not Muslims can respect one factor only at the expense of the other. With the intensification of calls for Islamisation, often understood as reviving elements of Islamic law as it was interpreted by medieval jurists, it seems that human rights are increasingly vulnerable to being curbed in the interests of upholding clashing Islamic criteria. At the same time, a segment of Muslim opinion has been more assertively insisting that supposed conflicts between human rights and Islamic values are based on false premises, that it is perfectly consonant with Islamic principles to have strong constitutional provisions securing human rights.

As the intense controversies swirling around the relevant principles in the recently-produced Afghan and Iraqi Constitutions demonstrate, contending factions believe that what is placed in constitutions defining the roles of human rights and Islam matters greatly. Despite assertions by progressives that human rights and Islam share similar values, it is obvious that the two are mostly seen as an oppositional pair, with any victory in terms of upholding human rights according to international standards being read as a defeat for the claims of Islamic law as traditionally interpreted, and vice versa.

This is not to say that observers are expecting that governments will automatically adhere to the letter of constitutional texts that officially accord primacy either to human rights or to rules of Islamic law; people realise that in the Middle East, governments may often disregard their own constitutions. However, the perception persists that constitutional principles signal the basic orientation in government policy and whether or not it will favour upholding Islamic tradition at the expense of international law, or vice versa.

In the region as a whole and often within individual countries, many different constitutional formulations have been offered, ranging from nominal provisions for human rights that are negated by superimposed Islamic criteria, to strong commitments to international human rights law that are minimally compromised by invocations of Islam. An awkward compromise is seen in some texts that accord equal weight to both, simultaneously promising adherence to international human rights law and respect for Islamic law, heedless of the contradictions that this normally entails. The instances of stark incoherence call to mind Arjomand's observation that more recent constitutions tend to be more syncretic, including larger numbers of 'heterogeneous and potentially conflicting principles of order'.[27] Of course, in cases where constitution drafters leave serious contradictions between provisions delineating the religion-state relationship and provisions setting the scope of citizens' rights, they are in effect displacing controversies that the constitution should resolve, relegating them in some instances to the courts but more often to the political arena, where rival forces will continue to do battle.

As has been indicated, disputes over provisions in Middle Eastern constitutions dealing with human rights and Islam are part of broader political struggles. These disputes take place in a region where both secular and Islamist ideologies have their supporters and critics and where wrenching political upheavals are common. For constitutions in the region to treat human rights and Islam with greater clarity and for these treatments to stabilise rather than shifting dramatically when regimes change, the corresponding political systems as well as the prevailing notions of how human rights relate to Islam will have to evolve to a new stage where greater coherence and consistency are achievable.

---

[27] SA Arjomand, 'Constitutions and the Struggle for Political Order: a Study in the Modernization of Political Traditions' (1992) 33 *Archives europeennes de sociologie/ European Journal of Sociology* 75.

5

The Guardian of the Regime: the Turkish Constitutional Court in Comparative Perspective

HOOTAN SHAMBAYATI

MANY MODERN CONSTITUTIONS, including those included in this volume, reflect ambitious programmes for transforming existing social, economic and political interests through political engineering. In countries like Iran and Turkey the underlying ideal of the constitution is not the protection of the existing nation but nothing less than the creation of a new nation. As Arjomand has noted, this desire for social engineering through constitutionalism is a characteristic of ideological constitutions found in many developing countries.[1]

The attempt to transform the nation, however, is often at the expense of powerful actors and is opposed by significant portions of the society. As a result the state emerges as an 'enlightened' institution whose job is not only designing a system that will bring the 'nation to the level of contemporary civilization'[2] but also a system that will protect the civilizing project against its 'enemies', even when those enemies are a majority in the polity. The Islamic revolution of 1979 in Iran adopted this project by proposing a new order of a different kind. For Turkish leaders, 'contemporary civilization' is Western and secular. For their Iranian counterparts, it is Islamic and theocratic. For both, the mission is the transformation of the nation.

In this chapter, I argue that the civilizing mission of the state in Turkey has led to the creation of a regime with guardians where elected and unelected institutions jointly exercise power. The presence of guardians requires the creation of institutions such as constitutional courts that serve to preserve

---

[1] SA Arjomand, 'Law, Political Reconstruction and Constitutional Politics' (2003) 18 *International Sociology* (March) 7–32.

[2] This oft-repeated phrase is from a speech delivered by Ataturk on the Occasion of the Tenth Anniversary of the Foundation of the Turkish Republic, 29 October 1933, available at www.allaboutturkey.com/ata_speech.htm

the above politics posture of the guardians by putting a distance between them and day-to-day politics. What distinguishes these institutions from their counterparts in consolidated democracies is that despite their political importance they are isolated from elected institutions and their primary role is to protect the ideological dominance of the guardians.

The case of Turkey is, however, by no means unique, and extra-political institutions are a characteristic of many regimes with guardians. As Haggard and Kaufman have argued, regimes with guardians create 'insulated decision-making structures that can be counted on to pursue [the guardian's] policy agenda'[3] without relying on elected institutions. To demonstrate this, I will offer a brief discussion of the Iranian system and the role of that country's Guardian Council. In Iran, the division of sovereignty between an elected parliament and president representing the will of the people and the Supreme Leader representing the alleged will of God has created a political system that relies heavily on extra-political institutions. My comparison highlights the similarity of the two political systems with guardians despite their diametrically opposite ideologies.

THE TURKISH CONSTITUTION: DEMOCRATIC DEFICIT

In 1945, Turkey abandoned the single-party system that had been in place since the establishment of the Republic two decades earlier. Five years later, the opposition Democrat Party (DP) won an overwhelming majority in parliamentary elections and replaced the Republican People's Party (RPP) as the governing party. Turkey's first experience with democracy came to an end in May 1960 when the military overthrew the DP government. The return to civilian government and multiparty politics was swift, but before leaving office in 1962, the military government put in place a new constitution which governed Turkey for the next two decades and in some surprising ways established the basis for the post-1982 constitutional system. Although many students of Turkish politics agree that the 1982 Constitution is illiberal in nature and imposes severe restrictions on rights and liberties, they tend to view the 1961 Constitution as liberal. As the discussion below suggests, however, many of the restrictive institutions of the 1982 Constitution have their roots in the 1961 document.

As Ergun Özbudun notes, the 1961 Constitution 'reflected the basic political values and interests of the state elites'.[4] Believing that the DP governments had abused governmental power, the framers of the new constitution

---

[3] S Haggard and RR Kaufman, *The Political Economy of Democratic Transitions* (Princeton, Princeton University Press, 1995) 121.

[4] E Özbudun, *Contemporary Turkish Politics: Challenges to Democratic Consolidation* (Boulder, Rienner, 2000) 54.

tried to divide sovereignty and the exercise of political power among various institutions. Accordingly, Article 4 of the 1961 Constitution read:

> Sovereignty is vested in the nation without reservation and condition. The nation should exercise its sovereignty through the authorised agencies as prescribed by the principles laid down in the Constitution.

The official webpage of the Turkish Constitutional Court interprets the second sentence as 'putting an end to the principle of the supremacy of Parliament'.[5] This concept is also present in the 1982 Constitution, where the exact wording of its 1961 predecessor is repeated in Article 6. As the webpage continues, 'With the adoption of this new principle the Turkish Grand National Assembly ceased to be the sole organ empowered to exercise sovereignty on behalf of the nation'.[6] The result has been the creation of a bifurcated political system based on the division of sovereignty between elected institutions and unelected guardians.

The Turkish political system is a hybrid of electoral democracy and authoritarian tendencies, where elected institutions share the exercise of sovereignty with non-elected and democratically unaccountable actors. This dichotomy has resulted in a sharp distinction between what the Turkish public identifies as the state (*devlet*), composed of the military, security agencies and the judiciary, and the government (*hükümet*), composed of the parliament and the cabinet.

To put into operation the division of sovereignty, the 1961 Constitution created a number of institutions that were further strengthened under the 1982 Constitution. Most important among these institutions are the National Security Council and the Constitutional Court. In addition, a number of other 'illiberal' institutions like the State Security Courts and the Council of Higher Education were first introduced in the 1970s and achieved constitutional status in 1982.

Originally thought of as a forum for the exchange of views between civilian institutions and the military establishment, the role of the National Security Council (NSC) was strengthened in the 1970s and then again by the 1982 Constitution. Article 118 of the 1982 Constitution enumerates the membership and the duties of the NSC. In its original version, which remained in effect until 2001, it read:

> The National Security Council shall be composed of the Prime Minister, the Chief of the General Staff, the Ministers of National Defense, Internal Affairs, and Foreign Affairs, the Commanders of the Army, Navy, and the Air Force, and the General Commander of the Gendarmerie, under the chairmanship of the President of the Republic.

---

[5] See www.anayasa.gov.tr/engconst/COURT.HTM
[6] *Ibid.*

Depending on the particulars of the agenda, Ministers and other persons concerned may be invited to meetings of the Council and their views be heard.

The National Security Council shall submit to the Council of Ministers its views on taking decisions and ensuring necessary coordination with regard to the formulation, establishment, and implementation of the national security policy of the State. *The Council of Ministers shall give priority consideration to the decisions of the National Security Council* concerning the measures that it deems necessary for the preservation of the existence and independence of the State, the integrity and indivisibility of the country, and the peace and security of society. (emphasis added)

While the 'decisions' of the NSC are theoretically only advisory, and the final decision for their implementation is left to the council of ministers and the parliament, it is clear that the framers of the constitution conceived of the NSC as an important actor in the decision-making process.[7]

Over the years the council has used a very inclusive definition of security and has discussed all kinds of issues concerning domestic and foreign policy. At times, this has resulted in major confrontations between the civilian governments and the military-wing of the NSC. In 1997, for example, the military forced the resignation of the government led by the Islamist Refah party, even though the party was the largest single party in the parliament. It is also worthy to note that the economic crisis of 2001, which resulted in the rapid devaluation of the Turkish currency, was triggered by a confrontation between the President and the Prime Minister during an NSC meeting.

Although the role of the military in Turkish politics has been extensively studied and has been the subject of much discussion, the NSC is not the only constitutional institution that shares in the exercise of sovereignty. As Pereira notes, 'military strength and autonomy cannot be achieved by the military alone but must be nurtured and sustained by legal and legislative projects that convert parts of the judiciary and the congress into defenders of the status-quo'.[8] An equally important, but much less commented upon institution, is the Constitutional Court.

THE CONSTITUTIONAL COURT AND THE JUDICIALISATION OF TURKISH POLITICS

When sovereignty is divided between elected and non-elected institutions, conditions are ripe for judicialisation of politics, or the expansion of the

---

[7] In preparation for Turkey's eventual entry into the European Union the parliament has adopted a number of constitutional amendments with the aim of reducing the military's role in politics. Accordingly, in 2001 the composition of the NSC was changed to increase the number of civilian members and to emphasise the council's advisory role. In addition, a civilian replaced the council's military Secretary-General.

[8] AW Pereira, 'Virtual Legality: Authoritarian Legacies and the Reform of Military Justice in Brazil, the Southern Cone, and Mexico' (2001) 34(5) *Comparative Political Studies* (June) 557.

judiciary's role in the political arena.[9] The adoption of a system based on divided sovereignty signifies a schism in the ruling coalition concerning the nature of sovereignty. Judicialisation of the political arena can be an attractive way for constitutional drafters to deal with this problem. As Hirschl has noted, the political empowerment of the courts is a form of 'hegemonic preservation', where a political elite that is losing its dominance tries to protect its values and interests by empowering a sympathetic judiciary.[10] Although Hirschl does not apply his model to transitions from military rule, this scenario seems to be particularly likely in such transitions. Whereas civilian authoritarians can regroup in the post-transition era and compete in democratic elections, that route is not available to military regimes. An outgoing military regime must ensure the continued protection of its institutional interests before leaving office.

Although national security councils, or similar institutions, can go a long way in meeting this goal, they also run the danger of undermining the above-politics posture of the military-as-institution. As one of the legal advisors to the Chilean military junta and one of the primary authors of the that country's 1980 Constitution noted, 'everyone is in agreement not to develop a formula that, in fact, implies the politicization of the armed forces, since it is evident that if one seeks to preserve an institution's character as permanent safeguard one should take precaution not to waste it upon the contingent'.[11] As the Turkish experience shows, in transitions from military rule, the empowerment of the judiciary is a mechanism to minimise the need for direct participation of the military in day-to-day politics while at the same time protecting the outgoing regime's interest under civilian rule. Military regimes might have strong incentives to adopt judicial review as an 'insurance policy'.[12]

THE TURKISH CONSTITUTIONAL COURT: INSTITUTIONAL DESIGN

What distinguishes the post-1982 Turkish Constitutional Court from its European counterparts is its 'apolitical' appointments procedure and its eagerness to override the parliament.[13] Between 1982 and 2000, the Court

[9] H Shambayati, 'A Tale of Two Mayors: Courts and Politics in Turkey and Iran' (2004) *International Journal of Middle East Studies* (May) 253–75.

[10] R Hirschl, *Towards Juristocracy: the Origins and Consequences of the New Constitutionalism* (Cambridge, MA, Harvard University Press, 2004).

[11] Cited in R Barros, *Constitutionalism and Dictatorship: Pinochet, the Junta, and the 1980 Constitution*, Cambridge Studies in the Theory of Democracy (Cambridge, Cambridge University Press, 2002) 244.

[12] As Ginsburg notes, 'by serving as an alternative forum to challenge government action, judicial review provides a form of insurance to prospective electoral losers during the constitutional bargain'. T Ginsburg, *Judicial Review in New Democracies: Constitutional Courts in Asian Cases* (Cambridge, Cambridge University Press, 2003) 25.

[13] There are very few scholarly studies devoted to the Turkish Constitutional Court. Among the more important ones are Z Arslan, 'Conflicting Paradigms: Political Rights in the Turkish

annulled 72 per cent of the cases it received for abstract review. In addition, since 1983 it has closed 18 political parties, including three political parties with representation in the parliament. At the same time, since 1982 the parliament has had no role in appointments to the Court.

The Court began operations in 1962 with 15 permanent members appointed by the bicameral parliament (three Grand National Assembly, two Senate), the high courts, and the President of the Republic. Like its counterpart in other countries, the military regime that came to power in September 1980 did not openly interfere with the Constitutional Court, although it did appoint some new members to the Court.[14] The military regime, however, suspended the constitution and exempted its own decisions from review by the Court.

The framers of the 1982 Constitution reduced the number of justices to 11 regular and four substitute members. Most importantly, they eliminated the five justices appointed by the parliament and increased the number of justices nominated by the military courts from one to two. The President of the Republic, a 'nonpartisan' official elected by the unicameral parliament,[15] appoints all justices of the Constitutional Court from among candidates nominated by other high courts and the Higher Education Council.[16] Seven out of the 11 seats on the Court are reserved for the judiciary. The president also appoints one justice from among the teaching staff of the universities nominated by the Higher Education Council and three justices from among high civil servants and lawyers. It is not unusual for some of these appointees to be retired military judges. Justices of the Constitutional Court have to be at least 40 years old at the time of their appointment and retire at age 65. This apolitical appointment procedure of the Turkish Constitutional Court betrays the framers distrust of politicians and political institutions. Under the 1982 Constitution, and in sharp contrast with other Western democracies, the parliament has no role in appointments to the Constitutional Court.[17]

Constitutional Court' (2002) 11 *Critique: Critical Middle Eastern Studies* (Spring) 9–25; D Kogacioglu, 'Dissolution of Political Parties by the Constitutional Court in Turkey: Judicial Delimitation of the Political Domain' (2003) 18 *International Sociology* (March) 258–76; D Kogacioglu, 'Progress, Unity, and Democracy: Dissolving Political Parties in Turkey' (2004) 38(3) *Law and Society Review* 433–62.

[14] For other examples, see CN Tate, 'Courts and Crisis Regimes: a Theory Sketch with Asian Case Studies' (1992) *Political Research Quarterly* 311–38; see also R Barros, *Constitutionalism and Dictatorship: Pinochet, the Junta, and the 1980 Constitution* (Cambridge, Cambridge University Press, 2002); JC Sutil, 'The Judiciary and the Political System in Chile: the Dilemmas of Judicial Independence during the Transition to Democracy' in I Stotzky (ed), *Transition to Democracy in Latin America: the Role of the Judiciary* (Boulder, Westview, 1993).

[15] The 1982 Constitution abolished the Senate.

[16] This controversial body was established after the 1980 coup and has the duty of supervising institutions of higher education. Its members are appointed by the President of the Republic and include a nominee of the chief of staff of the military.

[17] The change in the judicial appointment procedures was part of an overall attempt to augment the powers of the presidency. The framers of the 1982 Constitution conceived of the presidency as a watchdog over the popularly elected institutions. They also hoped that by

Another distinguishing feature of the Turkish Constitutional Court is the role of the military in appointments to the Court. Two justices of the Constitutional Court are appointed from among members of the High Military Administrative Court (*Askeri Yüksek Idare Mahkemesi*) and the Military Court of Cassation (*Askeri Yargitay*) based on nominations by the plenary session of the two institutions. Although these justices resign their military commission before assuming their seat on the Constitutional Court, they are products of the military's justice system and the manner of their nomination can provide the military with a mechanism to influence the composition of the Court.[18] Technically, the military could also influence the nomination of the candidates put forward by the Higher Education Council, a controversial body established after the 1980 coup to supervise civilian (but not military) institutions of higher education. Until 2004 a representative of the Chief of Staff sat on the Council's governing board.

Both Dicle Kogacioglu and Nathan Brown see some virtue in apolitical judicial appointment procedures. Kogacioglu has argued that the appointment procedure of the Turkish Constitutional Court has enhanced the legitimacy of the Court in the public's eye.[19] Similarly Brown, using the example of Egypt's Supreme Constitutional Council, advocates isolating the courts from the Arab executives and legislatures in order to enhance judicial independence and increase the possibility of the courts standing up to the other branches. He is, however, quick to add that none of the Arab countries are democracies.[20]

Isolating the judiciary from executives and legislatures might be desirable if those branches themselves are not democratic. In democracies, on the other hand, a partially politicised appointment procedure is not only necessary for establishing democratic legitimacy of judicial review but also for producing more democratic results. Deepening democracy and preservation of judicial independence require measures to reduce the dangers of ideological uniformity on the bench. As Russell has noted, 'to guard against

augmenting the powers of the President they would allow for the continued participation of the military in policy-making after the transition to civilian rule. A provisional article of the constitution declared that General Evren, the leader of the 12 September 1980 military coup and one of the main authors of the constitution, would become President of the Republic upon the ratification of the constitution. Furthermore, the framers hoped that the pre-coup tradition of electing recently retired military commanders to the presidency would continue after the transition to civilian rule. Until the election of Turgut Ozal as President in 1989, Celal Bayar (1950–1960) had been Turkey's only civilian President.

[18] The role of the military in appointments to the Constitutional Court is to some extent reminiscent of the role of the Chilean military in appointing two out of seven members of that country's Constitutional Tribunal under the 1980 Constitution. In that country, however, the Constitutional Tribunal has more limited political functions.

[19] D Kogacioglu, 'Progress, Unity, and Democracy: Dissolving Political Parties in Turkey', above n 13, at 441 n 22.

[20] NJ Brown, *Constitutions in a Non-Constitutional World* (Albany, State University of New York, 2002) 150–2 and 159.

a politically unbalanced judiciary, liberal democracies are well advised to build social and political pluralism into their judicial appointing arrangements'.[21]

The apolitical appointment procedure of the Turkish Constitutional Court has produced a remarkably homogeneous court where not only most members are jurists but they also have had very similar educational backgrounds and life experiences. As a consequence, although the Court has emerged as a powerful political actor and has not shied away from confronting the parliament, it has been more cautious in dealing with the state.

Acting like a Senate

The Turkish Constitutional Court sees its primary role as 'counterbalanc[ing] political institutions and especially Parliament in order to avoid an abuse of powers'.[22] To make this possible, the 1961 Constitution adopted a very liberal definition of standing and authorised the President of the Republic, political parties represented in the parliament, one-sixth of the members of each house of the legislature,[23] and any political party which had mustered at least 10 per cent of the votes in the last national election, to petition the Constitutional Court for abstract review. In addition, the plenary sessions of the high courts and the universities were allowed to petition the Court 'in cases concerning their duties and welfare' (Article 149). This liberal definition of standing meant that in the polarised political environment of the 1960s and the 1970s, a large number of laws and regulations were referred to the Court.[24] Between 1962 and the September 1980 military coup, the Constitutional Court received an average of 19 cases per annum for abstract review. It found grounds for unconstitutionality in 37 per cent of these cases.

The involvement of the court in the political arena encouraged further polarisation of the political life and opened the court to charges by

---

[21] PH Russell, 'Toward a General Theory of Judicial Independence' in PH Russell and DM O'Brien (eds), *Judicial Independence in the Age of Democracy* (Charlottesville, University Press of Virginia, 2001) 17. See also chapters by Guarnieri, Kommers and Corder in the same volume.

[22] See www.anayasa.gov.tr/engconst/COURT.HTM

[23] The 1961 Constitution created a senate to reduce the powers of the lower house, the Grand National Assembly. The senate was abolished by the 1982 Constitution.

[24] Turning to the courts at times of political crisis is not unique to Turkey. For examples from other countries see J Linz, *The Breakdown of Democratic Regimes: Crisis, Breakdown, and Reequilibrium* (Baltimore, Johns Hopkins University Press, 1978); CN Tate, 'Courts and the Breakdown and Recreation of Philippine Democracy: Evidence from the Supreme Court's Agenda' (1997) *International Social Science Journal* (Special Issue: Democracy and Law) 279; A Valenzuela, *The Breakdown of Democratic Regimes: Chile* (Baltimore, Johns Hopkins University Press, 1978).

politicians that the Constitutional Court was usurping the powers of the parliament and was making it impossible for the government to function properly.[25] As Dodd notes:

> the Constitutional Court and the Council of State, manned by the most enlightened of those who represented the tradition of the Ataturkist state, might well have been able to establish a rapport with a stable majority government. In conditions of unstable government and intense political rivalry it was difficult for these institutions not to be seen to be engaged in the political struggle.[26]

Between its establishment in 1962 and the military coup of 1980, the Court was occasionally willing to annul some of the more restrictive legislation favoured by the state. In 1975, for example, the Court struck down most of the provisions of a law that attempted to decrease the autonomy of universities and establish a council to oversee all institutions of higher education. Similarly, a year later the Court ordered the closure of State Security Courts. Both institutions were resurrected after the 1980 coup and were given constitutional status in the 1982 Constitution.

The framers of the 1982 Constitution reacted to the Court's controversial decisions by changing the appointment procedures and the rules of standing. Under the system in place since 1982, the power of referral belongs to the President of the Republic, the parliamentary group of the main party in government, the main opposition party (the largest parliamentary party outside of government), or one-fifth (at present 110) of the members of the unicameral parliament.[27]

Parliamentary deputies and the President submit most petitions for abstract review. In general, however, the President can use his veto power to stop 'unacceptable' legislation. Although overriding a presidential veto is relatively easy,[28] depending on the relationship between the President and the government, the parliament usually defers to the presidential judgement and amends the provisions in question.[29] As in other countries with

---

[25] F Ahmad, *Turkish Experiment in Democracy, 1950–1975* (Boulder, Westview, 1977) 245; CH Dodd, *Crisis of Turkish Democracy* (Huntingdon, UK, Eothen Press,1990) 34.

[26] Dodd, above n 25, at 64–5.

[27] Abstract review procedures in Turkey are a posteriori. The legislation in question must first be implemented before its constitutionality can be challenged. Institutions with standing have to file their petitions for the annulment of the contested law or decree within 60 days after its publication in the *Official Gazette*.

[28] If the parliament passes the objectionable provisions without amendment for a second time the legislation becomes law without the President's signature.

[29] This was particularly true during the presidency of Turgut Ozal and Suleyman Demirel, two veteran politicians and former prime ministers, who continued to maintain a political base even after assuming the presidency. Turkey's current president, Ahmet Necdet Sezer, however, does not have an organised political base. A career judge who at the time of his appointment to the presidency was the president of the Constitutional Court, Sezer has relied more heavily on the Court.

Table 5.1: Abstract Review Cases Decided by the Turkish Constitutional Court

Year	Docket	New cases	Annulled	Objection rejected	Total cases decided	% Annulled
1984	6	6	0	2	2	0
1985	16	12	3	5	8	38
1986	18	10	7	3	10	70
1987	21	13	7	6	13	54
1988	17	10	9	2	11	82
1989	14	8	6	2	8	75
1990	19	13	6	4	10	60
1991	15	7	8	2	10	80
1992	10	5	6	1	7	86
1993	23	20	21	2	23	91
1994	19	19	17	1	18	94
1995	14	13	11	1	12	92
1996	17	16	8	2	10	80
1997	11	4	5	3	8	63
1998	5	2	1	3	4	25
1999	13	12	4	4	8	50
2000	34	29	21	2	23	91

Years	Ave. per year	New	Annulled	Rejected	Total	% Annulled
1962–1980	19	350	129	220	349	37
1984–2000	12	199	140	45	185	76

Source: Turkish Republic, State Institute of Statistics, *Judicial Statistics* (various years) and *Anayasa Mahkemesi*.

abstract review, most cases are brought before the Constitutional Court by the parliamentary opposition, a practice that increases the potential for the judicialisation of the political process.[30] The frequency with which the opposition has used this strategy led one president of the Court to complain that the Constitutional Court had become 'like a senate'.[31] This, however, has not stopped the Court from using its powers to strike down parliamentary acts and governmental decrees.

As Table 5.1 shows, the framers of the 1982 Constitution have succeeded in decreasing the workload of the Court. Whereas in the 1962–1980 period the Court received an average of 19 cases a year, in the 1983–2000 period that number was reduced to 12. The proportion of annulments however, has more than doubled from 37 per cent in the first period to 76 per cent in the second. The Court might not be deciding as many cases as it once did, but it has become a more activist court. To be sure many of the findings of unconstitutionality are based on minor technical points. Nevertheless, 76 per cent is an astonishingly high average.

---

[30] A Stone Sweet, *Governing with Judges* (New York, Oxford University Press, 2000) 50–1.
[31] *Hürriyet*, 15 May 2003.

Protecting Rights

Whereas abstract review is a mechanism designed to 'tame the parliament',[32] concrete review is intended to protect civil liberties. Claims of violation of civil liberties and rights are more likely to arise after a statute has been put into effect.[33] Turkish law does not allow for individual complaints to reach the Constitutional Court directly, but it does allow the parties to a conflict to raise claims of unconstitutionality of the applied statutes during the course of a trial. If the trial court is convinced that a constitutional question exists, it is required to stop the trial and refer the matter to the Constitutional Court. In such cases the Constitutional Court only decides the constitutional question before it. The original court then tries the facts of the case in light of the Constitutional Court's ruling.

The protection of rights through judicial action in Turkey faces three major structural obstacles. First, as in other countries based on the civil law system, the Constitutional Court only addresses the constitutionality of the law in question not its interpretation by the trial courts. The Constitutional Court only has the power to review the constitutionality of laws and decrees with the force of law, but it does not have the power to review decisions of the other courts. Although Article 153 of the Constitution declares that the decisions of the Constitutional Court 'shall be binding on the legislative, executive, and judicial organs, on the administrative authorities, and on persons and corporate bodies', it does not provide any mechanism for enforcing this provision. A citizen who feels his constitutionally guaranteed rights have been violated by an unconstitutional interpretation of an otherwise constitutional law has no recourse available other than relying on the goodwill of the appellate court.[34]

Secondly, the 1982 Constitution and Turkey's legal codes provide weak foundations for the protection of rights. The leaders of the 1980 coup believed that the political paralysis of the late 1970s and the breakdown of law and order had violated the rights of the state, and that the future political system had to protect these rights. In opening the 1981 Constituent Assembly, General Evren, the leader of the coup, noted:

> While trying to enhance and protect human rights and liberties, the state itself has certain rights and obligations as far as its continuity and future is concerned. We do not have the right to put the state into a powerless and inactive position. The state cannot be turned into a helpless institution ... Citizens should know

---

[32] A Stone [Sweet], *The Birth of Judicial Politics in France* (Oxford, Oxford University Press, 1992) 60.

[33] Stone Sweet, above n 30, at 113.

[34] This seems to be a common problem for Kelsenian courts. See A Örkény and KL Scheppele, 'Rule of Law: the Complexity of Legality in Hungary' in M Krygier and A Czarnota (eds), *The Rule of Law after Communism: Problems and Prospects in East-Central Europe* (Brookfield, VT, Ashgate, 1999) 66.

that freedoms of thought and conscience exist. There are, however, limits to these freedoms; there is also a state founded by individuals that together make up a collectivity. The state in question protects the individuals. This state, too, has a will and sovereignty of its own. Individual freedoms can be protected to the extent that the will and the sovereignty of the state are maintained. If the will and sovereignty of the state are undermined, then the only entity that can safeguard individual freedoms has withered away.[35]

Accordingly, the constitution recognised a long list of civil liberties but it also imposed severe restrictions on the exercise of those rights. Article 14 specified that:

> None of the rights and freedoms embodied in the Constitution shall be exercised with the aim of violating the indivisible integrity of the State with its territory and nation, of endangering the existence of the Turkish State and Republic, of destroying fundamental rights and freedoms, of placing the government of the State under the control of an individual or a group of people, or establishing the hegemony of one social class over others, or creating discrimination on the basis of language, race, religion or sect, or of establishing by any other means a system of government based on these concepts and ideas.[36]

Clearly, the protection of individual rights and liberties was secondary to the protection of the rights of the state.

Furthermore, until 2001, the constitution specifically barred the Constitutional Court from reviewing some of the more restrictive laws and regulations that were legislated by the military regime. Although this prohibition was removed in 2001 as part of a European Union harmonisation package, it is not yet clear what effect it might have on the activities of the Court. The constitution also bars the Court from revisiting an issue until 10 years have elapsed from the publication of the Court's original decision in the *Official Gazette*. This provision is intended to ensure the stability of law, but it has also made it more difficult for the court to quickly correct its 'mistakes'. Given the extent and speed of economic, political and social changes in Turkey over the past two decades, this provision might also have had the unintended consequence of widening the gap between the legal system and the realities faced by the society.

Thirdly, the Turkish Constitutional Court can only accept cases for concrete review on referral from other courts. All trial and appellate courts have the power to refer cases to the Constitutional Court, but some courts seem extremely reluctant to do so. The largest numbers of cases are referred by

---

[35] Quoted in M Heper, *The State Tradition in Turkey* (Beverly, Eothen Press, 1985) 131.
[36] In 2001, the parliament amended this article to read: 'None of the rights and freedoms embodied in the Constitution shall be exercised with the aim of violating the indivisible integrity of the state with its territory and nation, and endangering the existence of the democratic and secular order of the Turkish Republic based upon human rights'.

Table 5.2: Cases of Concrete Review Decided by the Turkish Constitutional Court (1983–1998)

Year	New	Annulled	Rejected	Returned*
1983	0	0	0	0
1984	6	0	2	0
1985	19	0	4	8
1986	14	0	16	4
1987	22	2	12	4
1988	52	3	7	11
1989	23	3	14	13
1990	27	1	14	7
1991	54	13	18	10
1992	43	3	22	9
1993	33	6	18	10
1994	34	5	12	8
1995	43	15	30	6
1996	61	11	19	7
1997	73	12	17	10
1998	56	17	39	6
1999	39	14	23	4
2000	57	3	12	6
Total	656**	108	279	223***
		(17.7%)	(45.7%)	(36.5%)

*Returned to the original court.
**610 cases were decided. Calculations are based on the number of decisions made.
***Returned (123) or refused to hear (100).

Source: Turkish Republic, State Institute of Statistics, *Judicial Statistics* (various years).

the administrative courts and concern various administrative and economic reforms. Particularly disturbing is the very small number of cases referred by the State Security Courts. In over 600 decisions by the Constitutional Court, only four have concerned cases referred directly by the SSCs.[37] In part, this is due to the fact that until 2001 some provisions of the anti-terror law were exempt from constitutional review. More important, however, seems to have been the general reluctance of these courts to refer cases for constitutional review.

Between 1984 and 2000, the Constitutional Court received 656 referrals from other courts and delivered decisions in 610 cases. The Court's decisions in these cases are summarised in Table 5.2. The possibility of success in declaring a law unconstitutional through the process of concrete review is low. Of the 610 decisions, only 108 (18 per cent) have struck down a law or regulation; 46 per cent of the claims of unconstitutionality were rejected, while the Court refused to render a decision in 37 per cent of the

---

[37] Cases from trial courts, including SSCs, can be referred to the Constitutional Court either directly by the original court or the appellate court. It is difficult to determine the number of cases from the SSCs reaching the Constitutional Court through the Court of Cassation.

cases, either due to the absence of a substantial constitutional question or for other reasons.

The relatively low success rate of concrete review points to the failure of the Court to emerge as a guardian of individual rights and civil liberties against encroachments by the state. Although the Constitutional Court occasionally has expanded rights, it has not been able to appropriate for itself the role of the protector of civil liberties against encroachments by the state. This is also affirmed by the poor performance of Turkey before the European Court of Human Rights (ECtHR).[38] This discrepancy points to two very different conceptions of 'rights' by the ECtHR and the Turkish judiciary. The ECtHR emphasises individual rights and civil liberties. The Turkish judiciary, on the other hand, follows an ideology-based paradigm favouring the state.[39] As a former president of the Constitutional Court put it, 'The state that does not protect itself is not a state'.[40] A similar sentiment was repeated in April 2005 when the sitting president of the Court used the opening of the Court's judicial year to threaten the ruling Justice and Development Party with dissolution if it attempted to lift the ban on headscarf-wearing female students at universities.[41]

Supervision of Political Parties

When sovereignty is divided between elected and non-elected institutions, the political system is particularly susceptible to anti-systemic movements. As Brumberg notes, these political systems lack a hegemonic ideology and 'can become vulnerable to efforts by competing social forces to radically redefine [their] ideological foundations'.[42] Unwilling to accommodate new social movements and unable to defeat them at the polls, elements within the system might turn to the courts in an effort to suppress, or at least to undermine, the challengers. As it will be shown below, the Turkish political system, like its Iranian counterpart, has relied very heavily on the courts to suppress political movements that have challenged the hegemony of the ruling elite.[43]

---

[38] Many of the cases concerning civil liberties arise from the situation concerning the Kurdish movement. The fight against Kurdish separatism and Islamic fundamentalism has led to numerous allegations of violations of individual rights and civil liberties. In such cases the Turkish courts have often deferred to the security personnel.

[39] Z Arslan, 'Conflicting Paradigms: Political Rights in the Turkish Constitutional Court' (2002) 11 *Critique: Critical Middle Eastern Studies* (Spring) 9.

[40] YG Özden, 'Opening Speech by Yekta Güngör Özden, President of the Turkish Constitutional Court', reprinted in YG Özden and E Yildiz (eds), *Constitutional Jurisdiction 9: Papers Presented at the International Symposium held at the Thirtieth Anniversary of the Constitutional Court of Turkey, April 25–27, 1992* (Ankara, 1993) 22.

[41] *Hürriyet*, 24 April 2005.

[42] D Brumberg, *Reinventing Khomeini: the Struggle for Reform in Iran* (Chicago, University of Chicago Press, 2001) 34.

[43] See Shambayati, above n 9.

Officially the Turkish state is based on Kemalism, a loosely defined ideology named after the founder of modern Turkey, Mustafa Kemal Ataturk. However, most observers of Turkish politics agree with Zürcher that 'Kemalism never became a coherent, all-embracing ideology, but can best be described as a set of attitudes and opinions, which were never defined in any detail'.[44] This has allowed the periodic rise of movements that have used both democratic and undemocratic means to challenge the state's definition of Kemalism, particularly with respect to secularism and nationalism.

Since its foundation in 1962, the Court has closed 24 political parties. Of these, six were closed before the 1980 coup and the rest since the return to party politics in 1983 (Table 5.3). The Court has been particularly active since 1991, a date that in many ways signals the return to true civilian politics.[45] The frequency of party closures in Turkey puts it in a unique category among democratic countries and requires further explanation. In

Table 5.3: Political Party Closures (1983–2003)

Year	New cases	Closed	Rejected
1983	6	1	5
1984	2	0	2
1985	1	0	1
1986	0	0	0
1987	1	0	1
1988	2	0	1
1989	0	0	1
1990	2	0	0
1991	2	2	1
1992	2	1	0
1993	4	3	0
1994	1	3	0
1995	1	1	0
1996	3	1	0
1997	2	2	1
1998	0	1	0
1999	2	1	0
2000	0	0	0
2001	0	1	0
2002	1	0	0
2003	1	1	0
Total	32	18	13

Source: Turkish Republic, State Institute of Statistics, *Judicial Statistics* (various years) and *Anayasa Mahkemesi*.

[44] E J Zürcher, *Turkey: A Modern History* (London, IB Tauris, 1994) 189.
[45] Although technically Turkey had returned to civilian rule in 1983, the leader of the military coup had remained as the President of the Republic until 1990. Furthermore, until the referendum of 1987 the constitution barred the pre-coup political leaders from active participation in politics.

fact, the closure of political parties in Western democracies is so rare that in 1988 Alexander von Brüneck could argue, 'This function of constitutional courts has in recent times lost much of its significance'.[46] This, of course, has somewhat changed in recent years. Nevertheless, party closures are extremely rare in established democracies.[47]

One factor that might explain the difference between Turkey and other Western democracies is the low political cost of party closures for the government in power and for the political system as a whole. As I will argue in this section, both the Turkish Constitutional Court and political institutions have devised a number of mechanisms to reduce the potential political cost of party closures.

First, unlike in either Germany or Spain, the elected government and parliament have no role in closure of political parties. Under Article 69 of the Constitution the power to bring suits for the closure of political parties or for the issuance of warnings to them is given to the Chief Public Prosecutor of the Court of Cassation (*Yargitay*) who acts as the Chief Public Prosecutor of the Republic in cases before the Constitutional Court. The Chief Public Prosecutor is a professional prosecutor appointed by the President of the Republic from a list of nominees prepared by other prosecutors. It is not possible to hold him/her democratically accountable. Nor is it possible to hold the members of the Constitutional Court or those who have appointed them accountable.

Furthermore, prosecutors have little fear of failure when asking for the closure of political parties. Since 1989, the Constitutional Court has acted on 20 petitions for party closures. It has granted the petition on 17 occasions (Table 5.3). When the prosecutor asks for the closure of a political party

---

[46] A von Brüneck, 'Constitutional Review and Legislation in Western Democracies' in C Landfried (ed), *Constitutional Review and Legislation: an International Comparison* (Baden-Baden, Nomos, 1988) 242–3.

[47] The Western country most often cited for the closure of political parties is Germany. Article 21, para 2 of the German Constitution reads, 'Parties which, by reason of their aims or the behaviour of their adherents, seek to impair or abolish the free democratic basic order or to endanger the existence of the Federal Republic of Germany are unconstitutional. The Federal Constitutional Court decides on the question of unconstitutionality'. Using this article the German Constitutional Court closed the neo-Nazi Socialist Reich Party (SRP) in 1952 and the Communist Party in 1956. Neither of these parties was a major political force at the time of its closure, although the SRP occupied two seats in the federal parliament, and both parties reappeared in later years under different names and with more moderate programmes. Since 1956, the German courts have not closed any political parties. In 2003, the court rejected a joint petition by the government and the two houses of parliament to close the neo-Nazi National Democratic Party (*Nationaldemokratische Partei Deutschlands* (NPD)). The other example of party closure in a Western democracy is the Spanish Constitutional Court's decision to outlaw the Basque party Batasuna in 2003. On the closure of political parties in Germany, see John E Finn, *Constitutions in Crisis: Political Violence and the Rule of Law* (Oxford: Oxford University Press, 1991) 191–3; DP Kommers. *The Constitutional Jurisprudence of the Federal Republic of Germany* (Durham, Duke University Press, 1989). For the Spanish case, see L Turano, 'Spain: Banning Political Parties as a Response to Terrorism' (2003) 1:4 *International Journal of Constitutional Law* 730–40.

there is an 85 per cent chance that his request will be granted (Table 5.3). The prosecutor's success rate is even higher when he asks the Constitutional Court to issue a warning to political parties. In such cases the prosecutor can expect a favourable outcome for 95 per cent of his petitions.

Given the frequency of party closures, it is not surprising that both the parliament and the Court have taken a number of steps to reduce further the potential costs of closures. For example, in its original version, Article 84 of the Constitution read:

> The membership of a deputy, whose acts and statements are cited in a judgment of the Constitutional Court as having caused the dissolution of a political party and *that of other deputies who belonged to the party* on the date when the action for dissolution was brought, shall end when the Presidency of the Turkish Grand National Assembly is notified of the dissolution order. (emphasis added)

This meant that when a political party was closed all the deputies from that party in the parliament lost their seats, threatening the parliament with automatic dissolution due to lack of quorum. In 1995, the Constitutional Court closed the pro-Kurdish Democrat Party (DEP). At the time, DEP had a small number of deputies in the parliament. After much wrangling DEP deputies eventually lost their parliamentary immunities and were put on trial.[48] Some, including the much-celebrated Layla Zana, were convicted and imprisoned.[49]

Although the number of DEP deputies was not large enough to threaten the continuation of the parliament, the Constitutional Court's willingness to close a party with representation in the parliament raised the possibility that the closure of political parties might potentially threaten the parliamentary term. Accordingly, in July 1995 the parliament amended the relevant clause of Article 84 to limit the loss of membership to only those deputies 'whose acts and statements are cited in a judgment of the Constitutional Court as having caused the dissolution of a political party'.

The wisdom of this change became apparent when the Court closed the pro-Islamist Welfare Party and its replacement the Virtue Party in January 1998 and June 2001, respectively. At the time of its closure Welfare was the largest party in parliament and in fact until June 1997, when it was forced to resign under pressure from the military, it had been the party in power. Virtue, which had replaced Welfare after the latter's closure, was the main opposition party in 2001. Under the amended version of Article 84, the Constitutional Court chose to hold a very small number of deputies

[48] NF Watts, 'Allies and Enemies: Pro-Kurdish Parties in Turkish Politics, 1990–94' (1999) 31 *International Journal of Middle East Studies* (November) 631.
[49] In 2001, ECtHR ordered new trials for the jailed deputies. Eventually the Turkish parliament amended the law to allow new trials in response to ECtHR rulings and the four deputies still in jail were retried and eventually released in 2004.

responsible for the closure of the two parties, preventing the dissolution of the parliament.

The parliament and the Court have also taken further steps to minimise the cost of party closures. A common phenomenon in Turkish politics is the appearance of what may be called reserve parties. When a political party faces closure some of its members resign to form a new party and as the date for closure gets closer elected officials belonging to the threatened party move to the new party. This strategy was made possible by the 1995 constitutional amendments and the Court's deliberate interpretations. In its original version Article 69 of the Constitution read:

> The founding members and administrators at every level of a political party which has been permanently dissolved shall not become founding members, administrators, or comptrollers of a new political party; nor shall any new political party be founded, the majority of whose members are former members of a political party previously dissolved.

This clause, however, proved unenforceable and was amended by the parliament, thus allowing the members of the closed party to join a new party.

The strategy of setting up reserve parties has been particularly popular with pro-Kurdish and Pro-Islamist political parties that have a social base. The main pro-Kurdish political party, the Democratic People's Party (*Demokratik Halk Partisi*, better known by its Turkish acronym DEHAP), for example, which controls a number of municipalities in the Kurdish populated regions of south-eastern Turkey, was set up when it became clear that the party's predecessor, the People's Democratic Party (*Halkin Demokrasi Partisi* or HADEP) was on the verge of closure. HADEP itself had risen from the ashes of three earlier closed pro-Kurdish parties. On the same day that HADEP was closed (13 March 2003) the Chief Public Prosecutor filed a petition for the closure of DEHAP. Similarly, the Justice and Development Party, which is the ruling party at present (November 2005) is a successor to the closed Virtue Party (closed by the Court in 2001), which was a successor to the closed Welfare Party (closed by the Court in 1998), which was a successor to the closed National Salvation Party (banned after the 1980 coup), which was a successor to the closed National Order party (closed by the Court in 1971).

In October 2001, under pressure from the European Union, the parliament once again amended the constitution to tighten conditions under which parties can be closed. According to Article 68, political parties can still be closed if their:

> statutes and programmes, as well as the activities ... [are] in conflict with the independence of the state, its indivisible integrity with its territory and nation, human rights, the principles of equality and rule of law, sovereignty of the nation, the principles of the democratic and secular republic; they shall not aim to protect or establish class or group dictatorship or dictatorship of any kind, nor shall they incite citizens to crime.

According to Article 69, 'A political party shall be deemed to become the centre of such actions only when such actions are carried out *intensively* by the members of that party' (emphasis added).

Furthermore, under the new arrangement, the closure of a political party would require a three-fifths (7 out of 11) vote. Also, the Constitutional Court now has the option of imposing monetary fines and/or to deny state aid to the offending party. What effect these changes will have on party closures is not clear. Although the overall number of party closures might decline, as the closure of HADEP in 2003 shows, it is unlikely that it will change the Court's attitude toward pro-Kurdish, pro-Islamist, or other ideologically motivated and/or ethnically organised political parties.

Although the Court vehemently opposed these changes and issued a public statement warning the government that the changes would leave Turkey defenceless against separatist (pro-Kurdish) and reactionary (Islamist) movements, these changes should not be viewed as an attack on the Court's powers.[50] The Court still has the right to close political parties. Furthermore, the members of the Court themselves have been complaining about the high number of party closures in Turkey.[51]

In short, The Turkish Constitutional Court is an activist court that has not shied away from engaging in political controversies. The record of the Court clearly indicates its willingness to 'tame the parliament'. At the same time, the Court has been more reluctant in acting against the state. At best, its record has been modest in 'taming the state'. If, as Saïd Arjomand suggests, the Iranian Council of Guardians is the guardian of *shari'a* and the Egyptian Supreme Constitutional Council is the guardian of the constitution,[52] the Turkish Constitutional Court, to quote its former president, is 'the guardian of the regime'.[53]

DIVISION OF SOVEREIGNTY AND THE STATE STRUCTURE IN IRAN

A comparison with Iran is, however, much more illuminating than one with Egypt. The political system of the Islamic Republic of Iran, as Daniel Brumberg has noted, is an example of 'dissonant institutionalisation'. As Brumberg notes, 'dissonant institutionalization occurs when competing images of political community and the symbolic systems legitimating them

---

[50] 'Anayasal Muhtira' (Constitutional Memorandum), *Milliyet*, 23 January 2001; *Turkish Daily News*, 24 January 2001.

[51] 40. Kurulus, Günü Töreni Açilis Konusmasi (Speech of the President of the Constitutional Court on the Occasion of the Beginning of the Court's 40th Term), 25 April 2002, available at www.anayasa.gov.tr/ydonum/k40.htm (visited 26 March 2004). See also, *Turkish Daily News*, 26 April 2002.

[52] SA Arjomand, 'Islam and Constitutionalism: the Significance and Peculiarities of Twentieth-Century Iran', ch 2 in this volume.

[53] YG Özden, 'Opening Speech by Yekta Gungor Ozden, President of the Turkish Constitutional Court' (Ankara: The Constitutional Court of Turkey, 1993) at 9.

are reproduced in the formal and informal institutions of state and society'.[54] The 1979 Iranian Constitution officially recognises the power of the people and the role of elections in legitimising the state. At the same time, it declares that 'absolute sovereignty belongs to God' (Article 56) and subjects elected institutions such as the presidency and the parliament to control by the Supreme Leader of the Revolution (*vali-ye faqih*), an undemocratically and indirectly selected official representing the will of God.[55] This institutionalisation of competing ideologies has produced a political structure composed of contradictory elements. The system's democratic elements encourage change, while its authoritarian features try to limit the impact of that change.[56]

The Islamic Republic has tried to manage the resulting tensions through a number of extra-political institutions. One of the most important of these institutions is the controversial Council of Guardians.[57] According to the Constitution, the Council was established 'to safeguard the Islamic ordinances and the Constitution, [and] to examine the compatibility of the legislations passed by the Islamic Consultative Assembly with Islam' (Article 91). In addition, the Council has the responsibility to supervise elections for the Assembly of Experts, the presidency and the parliament (Article 99).

The Council of Guardians is a combination upper house of the parliament and constitutional court. Two aspects of the Council's powers, however, distinguish it from conventional upper houses found in other countries. First, the Council does not have the power to initiate legislation on its own. Similarly to a constitutional court, it can only review legislation adopted by the parliament (*majlis*). Secondly, the Council has the exclusive power of constitutional review. What distinguishes the Council from a proper constitutional court, as the term is generally understood in other political systems, is that legislation adopted by the *majlis* cannot become law without the consent of the Council that it meets both the requirements of Islamic law and the Constitution.

It is also clear that the Constitution sees the Council of Guardians as superior to the parliament. Article 93 of the Constitution specifically states

---

[54] Brumberg, above n 42, at 33–4.

[55] On the political structure of the Islamic Republic of Iran, see inter alia W Buchta, *Who Rules Iran? The Structure of Power in the Islamic Republic* (Washington, DC, Washington Institute for Near East Policy, 2000); HE Chehabi, 'The Political Regime of the Islamic Republic of Iran in Comparative Perspective' (2001) *Government and Opposition* 36; M Kamrava and H Hassan-Yari, 'Suspended Equilibrium in Iran's Political System' (2004) *The Muslim World* (October) 94.

[56] Brumberg, above n 42, at 5.

[57] SA Arjomand, 'Civil Society and the Rule of Law in the Constitutional Politics of Iran under Khatami' (2000) 67(2) *Social Research* (Summer) 283–301; A Gheisssari and V Nasr, 'Iran's Democracy Debate' (2004) 11(2) *Middle East Policy* (Summer) 94–105; Mehrangiz Kar, 'The Deadlock in Iran: Constitutional Constraints' (2003) 14(1) *Journal of Democracy* (January) 132–36; AW Samii, 'Iran's Guardian Council as an Obstacle to Democracy' (2001) *Middle East Journal* (Autumn) 55.

that 'The Islamic Consultative Assembly does not hold any legal status if there is no Guardian Council in existence, except for the purpose of approving the credentials of its members and the election of the six jurists on the Guardian Council'. Furthermore, the members of the Council can take part in parliamentary debates while the reverse is not true for the members of the parliament.

The Council is composed of six clerics and six non-clerical jurists. The first group are appointed directly by the Supreme Leader while the parliament appoints the non-clerical jurists. The parliament's role in influencing the composition of the Council is severely limited by the constitutional requirement that the non-clerical jurists be nominated by the Head of the Judiciary, himself appointed by and responsible to the Supreme Leader. All 12 members determine compatibility of legislation with the Constitution. However, only the clerics on the Council can determine compatibility with Islamic law. Furthermore, decisions of the Council concerning conformity with Islamic law require the support of only a simple majority of the clerical members while those concerning constitutional issues require the affirmative vote of three-fourths of the entire body. In other words, although the lay jurists on the Council have no role in determining conformity with Islamic law, the support of at least three of the clerical members is needed in determining constitutionality. Members of the Council serve for renewable six-year terms (Articles 91–99).

One consequence of the structure of the Council of Guardians and its role in the legislative process has been the institutionalisation of a high level of tension between the parliament/presidency and the Council of Guardians. These tensions reached a high point during the presidency of Mohammad Khatami (1997–2005), when the Council rejected 111 out of his 297 legislative proposals, including some concerning the powers of the Guardian Council itself.[58] Similarly, the Council used its supervisory powers to disqualify many reformist candidates from standing in parliamentary and presidential elections. At the same time, the courts and the judiciary joined the battle between the reformers and more conservative elements by banning numerous reformist newspapers and imprisoning reformist intellectuals and activists.

It would be a mistake, however, to contribute the tensions inherent in Iran's political system to ideological differences between the reformers and the conservatives. Reforms, of course, test the boundaries of the constitutional system. However, tensions between the parliament and the Guardian Council were not unique to Khatami's tenure and have their roots in the institutional structure of the Islamic Republic. In fact, these tensions first appeared under Khomeini himself and eventually led him to decree into

---

[58] L Secor, 'Fugitives: Young Iranians Confront the Collapse of the Reform Movement', *New Yorker*, 21 November 2005, 64.

existence the Expediency Council charged with the task of settling the differences between the parliament and the Guardian Council.

The Supreme Leader appoints all members of the Expediency Council (*majma`-e tashkhis-e maslahat*) and the Council reports to him directly.[59] The heads of the three branches of government and the clerical members, but not the lay members, of the Guardian Council are members of the Council. The Expediency Council also includes a number of other religious and political personalities appointed by the Supreme Leader. Furthermore, depending on the issues on the agenda, other individuals can be invited to take part in the deliberations of the Council.

The Expediency Council has two primary functions. First, it is to resolve the differences between the Majlis and the Council of Guardians. Secondly, it is to act as an advisory Council to the Supreme Leader. The Council establishes the overall policy orientation of the Islamic Republic that the other organs are required to follow. In this regard, the Expediency Council is somewhat similar to the Turkish National Security Council discussed above, which also serves as a forum for joint policy-making by the guardians and elected officials. Both institutions are recognition of the fact that the political system embodies a high level of tension between elected and unelected institutions that, if left unchecked, could paralyse the political system.

Though tempting, it would be wrong to attribute reliance on extra-political institutions to the peculiarities of the Iranian system or the needs of theocracy. As I have shown, reliance on extra-political institutions is characteristic of the systems where elected officials share power with unelected guardians, including the political system of secular Turkey.

CONCLUSIONS

The challenge for many developing countries is how to accept the ideals of popular sovereignty and universal suffrage as the basic organising principles of the polity while designing an institutional framework that would effectively deny the franchise to those segments of the society who oppose the project of the state elite. An earlier generation of constitutional framers could overcome this problem by formally denying the vote to certain groups in society. For designers of modern constitutions, however, there is no escape from the need to minimise formal limits on the right to participate in the political life of the community. This is not only true in democracies like Turkey, where the modern understanding of the term by definition includes universal suffrage, but also in countries like Iran, where public support is accepted as one of the main legitimating factors by the regime.

---

[59] See www.iranonline.com/iran/iran-info/Government/Expediency.html

The consequence has been the division of sovereignty between elected institutions and unelected guardians.

As I have shown in this chapter, despite their different regime types and opposing ideologies, in both Turkey and Iran elected institutions function side by side with guardians who see their own role as safeguarding the state project against powerful social interests, even when those interests form a majority in the polity. In Iran, the Supreme Leader sees himself as the guardian of the Islamic nature of the system, while the Turkish military sees itself as the defender of secularism. The heavy reliance on extra-political institutions such as Iran's Guardian Council and Turkey's Constitutional Court that characterises both political systems, hence, is not a function of theocracy or secularism. Rather, as I have tried to show in this chapter, it is a consequence of the division of sovereignty between elected and unelected institutions and is designed to limit the powers of elected institutions without undermining the above-politics posture of the guardians.

6

Constitution, Legitimacy and Democracy in Turkey

MEHMET FEVZI BILGIN

CONSTITUTIONS PROVIDE A blueprint for a country's political organisation, establish normative and legal frameworks for basic institutions and embody an implicit or explicit ideology that governs the course of public life. As a blueprint of political organisation, constitutions fundamentally define the contours of political power in a given society and elaborate how political power is distributed, used and released. Accordingly, constitutions also establish basic institutions of political power, and identify the way they work and rules and principles that apply to their operations. Moreover, and perhaps most importantly, constitutions articulate a public ideology or philosophy, whether it is explicitly laid out in or inherently embedded in the text itself in various forms. Constitutional documents are replete with symbols, equivocations, indications, referring, overtly or not, to a certain ideological or philosophical perspective of choice revered by the framers.

Essential features of a constitution as such say little about its legitimacy. Legitimacy of a constitution is based on its moral, legal and sociological foundations, components of which range from the way a constitution is framed, the authority it involves, the justification it carries, the legality it endows, the consent it refers to and the support it draws. These components together contribute to an overall legitimacy of a given constitution. Constitutions as such are seen as primary political documents, possessing a level of authority and influence in a given body politic, more than any other document. The more legitimacy they assume, the more sway they carry in political and public spheres of life, and the more influence they emanate in political and public culture of a given political community. By the same token, constitutions that do not possess a sufficient degree of legitimacy follow a different trajectory. When tenaciously implemented by political authorities, a constitution as such could assume a distinction as the epitome of immoral and illegitimate execution of power and authority, where publics, directly or indirectly, suffer under its unwarranted provisions. And when constitutions are not implemented, even if they possess a great amount of legitimacy in the public eye, they would merely hang on the wall of political consciousness as ornaments of deep but forlorn affection.

For a constitution to be perceived as legitimate by a public, the public have to have access to its content to begin with. This means that they have to have an effect on its formation, influence its characteristics and provide substance to its tenets, principles and provisions. This access takes many forms, beginning from its actual writing and its ratification, to providing a continuous check on its implementation by political authority, to legislating further in line with its provisions, to updating and amending its content when necessary. The public might use this access directly or through their representatives; but, they must have this access regardless, free of any conditionality. These measures, taken altogether, constitute the very foundation of democratic legitimacy, and reflect the long tradition of the ideas of sovereignty of the people, rule of law, divisions of power, basic rights and, most recently, deliberative democracy. Thus, for a democratic constitution to be truly legitimate, it must possess this spirit of democracy and honour essential principles of democracy. Hence, like the body politic and regime they establish, constitutions themselves must also derive from a democratic origin and contain democratic principles and rules throughout its text. All things considered, it must be a script of democracy.

In this chapter, I apply this notion of legitimacy to the constitution of Turkey. The current constitution of Turkey was introduced about two decades ago during the military rule under auspices of military authorities and contained substantial anti-democratic principles until recent amendments. Turkey has been experiencing democracy for a half a century, however, and has always been willing to pursue a democratic prospect. Accordingly, the post-constitutional politics in Turkey has rather been in the direction of democracy, whereby the moral authority and legal justifications of the constitution have been continuously questioned. What is more interesting in the case of Turkey is the fact that the people of Turkey had a non-democratic constitution despite the fact that they strongly favour and cherish democratic ideas and institutions. This aspect of the case offers a rarely observed or studied phenomenon: a democratic country with a non-democratic constitution. Therefore, Turkey offers a strong and interesting case study in terms of the issues of constitutional legitimacy, the relation between democracy and constitution and the implications of a non-democratic constitution, and warrants special attention.

INTRODUCTION: WHAT MAKES A CONSTITUTION LEGITIMATE?

Constitutions come with and introduce not only a package of political, legal and juridical provisions and institutions, but also a baggage of philosophical, ideological and cultural conceptions. Every new constitution is marked by myriad of notions that would effectively regulate the legal-political and politico-cultural spheres of a given society for an undetermined period of time. Constitutions that are made anew, or those that went through major revisions, are products of intense periods of 'high politics' when citizens engage higher law-making processes that result in fundamental alterations in the way public and political life works and the principles they abide by. Bruce Ackerman aptly called these periods 'constitutional moments'.[1] These are periods of substantial change and crisis when nations engage serious debates about constitutional issues. Consequently, 'a collective reassessment of values and principles results in a constitutional paradigm shift'.[2]

Thus, every new constitution comes with its own paradigmatic features, which tend to suppress those of old constitutions or constitutional systems and introduce new conceptions, new philosophies and a new direction for a given nation. Similarly, every new constitution denotes a preconstitutional period or system, with all its transformative features that culminate in a new foundation on which the polity rests: 'A fundamental change in the existing base, effected by popular revolution or similar cataclysmic political event, usually means a corresponding change in the basic constitutional system and the postulation of a new legal starting point, or *Grundnorm*, as the basic premise of a new legal starting point'.[3] But, as McWhinney adds, the new legal premise is actually a result of a 'pre-legal' or meta-legal' process where the constitutional question is addressed. Thus, in fact, every new constitution is also a political answer to the constitutional question. Consequently, every new constitution is a new political paradigm.

The most saliently observed political aspect of constitutions manifests in the process of constitution-making. This is the dynamic side of the 'constitutional moments' when the political drama unfolds in full force. Arjomand captured this sense of animated manifestation of politics in his description of *constitutional politics*: 'a broader macrosociological meaning as the politics of reconstruction ... where sociopolitical forces and institutional interests are aligned competing and heterogeneous principles of order'.[4] Politics of reconstruction might bring about new communities, lead to modernisation or launch a period of transition; but, nonetheless, it essentially carries the

---

[1] B Ackerman, *We the People: Transformations* (Cambridge, MA, Harvard University Press, 1998). Ackerman identifies three such moments in the history of the United States: the Founding, Reconstruction and the New Deal. Although Ackerman uses the term to denote some radical changes in constitutional conceptions, in the context of countries which tend to have constitutions writ anew rather than significant constitutional changes, I think it is safe to use the term also for periods of constitution-making which result in new constitutions.
[2] S Chambers, 'Deliberative Democratic Theory' (2003) *Annual Review of Political Science* 6, 309.
[3] E McWhinney, *Constitution-Making: Principles, Process, Practice* (Toronto, University of Toronto Press, 1981) 12.
[4] SA Arjomand, 'Law, Political Reconstruction and Constitutional Politics' (2003) *International Sociology* 18, 27.

spirit of a constitutional moment along with all possible consequences. Thus, politics and constitution are inseparably related; the nature and qualities of the latter are very much dependent on the forces and discourses manifest in the course of politics which eventually produce a constitution. Accordingly, constitutions appear as projects of pre-constitutional politics which, in turn, inform their very principles and provisions.[5] On the other hand, constitutions have their share of significant influence on the course of post-constitutional politics, be it 'normal politics' in Ackerman's sense, when the interpretative paradigm of a given constitution is not questioned, or subsequent periods of higher law-making, such as amending constitutional provisions while upholding the existing constitutional paradigm.[6] A constitution could effect an ultimate impact on politics by happening to be the centre of a conflict, and thus helping launch a subsequent phase of constitutional politics.

To conceive a constitution as a political project helps us move beyond the legal provisions it entails, and understand what it actually implies, or more particularly, what sort of public and political philosophy a constitution propagates. According to Raz, constitutions are defined by a combination of the following seven features: constitutions define the organisation of government; they stand for durability and stability; they are canonical in nature; they are superior to ordinary law; they are subject to judicial procedures which implement their superiority; they are difficult to change; and they generally reflect a popularly consensual belief about the way a polity should operate.[7] Such approaches are instrumental in defining essential features of a constitution and providing a well-defined framework to study its legal aspects or implications. But, then, they are ultimately of a legal nature, missing out deeper political meanings behind the legal provisions.

The political nature of constitutions is highlighted by Michelman[8] who sees them as products of consequential political processes whereby philosophical and ideological characteristics of political forces and discourses find a legally established refuge within the confines of a 'superior law'. They are fundamentally a kind of political statement because the political authorities or elites, who introduce constitutions, also exert their political intention at the

---

[5] See Shäfer on how memory of past conflicts influences future constitutional constructions: M Shäfer, 'Memory in the Construction of Constitutions' (2002) *Ratio Juris* 14.

[6] A helpful note on constitutional amendments was provided by Walter F Murphy, who claimed that to amend is essentially to correct, thus 'an "amendment" corrects or modifies the system without fundamentally changing its nature: An "amendment" operates within the theoretical parameters of the existing constitution'. WF Murphy, 'Constitutions, Constitutionalism, and Democracy' in D Greenberg *et al* (eds), *Constitutionalism and Democracy: Transitions in the Contemporary World* (New York, Oxford University Press, 1993) 14.

[7] J Raz, 'On the Authority and Interpretation of Constitutions: Some Preliminaries' in L Alexander (ed), *Constitutionalism: Philosophical Foundations* (Cambridge, Cambridge University Press, 1998) 153. In short, in Raz's terms, constitutions are, respectively, constitutive, stable, written, superior law, justiciable, entrenched and express a common ideology.

[8] FI Michelman, 'Constitutional Authorship' in L Alexander (ed), *Constitutionalism: Philosophical Foundations* (Cambridge, Cambridge University Press, 1998) 65.

utmost level of authority and with long-term implications. Thus, a constitution is an 'expression of an intentional historical-political act', whereby the very nature of this act effectively commands obedience to a constitution.[9]

Since constitutions are of political nature, namely they are political acts or expressions of political intentions, or outright political exertions of respective circumstances, their legitimacy cannot possibly be established solely by legal terms. Fallon[10] identifies three realms of legitimacy with respect to constitutions: legal, sociological and moral. Legal legitimacy of a constitution derives from the fact it is a lawful undertaking. Legal legitimacy of a constitution would derive from the legality of its ratification and the authority of its makers, and also its connection to a prior constitutional system. Fallon argues that legal legitimacy of a constitution might depend on its legality, but what makes a constitution truly legitimate is its sociological acceptance, namely its sociological legitimacy. In contrast to legal legitimacy, a constitution is sociologically legitimate when it is freely and categorically revered by a given public: 'A constitutional regime, governmental institution, or official decision possesses legitimacy in a *strong* sense insofar as the relevant public regard it as justified, appropriate, or otherwise deserving of support for reasons beyond fear of sanctions or mere hope for personal reward'.[11] Moral legitimacy of a constitution, on the other hand, is 'a function of moral justifiability or respect-worthiness', and derives from the fact that a constitution is appropriate, fair and reasonable and has not a both viable and better alternative.[12]

Fallon's categories of sociological and moral legitimacy might be merged into one which delineates the political character of the legitimacy of a constitution. Legitimacy defines the propriety of this condition. In this respect, from a political point of view, the sociological acceptance of a political power implies the fact that a given public is content with the societal distribution of power with all its legal implications. Thus, the distinction between sociological and moral legitimacy is not mutually exclusive, and usually the latter is embedded in the former.

Consider Habermas' definition of a legitimate constitution, which seems to capture both imperatives: 'The constitution sets down political procedures according to which citizens can, in the exercise of their right to self-determination, successfully pursue the cooperative project of establishing just (ie relatively more just) conditions of life'.[13] Ideally, for a constitution

---

[9] RS Kay, 'American Constitutionalism' in L Alexander (ed), *Constitutionalism: Philosophical Foundations* (Cambridge, Cambridge University Press, 1998) 31.

[10] RH Fallon Jr, 'Legitimacy and the Constitution' (2005) *Harvard Law Review* 118: 1787–1853.

[11] *Ibid* 1795.

[12] *Ibid*.

[13] J Habermas, *Between Facts and Norms: Contributions to a Discourse Theory of Law and Democracy* (Cambridge, MA, MIT Press, 1996) 263.

to be maximally justified with full consent of a given public, it must not only embody a socially approved philosophy along with its respective principles and provisions, but also enjoy accessibility from the public stance, throughout its formational processes. This is especially important considering the fact that a constitution is meant to be a long-standing document, which 'articulates the horizon of expectation opening on an ever-present future'.[14] This means that constitutions must be subject to public engagement when they are created, in the form of deliberation upon the principles and provisions and ratification of the text. The role of public then manifests itself in their maintenance and updating.

A legitimate constitution, then, is a product of a political undertaking, which is both socially acceptable and morally respected. An ideal description of such a constitution might go as follows: 'The exercise of political power is proper and hence justifiable only when it is exercised in accordance with a constitution, the essentials of which all citizens may reasonably be expected to endorse in the light of principles and ideals accepted by them as reasonable and rational'.[15] As a consent-based theory of justification, Rawls's constitutional contractarianism merges social acceptability and moral basis in a sophisticated manner. Here we have the basic components of legitimacy, whereby citizens endorse constitutional essentials according to the higher principles and ideals they uphold. The premise of this view is that citizens must have the ability, namely freedom and willingness, to endorse such essentials, and those essentials are not imposed externally in any form.[16] Consequently, citizens essentially become subject to their own making.

Legitimacy in the form of social consent on a moral basis constitutes the essentials of the modern idea of democratic legitimacy. Democratic principles postulate congruence or symmetry between political acts or decisions and those who are subject to or affected by those acts and decisions. Citizens must have a say in political processes, influence decisions and form institutions, in some form or another, depending on the depth of democratic culture and quality of democratic mechanisms in a given society. These engagements might range from a minimal participation in the form of voting to active pursuits of will-formation. Recent studies on the theory of deliberative democracy have helped deepen our view of democracy and extend it beyond 'voting-centric' visions of democracy to the 'communicative processes of opinion and will-formation'.[17] Deliberative democratic

---

[14] *Ibid* 384.

[15] J Rawls, *Political Liberalism* (New York, Columbia University Press, 1993) 217.

[16] These notions more or less correspond to what Michelman observes as three key components of Rawls' constitutional contractarianism: rational universalism, constitutional essentialism, and moral responsivism. See FI Michelman, 'Morality, Identity, and "Constitutional Patriotism"' (2001) *Ratio Juris* 14, 258–60.

[17] Chambers, above n 2, at 308.

theory has drawn attention to institutions, processes, venues and spheres of deliberation. Constitutions, as essential framework documents of political procedures, shape contours of public life and exert influence on lives of citizens more than any other political institution. If a constitution itself lacks those democratic credentials, naturally the institutions and procedures it sets down would not obtain a democratic character.

For a constitution to be democratic, democratic credentials of a constitution are to be manifest mainly in two areas: (1) its creation and (2) its content. By creation, I mean the processes of framing, deliberating, drafting and ratifying a constitution. The democratic aspect of framing a constitution would involve credentials of its framers, their authority and the process of framing. In this respect, a democratic creation requires an open process, in which the framing body, be it a convention, council or congress, fairly represents interests of the relevant public. Secondly, the framing process must be fairly open to deliberation. This would require an active public engagement in the design of a constitution. This is a crucial condition for the framing process, since 'constitutions are meant to provide a framework for the public life in a country, giving it direction and shape ... widespread knowledge of the constitution has to be secured. This requires knowledge not only of the text but of its significance'.[18] Deliberation, also, is not to be held out of mere formality; rather, it should serve as a means of articulation of various public interests and carry a genuine leverage. A framing process having such credentials is expected to produce a democratic constitution, since it is not reasonable for an engaging public to constrain themselves in a non-democratic fashion through a restrictive constitution. Lastly, a constitution needs to be enacted by a democratic body and ratified in a democratic fashion, whether by a national referendum or a similar process, but at the end carrying an approval rate representing a greater majority of the people.

Participatory constitution-making as such, however, is some sort of novelty in the world. The best recent example of it is the 1996 South African Constitution. The creation phase of that constitution took nearly six years, marked by full-scale cooperation among political and juridical authorities, an extensive media campaign and unrestrained public engagement. Not all democratic constitutions involve such democratic credentials in creation. Constitutions of the post-war Germany and Japan, in particular, were created under the auspices of the Allied Powers. The 1949 Basic Law of the Federal Republic of Germany was drafted by a constitutional assembly whose members were selected by the regions but not elected by the people. The Basic Law went into effect without being submitted to the public for approval. The 1947 Constitution of Japan was promulgated based on a draft imposed by the Allied Powers and went into effect, again, without being

---

[18] Raz, above n 7, at 175.

submitted to the approval of the Japanese people. The German and Japanese examples demonstrate that constitutions can be democratic without being democratically created.

This brings us to the second and more important aspect of a democratic constitution, which is its content. By this, I mean that a constitution must possess a democratic spirit in script, and this spirit must command all the body of rules and principles it enacts, and institutions it constitutes. It should embody basic principles of democracy and offer a genuine prospect of democracy for its own people. Here, democracy is defined from a broader and deeper perspective. In this respect, democracy is not simply 'a regime in which governmental offices are filled as a consequence of contested elections'.[19] These sorts of approaches to democracy as merely of power struggles through an electoral system, namely an 'electoral democracy',[20] lack the moral and philosophical substance the idea of democracy has come to represent. As Sunstein aptly puts, 'Democracy comes with its own internal morality ... which requires constitutional protection of many individual rights, including the right of free expression, the right to vote, the right to political equality, and even the right to private property, for people cannot be independent citizens if their holdings are subject to unlimited government adjustment'.[21]

The internal morality of democracy, the ideas of liberty and equality that constitute its foundations and the insights taken from ongoing practice of democracy in the world today, necessitate the existence of certain basic institutions accompanied by certain fundamental rights for a regime to be considered a democracy. The main ones are: limited government, rule of law, political equality, elected and accountable officials, free and fair elections, inclusive suffrage, civil liberties (personal autonomy, life, religion, opinion, expression, speech, association, assembly) and political rights (voting, running for offices, electing representatives, instituting parties and associations). Sunstein argues that the central purpose of a constitution 'is to create the preconditions for a well-functioning democratic order, one in which citizens are genuinely able to govern themselves'.[22] This purpose also defines how democratic a constitution is. A democratic constitution must reflect a democratic spirit in either its creation or its content. A democratically created constitution cannot possibly embody non-democratic principles. If a constitution is not democratically created, then it must unequivocally embody democratic ideas and honour principles of democracy throughout its content to be considered democratic.

---

[19] A Przeworski *et al*, 'What Makes Democracies Endure?' (1996) *Journal of Democracy* 7, 50.

[20] L Diamond, *Developing Democracy: Toward Consolidation* (Baltimore, Johns Hopkins University Press, 1999) 9–10.

[21] C Sunstein, *Designing Democracy: What Constitutions Do* (New York, Oxford University Press, 2001) 7.

[22] *Ibid* 6.

TURKEY'S CONSTITUTIONAL PREDICAMENTS

The story of Turkey's constitution began on 12 September 1980, when the armed forces intervened into the democratic process, abolished the parliament and government, and effectively instituted a military rule that would last about three years. The military intervention came amidst chaotic social and political developments and military leaders had justified their action under the guise of restoring order. The coup was the third in the last 20 years and this time the military seemed resolved more than ever to restore normality and defend the integrity of the state to the extent that recourse to further intervention would not be necessary. A year from intervention, preparations for a new constitution began to unfold and following an unusually long process of framing, by the autumn of 1982, the new constitution was ready to be submitted to a popular vote. Following its approval by an extraordinary majority in its favour (91 per cent), it was adopted on 7 November 1982 as the new constitution of the Republic of Turkey. The new constitution was the third constitution of the Republic, which was founded in 1923 and saw two preceding constitutions of 1924 and 1961; the latter was also framed during an earlier military rule.

In the autumn of 1983, a year after the enactment of the new constitution, democracy was restored and a new civil government came into power following general elections. Despite the restoration, the 1982 Constitution remained almost intact by 2001, when Turkey stepped into a new 'constitutional moment', as a result of the pre-candidacy status offered by the European Union in 1999 and the political criteria it had to satisfy in order to advance into accession negotiations.[23] The following years have seen—and continue to see—radical constitutional changes that significantly enhanced the sphere of fundamental and political liberties and moved the country closer to a genuine practice of a democratic system. Despite these positive developments, however, the fact that Turkey had to endure the 1982 Constitution in its original form for so long, albeit experiencing a technically democratic political system, and could initiate radical changes only after encouragement and pressure by the European Union, had a lot to do with the constitutional predicaments it had faced since the birth of the new constitution.

The Preamble to the 1982 Constitution stated:

Following the operation carried out on 12 September 1980 by the Turkish Armed Forces in response to a call from the Turkish Nation, of which they form an

---

[23] These criteria are known as Copenhagen criteria, which were laid down at the 1993 European Council and defined the condition of eligibility for membership in the European Union. According to its political criterion, membership requires that the 'candidate country has achieved stability of institutions guaranteeing democracy, the rule of law, and respect for and protection of minorities' (http://ec.europa.eu/comm/enlargement/towards_EU_membership/criteria_en.htm).

inseparable part ... This Constitution was prepared by the Consultative Assembly, given final form by the Council of National Security, which are the legitimate representatives of the Turkish Nation, and adopted, approved and directly enacted by the Turkish Nation.

These words narrate quite a smooth operation of constitution-making with all the legitimate authority vested in the constitution-makers. Unfortunately, this does not represent the whole picture and the creation phase of the constitution came with its own troubled trajectory along with respective textual consequences. More than anything, the representative character of the constitution-making body was utterly controversial. The Consultative Assembly was convened through extremely strict and selective process that excluded everybody who had a connection to any political party that existed prior to the intervention and who failed further clearance. The Constitutional Commission that actually prepared the constitution as part of the Assembly also reflected this choice and was thus chaired by a law professor favoured by the military establishment. As an additional security, and as the Preamble stated, the Council of National Security formed by the five top military generals gave the final form to the text. During the process of writing of the constitution, public discussion of its content was forbidden. These limitations also continued to a certain extent in the period following the completion of the text until the day of referendum. In the meantime, the head of state gave a series of speeches in various locations on the country and introduced the content of the constitution. But these were not intended to incite a public discussion; rather, they were only informative speeches and any criticism of their contents was strictly forbidden. Finally, the constitution was approved as expected.[24]

Under these constraints, the fact that 91 per cent of the public voted in favour of the constitution could only be interpreted with their desire to see the armed forces retreat to their barracks as soon as possible. In fact, the military leaders did not provide a clear pathway should the constitution be rejected. There was registered public concern that the military would continue to rule. Considering all these circumstances in the creation phase, the 1982 Constitution did not seem to satisfy the requirements of a democratic constitution: the representative quality of the constitution-making body was controversial; public engagement in the process was utterly minimal; articulation of different interests was not possible; the ratification process was designed in a way that effectively secured an approval. Consequently, these facts together contributed to the birth of a constitution that came with a package of non-democratic provisions and regulations which would

---

[24] E Ozbudun, *Türk Anayasa Hukuku* (Ankara, Yetkin Yayinlari, 1993); E Ozbudun, *Contemporary Turkish Politics: Challenges to Democratc Consolidation.* (Boulder, CO, Lynne Rienner, 1999); M Erdogan, *Turkiye'de Anayasalar ve Siyaset* (Ankara, Liberte Yayinlari, 2003); T Parla, *Turkiye'de Anayasalar* (Istanbul, Iletisim Yayinlari, 1991).

challenge the very essence of democratic politics in Turkey in the upcoming decades.

Democracy is not a new idea and practice in Turkey. Democracy and a multiparty system was introduced in 1946, and by 1950, the official state party was already replaced in government by a populist party that had won general elections by a wide margin.[25] During the periods of civil rule,[26] the multiparty system functioned fairly well, elections were held regularly, and transitions from one government to another occurred by the rules. Turkey was also a signatory country to major international human rights conventions. But all these facts did not help prevent frequent cessations of democratic rule nor dissipate the ever-persistent presence of authoritarian inclinations that haunted the political system.

There are myriad reasons behind all these democratic failures, but, it seems, the most prominent is the state tradition descended from the Ottoman Empire, that exhibits 'patrimonial' tendencies,[27] and tends to protect the state from the people rather than the other way around, a feature that marked the modern history of democracy. Thus, the state elites posed as guardians of the official ideology, acted on behalf of the state and aimed to keep it above and beyond the ramifications of democratic politics. From this point of view, the political regime should not be left alone, and the military interventions were seen as a means to 'regulate' democracy in Turkey.[28] As Evin succinctly put it, this statism generated its own self-fulfilling prophecy that manifestly dominated the whole political process: 'It was the state in the first place which had provided the framework for a democratic system with all the freedoms associated with it. However, the politicians had been unable to appreciate this system and moreover, had committed the sin of subverting it through manipulation for their own gains. The state giveth and the state taketh, too'.[29] This statist mindset along with the imperatives of guardianship achieved new highs in the 1980 intervention. Equally, this era was also the breeding ground for the 1982 Constitution, which ultimately came to represent those sentiments in an unfettered fashion.

[25] This places Turkey in the second wave of democratisation according to Samuel Huntington's classification: S Huntington, *The Third Wave: Democratization in the Late Twentieth Century* (Norman, OK, University of Oklahoma Press, 1991). The first wave of democratisation took place between the years 1828–1926, and the second between 1942–1962; the third wave started in 1974 and arguably is still continuing. See also Diamond, above n 20, at ch 2.
[26] That excludes periods of active military rule in 1960–61 and 1980–83, and forced government transitions in 1971 and 1997.
[27] M Heper, 'State and Society in Turkish Political Experience' in M Heper and A Evin (eds), *State Democracy and the Military: Turkey in the 1980s* (Berlin, Walter de Gruyter, 1988) 27.
[28] *Ibid* 6.
[29] A Evin, 'Changing Patterns of Cleavages before and after 1980' in M Heper and A Evin (eds), *State Democracy and the Military: Turkey in the 1980s* (Berlin, Walter de Gruyter, 1988) 208.

The 1982 Constitution, essentially, exhibited familiar attributes of transition from authoritarian to democratic, and military to civil rule. The securities against the imperatives of democratic processes, such as 'reserve domains of power', immunity against prosecution, and other related mechanisms, were in place. Linz and Stepan[30] argue that in the cases of authoritarian transitions, if the regime is led by a hierarchical military, depending on the strength of democratic forces, the length of democratic transition might be long and the extent of reserve domains of power imposed by the military as the price of extrication might be large. This was the case in the democratic transitions in countries such as Portugal, Chile and Brazil. In the Turkish case, during the 1980 intervention, the military presented quite a hierarchical structure, and did not repeat the quandaries of hierarchy it faced during the 1960 intervention.[31]

The 1980 intervention was planned in greater detail and the outline of the new constitution was arguably ready from the beginning: 'Also quite unlike its predecessors, the military seem to have determined in detail the basic constitutional principles that would be enacted, the type of institutions that would be established, the division of labor between the "state" and the government, and the sort of mechanisms that would be needed to ensure smooth functioning after the civil rule'.[32] As a result, the 1982 Constitution was drafted to maintain the military sway over politics. The short-term privileges were defined in a number of provisional articles aimed at regulating the transition. According to the first provisional article,[33] following the 'adoption by referendum of the constitution ... the Chairman of the Council of National Security and Head of State at the time of the referendum, shall assume the title of President of the Republic and shall exercise the constitutional functions and powers of the President of the Republic for a period of seven years'. In addition, provisional article 2 states that 'after the Turkish Grand National Assembly has convened and assumed its

---

[30] JJ Linz and A Stepan, *Problems of Democratic Transition and Consolidation: Southern Europe, South America, and Post-Communist Europe* (Baltimore, Johns Hopkins University Press, 1996) 59.

[31] For more on the role of the military in Turkish politics, see W Hale, *Turkish Politics and the Military* (London, Routledge, 1994); G Harris, 'The Role of the Military in Turkey: Guardians or Decision-Makers?' in M Heper and A Evin (eds), *State Democracy and the Military: Turkey in the 1980s* (Berlin, Walter de Gruyter, 1988).

[32] K Karpat, 'Military Interventions: Army-Civilian Relations in Turkey before and after 1980' in M Heper and A Evin (eds), *State Democracy and the Military: Turkey in the 1980s* (Berlin, Walter de Gruyter, 1988) 149.

[33] In the text, I am referring to the articles and clauses of the 1982 Constitution as they appeared in the original text in 1982, unless otherwise stated. The constitution saw many changes as a result of recent reforms, and current paper and online copies of the text reflect those changes. This makes it difficult to reach the text in original form and follow the progress subsequently recorded. To acquire the original text, the reader best refer to the *Constitutions of the Countries of the World*, a series edited by Gisbert H Flanz (and most recently by Rainer Grote and Rudiger Wolfrum), published since 1971 by Oceana Publications in New York, and continuously revised and updated.

functions, the Council of National Security shall become the Presidential Council for a period of six years'. In the following clauses, the functions of this Council were described as a higher body of legal approval, where almost all legislation that passed in the national assembly had to be confirmed. As a final touch, the President was granted a qualified veto power over constitutional amendments for six years.

The military influence over politics was not limited to these six to seven years of transitional prerogatives. Various articles of the constitution ensured an ongoing supervisory role for the military. Article 118 regulated the National Security Council as the highest advisory board for the state. The Council was comprised of the Prime Minister, three other ministers, the Chief of the General Staff and four other top military commanders, and the President, who acts as the chairman. As is obvious from the composition, the military side prevailed over the civilian side. According to the constitution, the Council 'shall submit to the Council of Ministers its views on taking decisions and ensuring necessary coordination with regard to the formulation, establishment and implementation of the national security policy of the State'. The Council of Ministers, in turn 'shall give priority consideration to the decisions of the National Security Council concerning the measures that it deems necessary for the preservation of the existence and independence of the State, the integrity and indivisibility of the country and the peace and security of society'. The wide range of issues that fall into the interest of the Council ensures the supremacy of the military views over the deliberation of the Council and thus political processes. The constitution also provided other privileges to the military in the form of immunity from various legal control mechanisms and significant influences in the judicial processes. All these provisions helped establish the fact that 'in Turkish politics the military became a factor which should be taken into the consideration by the elected civilians'.[34]

Considering the fact that most of these prerogatives were weakened during the 2001–2004 reforms only after almost two decades of civilian rule and within the galvanising spirit of the European Union candidacy, this exhibits the thickness of the authoritarian mantle covering Turkish politics and the difficulty of challenging the obstacles enervating the prospect of democracy. Linz and Stepan succinctly pointed out this problematique, and argued that if a 'constitution *de jure* enshrines nondemocratic 'reserve domains' insisted upon by the outgoing nondemocratic power-holders, then the transition by our definition cannot be completed until these powers are removed'.[35] Thus, the fact that democracy was restored in Turkey in 1983 and the constitutionally predetermined time span of transition ended in

---

[34] E Ozbudun and S Yazici, *Democratization Reforms in Turkey (1993–2004)* (Istanbul, TESEV Publications, 2004) 37.
[35] Linz and Stepan, above n 30, at 82.

1989 did not result in a genuine transition towards a fully-fledged democracy. The constitutional legacy of the intervention continued to haunt the national politics; the wide range of privileges and prerogatives granted in the constitution ensured an ongoing check on civilian politics. Conversely, the fact that one major area of concentration in the recent reforms has been to remove this legacy, shows the willingness of democratic forces, which were constitutionally fettered, to engage transformations of this magnitude when the opportunity strikes.

Besides exhibiting vestiges of authoritarian tendencies as such, the 1982 Constitution also presented an ideological discourse that at times goes manifestly against the democratic grain. The constitution makes frequent references to ideas and concepts that could be subject to democratic contestation in many instances. Apart from the explicit usage of ideological language, there is also an implicit ideological tone that prevails throughout the text. In this respect, the 1982 Constitution is a product of 'the era of ideological constitutions', as Arjomand argues, when constitutions are considered 'as instrument of social transformation according to total ideologies and their offspring ... marked by the subservience of narrowly conceived rule of law and legality to the dominant ideology of the regime'.[36] The ideology of the 1982 Constitution might be called *statist republicanism*. The term aims to combine two trains of thought, namely political statism in the sense of exalting the state and proscribing an interventionist role for the state, and republicanism in the sense of subordination of different interests to a common weal, say to the interests of citizens in general. In statist republicanism, however, the emphasis moves onto the state and thus different interests are subordinated to the general interest of the state. Consequently, *res publica* is embodied in the state, separated from and above the public that constitutes it.

In the 1982 Constitution, this ideology of statist republicanism manifested itself in different forms and words—most explicitly in the Preamble by referring to 'the sacred Turkish State'—but ultimately ran a consistent discourse throughout the constitution. The constitution made recurrent references to 'indivisible integrity of the state with its territory and nation', 'national security or sovereignty' and 'fundamental characteristics of the State', in various sections regulating not only political, but also associational, social, cultural and economic life, and mostly at the expense of individual rights and pluralism. As Erdogan argues, by referring to the integrity of the state with its territory and nation, and thus the state having a nation and a territory, the constitution defined the state above the social consent of its citizens. This protective stance, embodied in many institutions including the infamous State

---

[36] Arjomand, above n 4, at 9. According to Arjomand this era lasted from 1917 to 1989. This era was preceded by the pre-modern constitutions (eighteenth century), modern constitutions (late eighteenth century), and constitutions of modernisation (early twentieth century), and was followed by the era of 'new constitutionalism' since 1989, marked by an increasing salience of constitutional courts. Arjomand argues that in 1920, Turkey entered the fourth phase but stalled there until recent constitutional reforms.

Security Courts, purported to 'protect' the state from society.[37] Part of this ideology was a vision of social engineering—most evidently in the section where the constitution, in great detail, regulated all aspects of education in view of this ideological foundation—that is seen as crucial to maintain those 'fundamental characteristics of the State'. The Preamble presented a vision of society converged on common 'ideas, belief, and resolutions', united 'in national honour and pride, in national joy and grief, in their rights and duties towards their existence as a nation, in blessings and in burdens, and in every manifestation of national life'. This vision of society as a 'homogenous entity' displays a significant departure from a democratic vision of *e pluribus unum*. In fact, there is not a single reference to pluralism or diversity of any sort in the constitution.

This ideological foundation manifestly influenced the discourse of rights in the constitution. One might argue that the most prominent legacy of the 1982 Constitution was the reversal of all kinds of democratic gains in the form of basic and political rights since the introduction of democracy in Turkey. This was evident in the report submitted by the Constitutional Council to the Consultative Assembly, saying that the aim was to design 'a constitution that is appropriate for the necessities of the national fabric without breaking basic principles of democracy'.[38] The report implies that the relatively greater area of freedom provided by the earlier constitution was beyond the national capacity for democracy, and thus democratic rules needed to be modified so as to address this deficiency. During the internal deliberations at the Assembly, statements such as 'a regime of freedoms is not a regime of irresponsible actions; rights are first listed and then restricted to protect them', 'if a person abuses his rights he is going to pay for it, but if he uses them properly, then of course there is not a problem', were commonplace. In one instance, one of the members even declared that 'we call the regime we have founded "liberal democracy"'.[39] Apparently, a misconstrued conception of freedom led to the formation of the troubled discourse of rights in the constitution.[40]

---

[37] Erdogan, above n 24, at 131–2.
[38] O Kocaoglu (ed), *Gerekçeli ve Açiklamali Anayasa: Danisma Meclisinde Anayasa Goruşmelerinin Perde Arkasi* (Istanbul, Temel Yayinlari, 1993) 25.
[39] *Ibid* 302, 305, 365.
[40] It is striking to observe that the framers of the constitution tried to legitimise their own efforts by using such discourses of democracy, while the product they came up with at the end was unequivocally non-democratic. This reveals a trend in Turkey in which, subsequent to the first multiparty election in Turkey in 1950 and the overwhelming public support for democratic discourses, no claim of political legitimacy, be it secular, nationalistic or religious, dared to base itself on a foundation that principally denied democracy. Thus, the secular and nationalistic foundation of the 1982 Constitution was justified in the eyes of 'democracy-loving Turkish youth' by the declaration of the fundamental characteristics of the state as 'democratic, secular, and social' (Article 2). Similar references to democracy can be observed in political religious discourses, where religious demands are articulated in the form of democratic demands. The discourse of *Adil Düzen* (Just System) adopted by the pro-Islamic Welfare Party in the 1990s was presented as the genuine practice of democracy.

Arjomand argues that 'ideological constitutions often syncretically included an impressive bill of rights, but took back with one hand what they pretended to give with the other by subordinating them to higher ideological principles'.[41] This was pretty much the case with the 1982 Constitution that 'after listing a certain right and freedom, it eliminated it or emptied of its content in the guise of restricting it'.[42] The framers developed a sophisticated mechanism of restriction in which every single right and freedom was subject to general and specific restrictions. Even if a right did not seem to be limited in the first instance, another article of the constitution would indirectly fulfil the promise by imposing a general restriction either on its essence or its practice. According to the grounds of restriction explained in the annotated text, there existed two types of restriction. The first type referred to the usual limitation of freedoms where an individual cannot violate freedoms of others by using his own freedoms. The second type was called restriction by public reasons. This was expressed in the recurrent statement (first appearing in Article 13) stating that a right may be restricted 'with the aim of safeguarding the indivisible integrity of the state with its territory and nation, national sovereignty, the Republic, national security, public order, general peace, the public interest, public morals and public health'. This criterion constituted a 'general' restriction and for it to apply to a certain right, it did not need to be mentioned specifically for that right. The second criterion was called a 'specific' restriction, which, evidently, imposed some restriction specific to a certain right in addition to general restrictions already imposed.[43] For example, freedom of movement might be restricted for 'promoting social and economic development' (Article 23); freedom of expression and of the press could not be used in 'languages prohibited by law' (Articles 26, 28); freedom of association was limited to non-political activities (Article 33).

These broad restrictive principles apparently did not adequately satisfy the concerns of the framers, so that they added another article (Article 14) to the constitution in which they 'prohibited' abuse of fundamental rights and freedoms. In addition to the restrictive criterion of Article 13, this article prohibited the use of rights with the aim of 'placing the government of the state under the control of an individual or a group of people, or establishing the hegemony of one social class over others, or creating discrimination on the basis of language, race, religion or sect, or of establishing by any other means a system of government based on these concepts and ideas'. According to the rationale provided by the framers, the general and specific restrictions of rights may not adequately prevent inappropriate uses of rights, albeit their use is in accordance with the law. In this respect,

---

[41] Arjomand, above n 4, at 13.
[42] Parla, above n 24, at 29.
[43] Kocaoglu, above n 38, at 44–6.

a certain use of freedom 'might always bear a different intention, and this intention might incline to prohibited aims'.[44] Thus, the restrictive hand of the constitution extended not only to actions but also to intentions. In this respect, the rights and freedoms listed in the constitution were more of an 'endowment from the state', which existed under the rules and principles of the constitution. Despite the initial declaration that 'everyone possess inherent fundamental rights and freedoms which are inviolable and inalienable' (Article 12), the subsequent regulations cancelled out this understanding of natural rights at the expense of the individual and citizen and in favour of the state.[45]

The 1982 Constitution also imposed significant restrictions on political rights. The general theme of the constitution in this context was to virtually regulate and delimit democracy and politics to the smallest detail. It aimed to provide stability at the expense of democratic politics, and tried to *depoliticise* the nation through strict regulations and effective mechanisms. This intention was evident from the beginning and succinctly put by Kenan Evren, the head of state during the military rule, in one his speeches propagating the constitution:

> The new Constitution lays down a principle valid for all institutions ... a party will function as a party, an association as an association, a foundation as a foundation, a trade union as a trade union. Political activity is reserved for political parties. No institution which is not organized as a political party may engage in political activity. On the other hand, political parties should not interfere in areas reserved for trade unions, associations, professional organizations, and foundations.[46]

The constitution imposed severe restrictions on the organisation of the civil society not only in a political sense but also in a social sense. It made clear distinctions between associations, professional organisations and trade unions and effectively prohibited these groups to 'engage in political activities, receive political support from or give to political parties' (Article 33). On the other hand, the same article also prohibited 'joint actions' by these organisations. This was aimed at curbing the formation of larger organisations or social movements that could possibly challenge 'fundamental characteristics of the Republic'. These prohibitions were accompanied by additional restrictions on holding meetings and demonstrations.

Although the framers confined the domain of politics to political parties, the regulations imposed in the constitution made the formation and sustenance of political parties that are not in line with the ideological principles of the constitution extremely difficult. According to Articles 68 and 69, 'the

---

[44] *Ibid* 48.
[45] Erdogan, above n 24, at 136.
[46] Ozbudun, *Contemporary Turkish Politics*, above n 24, at 131.

statutes and programmes of political parties shall not be in conflict with the indivisible integrity of the state with its territory and nation'; political parties 'shall not organize and function abroad, shall not form discriminative auxiliary bodies such as women's or youth branches, nor shall they establish foundations'; civil servant and students 'shall not become members of political parties'; political parties 'shall not have political ties and engage in political cooperation with associations, unions, foundations, cooperatives, and public professional organizations'. Further limitations were imposed through the Code of Political Parties which was enacted just before the 1983 elections. These limitations on political activities, along with restrictions in freedoms of expression and assembly, envisioned a supposedly orderly practice of democracy in which political participation and engagement is limited and regulated.

The 1982 Constitution also backed its restrictive vision with effective judicial mechanisms. It established State Security Courts that were specifically designed to prosecute offences against those ideological and philosophical principles advocated in the constitution. Equivocal and evasive criteria such as 'integrity of the state with its territory and nation', 'national security', 'the public interest', 'public order', were used drastically to suppress individuals, associations and interest groups challenging constitutional essentials. The Constitutional Court, on the other hand, acted as the guardian of the constitution and relentlessly upheld the principles of its restrictive and democratically troubled vision. Contrary to the examples of activist constitutional courts in Eastern Europe and South Africa that worked as conduits for democratic reforms and advocated demands of democratic citizenries against the state,[47] the Turkish Constitutional Court opted to adopt 'defensive constitutional politics', in Arjomand's words,[48] and engaged in political activism to defend the ideological scruples of the constitution. This stance of the court was most significant in its decisions banning and dissolving political parties. According to the constitution, the power to ban parties is vested in the Constitutional Court. The Court has dissolved 18 parties since 1983. Kogacioglu, who investigated the banning decisions, argues that 'decisions to ban a political party on constitutional grounds constitute a defining moment of demarcating and affirming concrete boundaries of legitimate action'.[49] In this respect, the Court acted as auxiliary to constitutional restrictions, and confined politics to a predetermined sphere of legitimate action.

---

[47] See KL Scheppele, 'Constitutional Negotiations: Political Contexts of Judicial Activism in Post-Soviet Empire' (2003) *International Sociology* 18; L Solyom, 'The Role of Constitutional Courts in the Transition to Democracy' (2003) *International Sociology* 18; H Klug, *Constituting Democracy: Law, Globalism and South Africa's Political Reconstruction* (Cambridge, Cambridge University Press, 2000).

[48] Arjomand, above n 4, at 27.

[49] D Kogacioglu, 'Progress, Unity, and Democracy: Dissolving Political Parties in Turkey' (2004) *Law and Society Review* 38, 434.

In summary, the 1982 Constitution of Turkey was a product of an authoritarian mindset and included severe impediments to democratic prospects in Turkey, in the form of ideological baggage, significant restrictions of rights and liberties and a confined domain of political action. The constitution substantially failed in terms of its democratic credentials in its creation and content. The creation phase of the constitution was a closed process, prohibiting broad public engagement and participation. The public had to abstain from any deliberative initiation and only vote for a text prepared by a consultative body of the least representative character and imposed by the military administration. Under these circumstances, the extraordinarily high level of approval given to the constitution only raised doubts about the real motive behind this approval. In terms of its content, the 1982 Constitution reflected a particular ideology, statist republicanism, which was not at all sympathetic to democratic ideas and principles. The constitution placed the state before the citizen and required the latter to show absolute loyalty to the former, without providing any moral grounds. Power domains reserved for the military establishment only helped exacerbate the trajectory of democratic prospects. Broad restrictions and regulations in the area of civil and political rights and freedoms and the demarcated nature of politics promoted by the constitution, together fulfilled a political vision that was far from a genuine and internally moral view of democracy.

RECLAIMING DEMOCRACY

Because of its unimpressive democratic credentials, the 1982 Constitution raises significant questions of legitimacy. By imposing many non-democratic legal mechanisms and institutions, the constitution seemed reluctant to give society a chance to appreciate its essence. More than anything, the composition itself was a creation of a closed process, and thus a product of imposition. In this respect, it was not possible to establish an unreserved social acceptance of the political intention behind this product. Therefore, the 1982 Constitution faced a serious problem of political legitimacy due to its creation and content, and this in turn prevented it from being an expression of social and political consent.

This democratically and politically controversial nature of the 1982 Constitution had become a subject of ongoing efforts aiming to overcome its limitations in the subsequent era of civilian rule. As Kay suggests, over time constitutions become politically unacceptable, and when they stand unchanged they become 'incorrigibly unsuitable for the polity it is meant to govern'.[50] In the Turkish case, the political acceptability of the constitution was controversial from the outset. But the limitations the constitution

---

[50] RS Kay, 'Constitutional Chronomy' (2000) *Ratio Juris* 13, 43.

imposed on the civilian authorities made it impossible to make radical changes in a short span of time. As Genckaya argues, 'although a great majority of political circles unanimously criticized the anti-democratic statements and mechanisms set forth in the constitution, until recently the Grand National Assembly of Turkey did not attempt to replace it by a totally new constitution'.[51] This indicates that the political intention to democratise the constitution was present from the beginning. This, in turn, suggests that the democratic deficiencies of the constitution in original form were well known, and so its political acceptability and legitimacy was always in question. Accordingly, the desire to change the constitution has always been at the forefront of Turkish politics, if not always successful. Since its inception in 1982, the constitution has been subject to a gradually increasing wave of amendments.[52] All amendments were adopted through broad consent among political parties, namely 'inter-party agreements in parliament', since none of the parties was individually strong enough numerically to adopt the amendment single-handedly.[53] Consequently, one-third of the constitution has been effectively amended up to the present day. The wave of change has also progressed from minor and regulative changes to major and radical changes that substantially modified the original philosophical and ideological vision of the constitution.

It is telling that the first serious attempt to amend the constitution was actually aimed at its strict amendment regulations. In 1987, after serious conflicts between the civilian government and the President, Article 175 which regulates the requirements for constitutional amendment was changed in favour of a relatively less strict mechanism. This move represented the intention of the civilian powers and the direction they would like to proceed, and was very important at a time when the vestiges of the transitional period were still present. A second broad attempt at democratisation took place in 1995 and produced amendments in 15 articles. Most importantly, it removed the sentences praising the military intervention in the Preamble, relaxed restrictions on the associations and allowed them to engage in political activities, allowed students and educators in universities to be party members, enhanced the activities of political parties in terms of creating women's and youth branches and foundations, and operating in foreign countries, and also relaxed the rules for banning parties. After 1995, the wave of amendments stalled until 2001, except for two regulative changes in 1999. The main reason behind this was the worsening relations between the civilian government and the military following an Islamist

---

[51] OF Gençkaya, 'Politics of Constitutional Amendment in Turkey, 1987–2002' in GH Flanz (ed), *Constitutions of the Countries of the World* (Dobbs Ferry, NY, Oceana Publications, 2003) 9.

[52] So far, the 1982 Constitution has been amended nine times in 1987, 1993, 1995, twice in 1999, 2001, 2002, 2004 and 2005.

[53] Ozbudun and Yazici, above n 34, at 14.

victory in the 1995 elections. Subsequently, the focus of politics shifted from democratisation to the protection of secularism. In 1997, the military establishment instigated a forced transition of government and increased its influence significantly on politics, short of taking over rule. This period of heightened military supervision over the government lasted arguably until the decisions of the European Union, first to grant Turkey a possibility of candidacy in 1999, and then to adopt accession partnership priorities for Turkey in March 2001.

The welcome decisions of the European Union shuffled the political balances, galvanised democratic forces in Turkey and shifted the locus of politics in favour of further democratisation and civilianisation. They led to the formation of broad coalitions among the political parties of divergent interests for further democratisation. One of the fundamental consequences of this development has been the change of mind on the religious front for which 'Turkey's endeavor to become a full member of the EU has become compatible with their aim of democratizing the Turkish political system'.[54] The prospect of EU candidacy also instigated an unprecedented activism in civil society toward democratisation, and increased public awareness toward the necessity of change in the legal structure. The segments of civil society that became increasingly vocal in the 1990s[55] has been 'the driving force behind most of the expansion of fundamental freedoms and the protection of human rights'.[56] The main expectation of this coalition of political, civil and social forces during this mobilisation has been 'that the authoritarian constitutional and legal norms which were inherited from the military government would be eliminated'.[57]

Consequently, the period of 2001–2004 has seen the most radical constitutional changes. Amendments have eliminated the restriction on freedom of speech in the Preamble to the constitution; repealed the general restrictions on fundamental rights and introduced protective clauses for such rights; relaxed sanctions on the abuse of fundamental rights; abolished the death penalty; improved privacy of individual life; considerably broadened the freedom of assembly; adopted equality of spouses; lifted the language ban on broadcasting; abolished the infamous State Security Courts; relaxed the rules regulating eligibility to parliament; and made it harder to ban

---

[54] B Duran, 'Islamist Redefinition(s) of European and Islamic Identities in Turkey' in M Ugur and N Canefe (eds), *Turkey and European Integration: Accession Prospects and Issues* (London, Routledge, 2004) 140.

[55] EF Keyman and A Içduygu, 'Globalization, Civil Society, and Citizenship in Turkey: Actors, Boundaries and Discoveries' (2003) *Citizenship Studies* 7.

[56] J Sugden, 'Leverage in Theory and Practice: Human Rights and Turkey's EU Candidacy' in M Ugur and N Canefe (eds), *Turkey and European Integration: Accession Prospects and Issues* (London, Routledge, 2004) 260.

[57] S Yazici, 'The Impact of the EU on the Liberalization and Democratisation Process in Turkey' in RT Griffiths and D Ozdemir (eds), *Turkey and the EU Enlargement* (Istanbul, Istanbul Bilgi University Press, 2004) 91.

political parties. In addition to these changes in the regulation of rights and liberties, the constitutional reforms have taken a significant direction towards elimination of the military legacy and influence over politics and the civilianisation of political society. Accordingly, further amendments in the constitution have increased the number of civilian members in the National Security Council and weakened the effect of its decisions on the government; enabled legal investigations of actions during the military intervention; and eliminated some judicial privileges of the military.

The gradual but ongoing changes to the constitution in the post-1983 era indicate that the non-democratic elements of the 1982 Constitution generated a deep problem of legitimacy that has become the locus of politics and a motive for democratic mobilisation in Turkey. Civil governments that were confined by reserve domains of military power have been scrambling to overcome these hurdles; legislators limited by difficulties in amending the constitution and the vast legal rules and regulations comprised in the constitution that indirectly confined law-making to minor issues, have been coalescing to make as radical changes as possible, notwithstanding the time and effort required to build agreements among diverse parties; and civil society, substantially hedged about with constitutional restrictions, has been trying to circumnavigate those regulations through bold actions and instruments. The ongoing democratic activism in this respect points to a perceived deficiency of democratic credentials and thus legitimacy of the constitution in the public eye that need to be effectively addressed, and to the political will to eliminate this deficiency to better correspond with the democratic demands raised by the civil society. Thus, it seems, democratically deficient constitutions that lack political legitimacy in social and moral terms are destined to become the subject of conflict rather consent, and to be perceived as obstacles to be sooner or later eliminated.

Brandon's analysis of the failure of constitutions is highly relevant for the present discussion. One such failure is the failure of constitutional discourse. Brandon argues that this occurs 'when a constitutional order is unable to speak coherently or more seriously, to sustain itself through constitutional interpretation or through discourse pertaining to its constitution'.[58] This has been very much the case in Turkey. The 1982 Constitution, on its face, promised to advance and protect democracy and the rights and freedoms associated with it. But subsequent restrictions and limitations substantially diminished the content of this promise. As a result, the constitutional order instituted by the constitution purported to be a democratic one while most democratic demands were effectively suppressed. This paradox is much evident in the various decisions of the Constitutional Court, in which it

---

[58] ME Brandon, 'Constitutionalism and Constitutional Failure' in SA Barber and RP George (eds), *Constitutional Politics: Essays on Constitution Making, Maintenance, and Change* (Princeton, Princeton University Press, 2001) 307.

denied reasonable manifestations of rights and liberties while claiming to protect and uphold them.

Reformers, politicians and civil society alike have all considered that, even though they could not create a new constitution and eliminate all the deficiencies, they still achieved a change to the point of no return. Thus, it is likely that a subsequent 'constitutional moment' in Turkey will produce a new and, most importantly, civil constitution.

CONCLUSION

I have tried to develop a notion of legitimate constitution in relation to the idea of democracy. As a blueprint of political organisation, constitutions provide most basic principles and ideas of legal and political structure and they aim to sustain this framework for generations to come. In this respect, the legitimacy of a constitution is an essential part of its content and an essential aspect of its promise. Constitutions which lack legitimacy do not command a sociological and moral authority in terms of their content and cannot fulfil a promise of any sort. I argued that the legitimacy of a constitution requires a social accessibility to the underlying political intention that creates it and to its content, and this, in turn, entails a congruent relation between a constitution and the relevant public. For a constitution to be legitimate it needs to express values and principles accepted by the society; and for a society effectively to express this acceptance, it needs to be free and able to judge and evaluate the credentials of a constitution.

A constitution is democratic only if its origin, namely its creation, and/or its content, is democratic. A democratic creation involves active public participation in the framing, designing and ratifying phases. A democratic content, on the other hand, involves appropriate principles and rules, rights and freedoms, institutions and mechanisms required for a genuine practice of a democratic regime.

The 1982 Constitution of Turkey, in its original form, reserved unusual domains of power for the military, contained severe restrictions on fundamental and political rights and freedoms, advocated a statist republican ideology that placed the state over the individuals, and confined the range of legal political actions to an ideologically demarcated domain. The origin of the constitution was also controversial; public participation and engagement were absent in the framing phase, and by the time of its approval, there was not a genuine opportunity to publicly deliberate upon its content. Consequently, the 1982 Constitution of Turkey posed serious challenges to the idea of democratic legitimacy and neither in its creation nor its content did it fulfil a truly democratic vision.

In the period following the restoration of democracy in 1983, the democratic deficiencies of the constitution quickly became subject to continuous political debate. The civilian governments and legislators began to amend the constitution in a process which was slow and cautious in the beginning, but gradually acquired pace, and was always moving toward a more democratic constitution. The constitutional reform process achieved a strong momentum in the 2000s, during a period of political opening and opportunity unfolded by the status of candidacy for membership offered to Turkey by the European Union. This recent wave of change has seen a number of amendments that scrapped most of the non-democratic statements of the constitution and substantially modified the philosophy underlying the constitution. In the period following the enactment of the constitution, the public perception that the constitution was democratically deficient and the political and social willingness for change have always been present. Coalitions that are extremely difficult to build due to party politics have been achieved during the amendment processes, and civil society has shown a great effort to raise demands for constitutional reform and sustain its pace. All these facts together indicate a strong relation between the legitimacy of a constitution and its democratic credentials, in which the public perception of a constitution determines not only its durability but also its authority. Constitutions that are perceived as democratic represent a ground of consent that is revered and respected by the public, while those that are perceived as democratically deficient or non-democratic fail to retain their social and moral authority and grow to be a source of conflict.

7

Crafting a Constitution for Afghanistan

BARNETT R RUBIN*

O N 4 JANUARY 2004, nearly all 502 members of the Constitutional
Loya Jirga (Grand Council) meeting in Kabul silently stood
to approve a new constitution for the 'Islamic Republic of
Afghanistan'. President Hamid Karzai signed and officially promulgated the
document on 26 January 2004, inaugurating Afghanistan's sixth constitution since King Amanullah Khan promulgated the first in 1923. Delegates
hoped that this relatively liberal Islamic constitution would provide a
framework for the long task of consolidating basic state structures, as the
country struggled to emerge from decades of anti-Soviet jihad, interfac-
tional and inter-ethnic civil war, and wars of conquest and resistance by
and against the radical Islamists of the Taliban movement. In his speech
to the closing session of the Loya Jirga, President Karzai explained why
he thought that the new constitution—which mandated a presidential system with a bicameral parliament, a highly centralised administration with
unprecedented rights for minority languages, and an Islamic legal system
safeguarded by a Supreme Court with powers of judicial review—would
meet the needs of a desperately indigent but proud country searching for a
period of stability in which to rebuild.

The constitution was the next to last step in the road map to
're-establishing permanent institutions of government' outlined in the
Bonn Accords of 5 December 2001. Afghans signed that agreement under
UN auspices as the United States was completing the job of routing the
Taliban regime that had given refuge to Osama bin Laden. The constitution provided a framework for the 'free and fair elections' to choose a 'fully
representative government' that completed that process. The process was

* My work on Afghanistan's constitution has been supported by the Open Society Institute
and the governments of Canada, Norway and the United Kingdom. This chapter benefited
from comments by Kawun Kakar and Donald L Horowitz. I thank them, noting that they bear
no responsibility for any statements in this chapter.

completed—somewhat belatedly—with the election of President Hamid Karzai in October 2004 and the formation of the National Assembly after September 2005 elections. But neither two and a half years (the original time frame of the Bonn Agreement) nor the eventual time frame of nearly four years could suffice to turn a failed state into a stable democracy. Whether the constitution, and with it the international effort in Afghanistan, could achieve its stated goals still depended on efforts beyond its scope, such as demobilising militias and eradicating the drug trade and other illicit activities. The Afghanistan Compact, a declaration agreed to at the London Conference on Afghanistan held from 31 January to 1 February 2006, committed more than 60 states and international organisations to a five-year programme of building a state and developing the economy in an effort to fill in the gaps left by the Bonn Agreement.

Unlike some post-war agreements, the Bonn Accords set out a process rather than a detailed settlement of major political issues. This reflected the time pressure under which the Accords were forged, which set a speed record as such things go. Afghanistan had been through 23 years of many-sided civil strife marked by the overt and covert involvement of regional and global powers, yet only nine days elapsed between the United Nations' opening of talks in the former West German capital and the affixing of signatures on 5 December 2001.

Once US President George W Bush announced on 1 October that the United States would support a political transition and a UN-coordinated reconstruction programme in Afghanistan, the pressure was on to cobble together a successor regime to the ousted Taliban movement, whose rule had sheltered al-Qaeda while that organisation made Afghanistan into its base for global terrorism. Four Afghan groups participated in Bonn.

The two most important were the Islamic United Front for the Salvation of Afghanistan, commonly known as the Northern Alliance (NA), which had received the bulk of American military assistance leading up to and during the military operations that began on 7 October, and the 'Rome group' representing exiled King Muhammad Zahir Shah, a resident of the Italian capital since his overthrow by a 1973 military coup. The NA represented force on the ground and a mixture of ethnic claims with those of politicised Islam, both Sunni and Shi'ite. Figuring prominently in NA ranks were members of such northern and central ethnic groups as the Tajiks, the Uzbeks and the Hazaras—all of which had armed and mobilised themselves during decades of warfare. Their Taliban foes represented a reassertion of the power of the historically dominant Pashtun ethnic group, this time in the guise of a harsh Islamic fundamentalist militia. Most of the NA groups had fought against the Soviets as *mujahideen* (holy warriors), though the main Uzbek group had begun as a tribal militia under the communist regime.

The Rome group, consisting of exiles mostly living in the West, brought with it the legitimacy of the ex-king, whose 40-year reign (1933–73) had marked the last time that Afghanistan had enjoyed any substantial degree of peace or stability. While long-suffering Afghans felt great sympathy for their former monarch, he had no political or military organisation in the country and nothing resembling a concrete programme. The ex-king seemed valuable to the United States and the United Nations as a possible source of historic continuity and a potential rallying point for Pashtuns, who had no armed organisations comparable to those of the NA. The Pashtun-led groups in the NA, including a radical Islamist formation under Abd al-Rabb al-Rasul Sayyaf, had no ethnic or tribal base of support in the southern heartland of the Pashtuns. The other two groups—known as 'Peshawar' and 'Cyprus' after places where they had met—included small, ad hoc groups based in Pakistan and Iran.

Despite this attempt at ethnic inclusiveness, the group assembled in Bonn did not represent the people of Afghanistan, either directly or indirectly. The UN veteran and former Algerian foreign minister Lakhdar Brahimi, who chaired the talks in his capacity as Secretary-General Kofi Annan's special representative, repeatedly stressed that no one would remember how unrepresentative the meeting had been if the participants managed to fashion a process that would lead to a legitimate and representative government.

THE PATH TO LEGITIMACY

The process that the Bonn participants agreed upon aimed at forming such a government. The approval of a new constitution and the holding of the elections were to be the final steps. Given the insecurity and disarray besetting Afghanistan, immediate direct elections would clearly be impossible. To fill the resulting gap, the Bonn Accords drew on an institution that had figured in the crafting of each of Afghanistan's five previous constitutions (1923, 1931, 1964, 1977 and 1987), the Loya Jirga. Previous rulers had summoned such meetings to legitimate key decisions. Mostly these earlier jirgas had been appointed, docile bodies. A few, such as the Constitutional Loya Jirgas (CLJs) of 1923 and 1964, had actively debated issues. And one, in November 1928, had actually rejected reform proposals put forward by King Amanullah and set the stage for the revolt that would drive him from his throne two months later.

The Loya Jirga developed as a state institution, but it harked back to large jirgas that Pashtun tribes had held in earlier centuries, when these tribes constituted both the main military force and, in effect, the electors of the king. During periods of turmoil when Afghans recognised no legitimate ruler, such jirgas had taken key national decisions. Drawing on these precedents, Zahir Shah's followers had developed a proposal for an Emergency Loya Jirga (ELJ) as a first step to reconstituting state power. The NA, despite the misgivings of some members, agreed to a UN-monitored ELJ as the legitimating device for the process of building a more representative government. Like all former constitutions of Afghanistan, the one drafted as part of the Bonn process was also to be approved by a Loya Jirga.

As an interim measure, the agreement reached at Bonn reinstated much of Zahir Shah's 1964 basic law, which had turned Afghanistan into a constitutional monarchy. While that constitution had provided guarantees of public liberty unprecedented in Afghan history, it had failed to establish a stable system of government. Over a mere ten years, the country had three elections and four governments, none of which succeeded in implementing needed reforms. Many Afghans greeted with relief the constitutional monarchy's overthrow and the establishment of a more authoritarian republic by Zahir Shah's cousin, Daoud Khan.

The Bonn Accords did not re-establish the monarchy, of course, but instead vested both executive and legislative power in the cabinet, to be headed by a president who would be head of state as well as chief of government. The 1964 Constitution had followed its predecessors in making Afghanistan an officially Sunni Muslim state. Religious rites performed by the state were carried out in accord with the Hanafi sect, one of the four main schools of jurisprudence followed by Sunni Muslims (Article 2). In cases where judges could find no provision in the constitution or written law to resolve a case, they were required to follow 'the basic principles of the Hanafi jurisprudence of the *shari'a* of Islam and, within the provisions set forth in this constitution, render a decision that in their opinion secures justice in the best possible way' (Article 102). Hence, as in most 'moderate' Sunni constitutions, the 1964 Constitution was supreme over a judge's interpretation of Islam. No law could be contrary to the 'basic principles of the sacred religion of Islam' (Article 64), but the king, not the judiciary or the *ulama* (Islamic scholars), had been the ultimate arbiter of this provision. The 1964 Constitution also declared Afghanistan a unitary state organised according to the 'principle of centralisation' (Article 108). As of late 2001, however, power was in fact anything but centralised, pointing to a disjunction between legal and ground-level realities that would soon become a focus of much political and constitutional controversy.

The participants in Bonn chose the personnel of an interim administration to serve under these provisions. Though the Accords claimed that considerations of 'professional competence and personal integrity' had guided the choice of interim officials, no one should be too surprised that they were mostly selected to offer patronage to different factions and to recognise the distribution of armed might on the ground. The interim administration's chairman, Hamid Karzai, was a Pashtun, originally from Kandahar but more recently residing in exile, who had ties to the king and who had come back to Afghanistan with American assistance to raise forces against the Taliban in its own southern bastion of Kandahar Province. The 'power ministries'—defence, interior and foreign affairs—all went to the leading faction within the NA, which also controlled the powerful intelligence service, developed in the 1980s on the model of the Soviet KGB. This faction, the Supervisory Council of the North (*Shura-yi Nazar* or SN), was based in the Tajik areas in and around the Panjshir Valley just north of Kabul. The SN's founder, military leader Ahmed Shah Massoud, had been murdered on 9 September 2001 by al-Qaeda suicide bombers posing as journalists. When Taliban and al-Qaeda forces fled Kabul under American bombing on 17 November, the SN had moved in and begun placing its own candidates in key posts.

Most Afghans probably saw the government chosen at Bonn as tilted in favour of the heavily Panjshiri SN. The Bonn process was designed to make the government gradually more representative. The first step was to be the holding of an ELJ by June 2002, with the mission of electing a head of state and approving what the Accords called the 'structure and key personnel' of a transitional administration. With UN and other international help, the government held the ELJ on time. The indirectly elected body of about 1,500 representatives voted to keep Hamid Karzai as Afghanistan's chief executive for another two years. After lengthy negotiations, Karzai named a government on 19 June 2002, the last day of the nine-day meeting. Many delegates objected that the ELJ had not in fact enabled them to vote on the 'structure and key personnel' of the transitional administration and that the new administration (named the Transitional Islamic State of Afghanistan) was not significantly more representative than its predecessor.

SHOW OF HANDS OR SHOW OF FORCE?

The same factors that limited the accomplishments of the ELJ bedevilled the constitutional process that followed. Afghanistan was and is not a place where a show of hands at a meeting can decide who will hold power. The American-led coalition gave commanders weapons and cash to fight the Taliban. The commanders used those resources to remobilise patronage networks into armed groups. These groups were then able to seize control of assets such as land, customs posts and businesses, as well as smuggling routes for drugs, lumber or gems. The mutually reinforcing personal control of armed groups and economic assets meant warlordism.

The warlords occupied the power vacuum left by the collapse of the state over decades and the destruction of the Taliban administration. Though international aid and troops ensured that the Karzai government would hang on in Kabul, the first post-Taliban year saw little in the way of effective efforts to widen the reach of President Karzai's writ or boost state-building. Even within Kabul, Karzai had only limited control over his own government, many of whose top officials led militias that had fought or were still fighting against the Taliban with American support. It was little wonder that he hesitated to dislodge such leaders.

The Karzai government's inability to guarantee the security of voters during the stages of voting for the ELJ, or of the delegates once elected, hampered the entire ELJ. In some districts, armed commanders occupied the polling places, and the United Nations cancelled or invalidated the elections. More commonly, intimidation was harder to prove, but just as clear to its objects. Agents of the security services worked inside the Loya Jirga tent. One Islamist leader (Abd al-Rabb al-Rasul Sayyaf) claimed that anyone criticizing '*mujahideen*' deserved the death penalty for blasphemy.

Fear of the intimidation tactics used by Islamists at the ELJ made the United Nations and the Karzai government cautious about opening the constitutional process to the public too early. Previous Afghan constitutions had been drafted in secret by governments that controlled the outcome. This was the first Afghan constitutional process where the outcome—even the form of government that would result—was open to political debate, and the UN insisted on introducing a measure of public consultation into the process. Brahimi also saw the UN's role as assuring that the constitution would create a 'workable' form of government and conform to basic international standards. Ultimately, the commission consulted Afghans in every province, in the refugee communities of Pakistan and Iran, and through tens of thousands of written questionnaires. Nonetheless, the government and UN thought it best to keep the content of deliberations confidential until the commission could make public a thoroughly vetted text.

The President first appointed a drafting commission of nine members, which completed a text based heavily on the constitution of 1964. A larger commission of 35 members reviewed the text, which was also shown to a few international experts and the government's National Security Council (NSC).[1] The government did not publish the text even during the public consultation sessions. The government published the commission's final draft, with changes incorporated at all these stages, on 3 November, only 37 days before the scheduled opening of the CLJ, which finally convened a few days late on 14 December 2003.

The CLJ went better than many had dared to hope it would. The UN had more time and experience in making the meeting secure, and the President and his supporters were better organised. Hence, warlords and *jihadi* leaders had lost some of the capacity to intimidate that they had exercised at the ELJ. The result was a constitution that reflected to a considerable extent the agenda shared by Karzai and those cabinet members who considered

---

[1] While many international experts offered advice of one sort or another to the commission, the author was one of three who worked with it closely. The other two were Yash Pal Ghai of Kenya and Guy Carcassonne of France. The author recruited other experts to draft papers on issues identified by the commission. These papers are available at http://www.cic.nyu.edu/afghanistan/constitution.html

themselves 'reformers'. The constitution, nonetheless, is a product of the fluid situation that is post-conflict Afghanistan. It remains to be seen whether measures crafted with an eye to the immediate demands of state-building will serve equally well the needs of long-term governance. We can explore this question by examining what the new Afghan constitution has to say on such key issues as the form of government, the place of Islam, the structure of the state, language and ethnic identity, and the judiciary.

Debate over these issues reflected historical realities as well as current dilemmas. Afghanistan began as a Pashtun empire ruled by tribal dynasts from Kandahar, and even today the ethnic question in its plainest form asks whether the state is to be the instrument of a mostly Pashtun elite, or a mechanism through which all citizens may equally take part in self-government. Both Loya Jirgas showed the strength of a supra-ethnic 'Afghan' national identity, but this national identity co-existed with strong ethnic identities, and ethnic politicians from different groups advocated different views of how to constitute the Afghan nation. Pashtuns have tended to want a strong and Pashtun-run central state. Tajiks have focused on power sharing in the central state, while Uzbeks and Hazaras have desired recognition of their identities and mechanisms of local self-government. Strengthening the central government was also a goal of those CLJ delegates who saw the regional warlords as illegitimate and who supported state-initiated reforms.

Among the strongest advocates of centralising reforms were Westernised Pashtuns. Their opponents, including non-Pashtun Islamist commanders, charged that an ostensibly 'non-ethnic' position actually served the interests of the largest group. All agree that Pashtuns are the largest group, but by how much, and whether they are a majority, are hotly contested issues.

Debate over basic institutions reflected assumptions about ethnic politics. Everyone took it for granted that the first elected president would be a Pashtun, and furthermore, one who enjoyed American approval—that is, Hamid Karzai. In a departure from the electoral system developed on the basis of the 1964 Constitution, which gave more weight to Pashtun areas, the new constitution provides that the new bicameral parliament's popularly elected lower house, the Wolesi Jirga, will be filled by deputies elected 'in proportion to population'. This reflects the contention by opponents of Pashtun domination that Pashtuns are not a majority. These opponents therefore expected that the Wolesi Jirga would be a mostly non-Pashtun body in which local and regional power-holders would exert great influence. In the event, the Wolesi Jirga appears to be almost evenly divided between Pashtuns and others. In a largely ethnic vote, it very narrowly elected Yunus Qanuni, a Tajik from Panjshir and close associate of Ahmad Shah Massoud, as chair in a contest largely along ethnic lines. About half of the members from all groups are affiliated to the groups that organised the resistance to the Soviet Union and the Taliban.

THE DEBATE OVER PRESIDENTIALISM

The draft constitution had called for a semi-presidential system until the NSC review stage (the last phase before the CLJ met). Drafting commission members had hoped that the probable combination of a directly elected Pashtun president and a non-Pashtun prime minister (chosen by the Wolesi Jirga, and possibly a Panjshiri), would provide ethnic balance. Hence the commission members resisted making the prime minister fully subordinate to the president, an essential element of stable semi-presidential systems.

For a long time, in keeping with the power-sharing model, the commission insisted that the prime minister, after being named by the president, would need to pass a confidence vote in the Wolesi Jirga before taking office. The argument that this would breed instability in a highly faction-alised and armed society by creating two executives with competing bases of power—the popular vote versus the support of parliament—led in September 2003 to the adoption of a more workable system in which the president's appointed prime minister would not need a vote of confidence to serve, but could be removed by a no-confidence vote.

Late in the joint review by the NSC and the drafting commission came a shift to full presidentialism. The office of prime minister was eliminated and the president received full power to appoint a cabinet (whose members could not be serving legislators) subject to parliamentary approval. Splits within the NA bloc and among the SN leaders in the cabinet had set the stage for this move, long resisted by the drafting commission. Major SN figures such as Education Minister Yunous Qanooni and Defense Minister Mohammed Qasim Fahim had taken different positions—the former had his eyes on a prospective premiership, while the latter aspired to become sole vice-president under Karzai—and the broader NA bloc had split as well. Qanooni found himself the cabinet's only supporter of the soon-to-be-rejected premiership option, while Fahim failed to deliver the support of any of his faction's CLJ delegates to the presidential system. The ethnic-Hazara Vice-President, Abdul Karim Khalili, however, delivered some support for the proposal, and Karzai then backed the idea of two vice-presidents, one of whom would presumably be Khalili.

The issue of governmental systems came into sharp relief at the CLJ as calls rang out for an up-or-down vote on presidentialism versus parliamentarism. Nearly all Pashtun delegates, joined by some members from other ethnic groups, came out for presidentialism. A bloc of non-Pashtun delegates, however, strongly supported a parliamentary system. Both sides made cases that mixed genuine public considerations with ethno-political ambitions. For Pashtuns and reformers, presidentialism provided a way for one of their own—everyone knew that the first incumbent would be Karzai—to emerge from the Bonn compromise with non-Pashtun armed factions as the popularly elected head of state. There would be no uncertainty about who held legitimate executive power in Kabul, and Washington would retain the benefit of having a clearly identifiable Afghan partner whom it knew well and indeed preferred. The largely non-Pashtun delegates who opposed presidentialism saw in it a risk of personal and ethnic dictatorship. A parliamentary system, they argued, would likely result in coalition governments that would be more representative and inclusive, safer from potential abuses of executive power, and hence more stable.

To some extent, the debate rehearsed standard arguments about the relative merits of presidential versus cabinet government, but with a twist: Afghanistan has been struggling to leave behind years of failed statehood. The challenge for any new government there is not to enact this or that policy so much as it is to found the basic institutions that must exist and function if the very idea of 'policy-making' is to mean anything at all. Afghanistan, in other words, needs to build a state.

Decades of internal warfare had left standing only the weakest of security institutions. The rule of law did not extend over much of the country, and political parties were feeble and embryonic. Some believe that a parliamentary system could better serve such a multiethnic country, though ethnic factions have also captured parliamentary systems. The presidentialists' argument persuaded those who worried that a parliament chosen under these arduous conditions was too likely to be a fragmented body dominated by warlords, local factions and even drug traffickers. In his speech to the CLJ's closing session, President Karzai cited post-1945 Italy and India since the Congress Party's decline as negative examples. Afghanistan's most urgent need is a functioning government. Presidentialism's advocates—who are not all Pashtuns-said that such a system, with its greater potential for what Alexander Hamilton called 'energy and dispatch', was more likely to bring such a government about.

Another bruising issue concerned qualifications for office. This revolved around the difficult relations between the elites who had remained in Afghanistan and those who were returning after decades of exile, in many cases having become citizens of developed countries where they found refuge, most often the United States. Two key cabinet members, Finance Minister Ashraf Ghani and Interior Minister Ali Ahmad Jalali, whom Karzai had appointed in 2003 as part of the process of broadening and professionalising the composition of the cabinet, belong to the latter group. By virtue of their roles, they have been on the front lines of building a state and opposing warlordism. Both are US citizens and had lived in the Washington, DC, area as officials of the World Bank and the Voice of America, respectively. Ghani, later mentioned as a candidate for both UN Secretary-General and President of the World Bank, was not appointed to the government President Karzai formed after his election. Jalali resigned his post and returned to the United States in July 2005.

During public consultations on the constitution, a powerful nativism surfaced, with people from all over the country calling for a ban on ministers holding dual citizenship. This feeling also crossed ethnic and partisan lines at the CLJ, but the President and international actors voiced strong opposition to such a ban. The compromise that was reached seems to keep the ban, but then provides that if the president nominates a minister with dual citizenship, the Wolesi Jirga will vote on it. Since the Wolesi Jirga has to confirm all ministerial appointments anyway, nothing new is added. The struggle over this issue, however, divided the cabinet and left more bruised feelings than any other question.

THE CONSTITUTIONAL STATUS OF ISLAM

The debate on the role of Islam involved numerous elements of the constitution, and the final result is a package deal that contains potential contradictions to spark future conflicts. More than almost any other issue, this one involved balancing outside actors' demands for the acceptance of international standards with the demands of domestic actors, notably Islamist politicians and the *ulama,* for a constitution that conforms to their understandings of Islam and empowers Islamic elites. From the start of the drafting, international actors made it clear that, while they accepted that the new constitution would declare Afghanistan an Islamic state, they did not want any explicit reference to *shari'a* in the text. In addition, the rising political influence of Shi'ite Afghans, mostly ethnic Hazaras, as well as the insistence of neighbouring Iran, required that the constitution for the first time make Islam alone, rather than the Hanafi sect, the state religion. Shi'ite jurisprudence enjoys near-parity in the current constitution, a milestone of sorts in national inclusiveness.

The final text passed at the Loya Jirga resulted from hard, late-stage bargaining among Islamists, President Karzai and international representatives, along with some adroit tactical moves.[2] In quiet negotiations, diplomats made clear to Islamist leaders what the international community's red lines were, and the final result reflected negotiation among many Afghan and international parties. The commission's draft named the state the 'Islamic Republic of Afghanistan', a move pushed through the commission by the chair, Vice-President Nematullah Shahrani, despite opposition from many members. At the CLJ, the Islamists did not oppose a presidential suggestion to change Article 2's sweeping statement that 'the religion of Afghanistan is the sacred religion of Islam' to the more qualified 'the religion of the

---

[2] The commission drafted the text in Dari and translated the working text into Pashto as needed. The UN provided unofficial English translations of the drafts for its own use and that of the international experts permitted to see the text. At the CLJ, the text was distributed in a bilingual edition in Dari and Pashto.

state of the Islamic Republic of Afghanistan is the sacred religion of Islam'. The Islamists also accepted a presidential proposal to expand the constitutional scope accorded the religious activities of non-Muslims. Whereas Article 3 had previously declared non-Muslims 'free to perform their religious ceremonies', after the President's suggestion it gave non-Muslims the broader-sounding freedom 'to exercise their faith'.

As part of the negotiated deal, Islamists also dropped their attempts to have the constitution cite Islam or *shari'a* as limits on Afghanistan's international human rights obligations. Article 7 unqualifiedly requires that the state observe the Universal Declaration of Human Rights and all covenants to which the government is a party, which include the major human rights covenants. Nor did Islamists ultimately oppose Article 22, which declares the legal equality of men and women without any of the qualifications found in *shari'a,* stating that 'the citizens of Afghanistan—whether women or men—have equal rights and duties before the law'. The women delegates to the CLJ-about 20 per cent of the total—made this passage their core demand.

In return, Islamists advanced their position on other important parts of the constitution. Article 3 contains a provision-which in some form is standard in the constitutions of predominantly Muslim countries- that bans laws contrary to Islam. Earlier drafts had reiterated the 1964 Constitution's decree that no Afghan law could be against the 'basic principles of the sacred religion of Islam and the values of this constitution'. At one point this phrase had been whittled down simply to 'Islam'. The final draft goes farther than did the 1964 document toward enshrining *shari'a* by specifying that laws cannot contradict any of 'beliefs and provisions *(ahkām)*' of Islam, the latter term a clear reference to the provisions of the *shari'a,* and by omitting the 1964 reference to other 'values of this constitution'.

This article promises to be more central to political life than in the past, as the constitution for the first time grants the Supreme Court the power to review the constitutionality of legislation, presidential decrees and international treaties. The President's team rejected the commission's proposal for a separate constitutional court, expressing the fear that it would resemble the Council of Guardians in Iran, but by granting the same power to the Supreme Court, a body that has always been dominated by *ulama* trained in Islamic jurisprudence rather than constitutional law, the President's advisors may have worsened their future predicament. For it is almost inevitable that conflicts will arise between the constitution's acceptance of international human rights standards and embrace of male-female legal equality, on the one hand, and the requirement that no law may contradict the 'beliefs and provisions' of Islam, on the other. When that happens, one may safely predict that political rather than purely interpretive considerations will shape the outcome.

The Islamists tried and failed to push a measure requiring that the president be male, but they made no objection to the constitution's requirement that at least one-quarter of lower-house seats and one-sixth of upper-house seats be filled by female legislators. Behind these numbers lay a notable victory for female CLJ delegates, who had successfully campaigned to double the lower house quota to 25 per cent by insisting on an average of two female deputies from each province.

While non-Pashtun delegates from northern Afghanistan failed to win any decentralisation measures, the CLJ debates marked a milestone in the recognition of cultural pluralism. Afghanistan's origin as an empire can be seen in its de jure unitary state: the administration was meant to enable the centre to control the periphery, not to help local communities exercise self-government. Provincial governors and district commissioners are appointed by the centre, and there was a long-standing practice of naming administrators who are not natives of the places they govern, which the current government is trying to revive. The new constitution retains this 'principle of centralisation'.

The constitution also provides for elected councils at all levels, elected mayors of municipalities, and potential devolution of some powers to councils through legislation. Whatever the law may say, however, the fact is that under the interim and transitional administrations most governors and military commanders received their posts because they already had locally-based power, rather than having power because of their official positions. A few, the major warlords, exercised power over several provinces. Uzbeks from northern Afghanistan, as well as Hazaras, though less insistently, wanted institutionalisation of aspects of this less centralised administration. While they had retreated from earlier demands for federalism, at the CLJ Uzbek delegates proposed that governors be elected rather than appointed. As a weaker alternative, they proposed that the centre appoint governors from among a pool of candidates proposed by provincial councils. Uzbek delegates explained that these proposals were designed to prevent the centre from imposing Pashtun governors on them. In the past such governors allocated land and assets to Pashtun settlers and engaged in other kinds of abuses.

The government, which had an active lobbying team on the floor of the CLJ, rejected all of these proposals. While some Pashtuns insist on centralism for ethnic reasons, many people of all ethnic groups genuinely fear the disintegration of the country. During the decades of war, regional commanders developed close ties to patrons in neighbouring countries. Kabul has less influence over parts of Afghanistan than do Iran, Pakistan or Uzbekistan. These commanders remain so potent that strengthening local government could simply mean strengthening them or other criminalised elements. Many serious Afghans argue that centralisation is needed now to help overcome the obstacle posed by extra-legal local power-holders— perhaps by persuading them that it is time to incorporate themselves into the state-building process that Kabul hopes to direct. Decentralisation or devolution can come later.

ACKNOWLEDGING AFGHAN DIVERSITY

Despite its rejection of administrative decentralisation, the constitution takes major steps forward in recognising Afghanistan's cultural diversity. During the drafting phase, a major issue was the relation of the two state languages, Pashto and Dari (Afghan Persian). In the past, while Pashto was the language of the dominant ethnic group, Dari was the language of urban life, high culture and the bureaucracy. While the rulers were Pashtuns, many could not speak Pashto, and Dari was the de facto language of government. The 1964 Constitution gave official status to both tongues, while mandating the state to 'implement an effective program for the development and strengthening of the national language, Pashto' (Article 35).

In 2003, the draft constitution recognised more linguistic pluralism than ever before: Pashto and Dari remained the official languages, but five others received recognition as official languages in areas where they are spoken, along with a guarantee of the freedom to broadcast or publish in any of them. For the first time, the draft also encouraged the development and teaching of all languages in areas where they were spoken. The relationship between Dari and Pashto became a major issue of controversy at the CLJ. A proposal to require the state to train employees to work in both languages fell before objections voiced by Tajiks, who feared that the provision was a threat to fire all functionaries not conversant in Pashto. They did agree, if reluctantly, that the national anthem should be in Pashto.

In the CLJ, the northern bloc that had called for parliamentarism also demanded recognition of the multiethnic character of Afghanistan, including official recognition of Turkic tongues (Uzbek and Turkmen) as national languages. Some leaders of this group even raised the issue of the meaning of 'Afghan', a noun that originally referred to Pashtuns but which this constitution, like that of 1964, defines as applicable to any and every citizen. For instance, they demanded that citizens be called 'Afghanistanis' and that the name of the currency be changed from the afghani to the paisa. These demands aroused a backlash from Pashtun delegates, who then sought to make Pashto the sole 'national' language again.

It would take a novel to do full justice to the manner in which this Gordian tangle of issues was at last resolved, but here I can sketch the results. After negotiations at the CLJ, the constitution recognises for the first time both the ethnic pluralism and the political unity of Afghanistan. As Article 4 states:

> The nation of Afghanistan is comprised of Pashtun, Tajik, Hazara, Uzbek, Turkmen, Baluch, Pashai, Nuristani, Aymaq, Arab, Kyrgyz, Qizilbash, Gujar, Brahui, and other ethnic groups. The word Afghan applies to every citizen of Afghanistan.

The constitution makes Pashto and Dari official languages. The national anthem is in Pashto, but its lyrics must mention all the ethnic groups listed in Article 4, and the chorus must contain the Islamic phrase '*Allahu akbar*' (Arabic for 'God is great', which also appears in the Dari lyrics of the anthem used from 1992 to 1996). Pashtun delegates long resisted making the Turkic language official, partly out of a desire not to hand a victory to the ex-communist Uzbek warlord Abdul Rashid Dostum. In the end, the CLJ settled on making Turkmen and Uzbek, along with Pashai, Baluch, Nuristani and Pamiri, additional official languages in areas where a majority speaks one of them rather than Pashto or Dari as its first language. In addition to keeping the national anthem in Pashto, the constitutional provision on language (Article 16) also states that Pashto nomenclature for certain institutions and titles must be retained in Dari and other languages as well.

One area about which there was unfortunately no controversy was the judiciary. This was a shame since in Afghanistan the judges have become a self-perpetuating caste. The Supreme Court is not only the ultimate appellate forum, now with the power of judicial review, but also the chief administrative organ of the judiciary. It controls judicial budgets and appoints, pays, promotes and disciplines the lower-court judges. While judicial nominees must win presidential confirmation, Karzai has never refused a candidate whom the Supreme Court has put forward. During the public consultations on the constitution, judicial corruption was an oft-heard complaint. The constitutional commission's leaders privately admit that the current system creates corrupt networks of judges. Yet the new constitution retains this system.

Judgeships form the main source of employment for the *ulama,* and neither the President nor the commission wanted to confront them. Given the expanded powers of the Supreme Court and the interest of the *ulama* in keeping a monopoly of the power to interpret Islam, the failure to create more constitutional space for judicial reform could prove a serious barrier against needed change in the future. The constitution requires the president to appoint a new Supreme Court within 30 days after the start of work by the National Assembly, and the rejection by the woles; Jirga of the first slate of appointees resulted in the naming of a bench that will be much more inclined to reform.

A GOOD START?

Given its difficult circumstances, Afghanistan is fortunate to have arrived at a result this positive. And yet the new constitution contains many obstacles to stable and effective governance. The pressure of time and inhibitions on public discussion due both to intimidation and self-censorship on sensitive issues prevented full discussion of many important questions. In some respects, Afghanistan has lost a one-time opportunity to rethink its social compact in depth. The elderly leadership of the constitutional commission sometimes seemed more intent on recovering lost traditions than on figuring out how to meet the demands of radically new conditions.

But perhaps the biggest challenge is the central paradox of post-conflict constitution-making. Societies emerging from civil conflict need to agree on rules for national decisions that seem reasonably fair to all or most parts of the society. A constitution is most often written—and the Afghan constitution is no exception—to be difficult to amend and to last for a long time. But before a constitution can last a century, it must first last a year. The historical moment when societies most need a constitution is also the one when they are least prepared to adopt it. Not only are their national capacities depleted by war and emigration, but it is uniquely difficult to draft for the ages when even the fairly immediate future is so uncertain.

The type of institutional or political structure needed for state-building may not be the same political structure that will later provide the best governance. One powerful minister, considered a stalwart supporter of presidentialism and centralisation, confided in private that he thought a more decentralised parliamentary system would ultimately be better for a stable and inclusive Afghanistan, but that adopting such options in the short term would delay or even prevent the building of urgently needed institutions.

Right now, the main challenge is to create a stable locus of authority. Yet broader inclusion and participation remain important goals, even if this is not the time to stress them above all else. So parliamentarism might some day be the better choice, and it may not be wise to lock decisions dictated by a temporary situation (decisions such as the option for presidentialism) into a hard-to-change constitution. Perhaps the Bonn Accords should have furnished an interim constitutional arrangement of more than two years. Perhaps the new constitution should also have been equipped with a 'sunset clause' or other mechanism to guarantee popular review after a certain period. Some post-conflict constitutions, such as that of East Timor, contain such provisions. Afghans to whom international advisors suggested such options, however, were wary of doing anything that could undermine a document already so beset with threats to its realisation and enforcement. In his final speech to the CLJ, President Karzai stated:

> [T]he constitution is not the Koran. If five or ten years down the line we find that stability improves, proper political parties emerge, and we judge that a parliamentary system can function better, then a Loya Jirga can at a time of our choosing be convened to adopt a different system of government.[3]

It seems likely that such a revision will indeed be necessary in five to ten years, if this document can last that long. That will depend on many things, some of which of course lie far outside the scope of the constitution itself. Yet among them will be the question as to whether Afghans can evade the pitfalls and contradictions that their new constitution contains.

---

[3] H Karzai, Address to the Closing Session of the Constitutional Loya Jirga, 4 January 2004. See www.unama-afg.org

8

From Interim to 'Permanent' Constitution in Iraq

ANDREW ARATO

'We're short of time—it's the fault of the Americans', Kurdish politician Mahmoud Othman said. 'They are always insisting on short deadlines. It's as if they're [making] hamburgers and fast food'. Othman added: 'If we'd had more time, it would have been possible to get Sunni participation. When October 15 comes, many won't even have seen the constitution.'[1]

INTRODUCTION

IRAQ NOW HAS its 'permanent' constitution, the second provisional one since the American invasion. Constructed to survive, the Iraqi interim constitution, the Transitional Administrative Law (TAL), did not technically outlive the present debacle of the making of a 'permanent' constitution it was supposed to regulate. As the result of the referendum of 15 October 2005, a new and supposedly permanent constitution has been in force since the National Assembly elected on 15 December 2005 had its first meeting. But, because of an extraordinary and illegal deal negotiated three days before that referendum to amend the proposed text, there will be a new parliamentary constitutional committee chosen to suggest a whole package of amendments that could modify anything and everything in the new draft whose own rules of amendment will be entirely suspended for four months. Instead, the package will have to be passed under rules almost identical to the very demanding ratification rules of the TAL! Even more remarkably, if things go at all well, the state structure that would emerge from such an amendment process would be identical with that of the TAL. If things go badly, then the constitution approved on 15 October 2005 will turn out not to have been provisional after all. In that case, Iraq may face an explosive

---

[1] T Marshall and L Roug, 'A Central Pillar of Iraq Policy Crumbling', *LA Times*, 9 October 2005.

break-up process that will be in no small part the result of imposed constitution making and exclusionary bargaining that could not be in the end reversed by the imposers and excluders themselves: the American occupying authorities.

This chapter will follow the history and logic of constitution making in Iraq, from the making of the TAL to the struggles over the writing of the permanent constitution. Three elements of the process will be emphasised: external imposition, exclusionary bargaining and attempts to assert as well as bind the sovereign constituent power of 'the Iraqi people'. In itself positive in terms of constitutionalist norms, binding the sovereign power of the people's representatives to give a political community a constitution raises fundamental problems of political legitimacy.[2] Neither external imposition[3] nor exclusionary political bargaining has a chance to solve these. According to the argument below, Iraqi constitution making stayed on its obstacle laden course only because of the very uneasy compromise among the principles of foreign imposition, exclusionary bargaining and popular sovereignty whose political embodiments were the American occupying authorities, the two major Kurdish political parties and the Shiʻite clerics initially under the leadership of the Grand Ayatollah Ali al-Sistani. The cost of the compromise was the Sunni exclusion, belatedly recognised by the Americans, that is the principal cause of the raging insurrection that could make constitution and constitutionalism ultimately an illusory exercise.

THE MAKING OF THE INTERIM CONSTITUTION

It is now well known that the executive organs of the American occupying authority, especially the Coalition Provisional Authority (CPA), and to an extent their superiors at home, have greatly occupied themselves not only with the tasks of Iraqi regime construction in general but with constitution making in particular. Resolutely refusing elections for a constitution making body, they were interested in the beginning in some dependent and controllable Iraqi entity producing a final text. Eventually they settled on the Interim Governing Council (GC), their own creation that had no legal

---

[2] I am currently working on a project dealing with 'post-sovereign constitution making', from the Spanish case to best developed paradigm of South Africa, and the mixed case of Iraq. What is fundamental to the paradigm is the establishment of a set of legitimate limits on the democratic power to make constitutions. Its main institutional elements are (legitimate) round-table type agreements, interim constitutions, legal continuity and democratic elections for the final drafting body. By post-sovereign I mean not that state sovereignty has become irrelevant, but that no organ embodies sovereign power while participating in constitution making.

[3] The denial of the legitimacy of external constitutional imposition has been considered obvious and fundamental since the very beginning of the modern idea of constitution and constitution making. See E Vattel *Law of Nations* (Philadelphia, T & J W Johnson & Co, 1883) ch 3, para 37.

or factual independence, and whose acts had to be ratified by the CPA to become in any sense binding. It was assumed very soon, if not from the very beginning, that the constitution so drafted would be offered to a popular referendum, most likely a rather constrained plebiscite, whose acceptance would be guaranteed more or less by a linkage to the restoration of (formal) sovereignty and the end of the (formal) occupation. This method of constitution making, the drafting of an executive-made, top-down constitution and its ratification through a constrained plebiscite, had it been carried through, would have resembled the Bonapartist version of sovereign constitution making that seems particularly appropriate in the case of the military exportation of democracy.

What is less well known, sadly enough, is that these efforts, especially but not only in the beginning, were not only misguided in terms of democratic theory but were also illegal under international law. If starting the war without new UN Security Council authorisation was the first major violation of international law by the United States, given Article 43 of the Hague Convention of 1907, changing the constitutional order of an occupied country under what was recognised by the United States itself as 'belligerent occupation' was going to be the second.[4] Security Council Resolutions that have been mentioned as providing relief from the Hague restriction have been at best deliberately ambiguous on the key issue.[5] From a legal point of view, the Coalition Provisional Authority remained the only source of authorisation for the TAL, since the nominal drafting instance, the Governing Council, was its creature, and could take decisions only under the CPA. In this sense, the 'agreement' of 15 November 2003 and the drafting of the TAL made no difference with respect to the earlier declarations that admitted American imposition more openly. The fact, however, that the TAL was not called a constitution, and more importantly, that it was established as an interim basic law fully replaceable by the constitutional product of a freely elected national assembly, arguably changed the legal situation. If the United States would still be imposing a basic law, it would be only a temporary one that would no longer violate the Hague Convention. Thus, the idea of an interim constitution, under whatever name, taken from the arsenal of recent post-sovereign democratic

---

[4] S Chesterman 'Occupation as Liberation' and A Arato 'Interim Imposition' in (2004) 18(3) *Ethics and International Affair* 51–64 and 25–50 resp; N Bhuta 'A New Bonapartism? Occupatio Bellica between Commissarial and Sovereign Dictatorship' in A Bartholomew (ed), *Empire's Law* (Pluto, 2005).
[5] While UN SC Res 1483 (point 4) called for the CPA to take measures 'through the effective administration of the territory' to enable Iraqis to freely determine their own future, it also (point 5) fully confirmed the validity of the Hague Regulations of 1907. UN SC Res 1511 reaffirmed 1483, but welcomed the creation of a Constitutional Committee by the Governing Council, without taking a stance concerning how a 'Constitutional Conference' would then be elected. UN SC Res 1546 positively mentions the formation of the interim government in which the UN participated, without authorising the TAL as the Kurds specifically sought.

efforts at constitution making was and remains the central aspect of the Iraqi constitution making process.[6] While the historical prototypes of this model were certainly not *externally* imposed, it is the interim character that was supposed to save the imposing power from the charge of international illegality that seemed to worry first and foremost its own lawyers.

The legal innovation was mainly in response not to these lawyerly worries, but, in several stages, to what I called the political factor. The Ayatollah Sistani refused to accept on democratic theoretical rather than international law grounds (*fatwā* of June 2003) *either* that an American appointed body could give Iraq a constitution, *or* that a co-opted National Assembly could exercise power as under the 15 November Agreement while an elected Constitutional Convention would draft a new document (*fatwā* of November 2003), *or* that elections be delayed until December or even March 2005, *or even* that the UN Security Council authorise the TAL that was not agreed to by any Iraqi body with an independent authority (letter of June 2004 to UN Secretary General). As a result of these protests, backed up by the threat of mass demonstrations and who knows what else, and UN mediation, the idea of an interim constitution was adopted, the co-opted caucuses were junked, elections were brought forward. The Security Council did not mention the TAL whose status remained uncertain till the meeting of the freely elected National Assembly.[7] What, however, Sistani did not achieve was the imposition of his own, classical populist-majoritarian sovereign model of constitution making.

Sistani's model was simple, and gained a lot of its power from the obvious illegitimacy and illegality of the American effort at constitutional imposition or 'sovereign dictatorship'. According to its evident logic, there was a constitutional break in Iraq, and there must be a new beginning for which there are no legal rules. No one has the authority to prejudge constitutional issues before new elections: not the Americans, because they are foreign, not the Iraqi politicians, because they are unelected and have not in any case achieved any credits in the work of liberation. All previous constituted powers are illegitimate. New legitimacy can only come from elections. There is inevitably a vacuum of legitimacy until there are elections, and elections therefore must be organised as soon as possible. Once elected, a constituent assembly could not be bound by any previous rules or restrictions: lesser authority cannot bind a greater one.[8] Simply put, this

---

[6] Arato, above n 4.

[7] For the details see Arato, 'Sistani v. Bush: Constitutional Politics in Iraq' in (2004) 11(2) *Constellations* 174–92 ; and Arato, above n 4.

[8] Arato, above n 7 at 175–8. Since the point has been misunderstood at a seminar discussion at New York University, let me state what should have been obvious: the paragraph articulates the logic of Sistani's position, not mine. My conception is post-sovereign as stated above n 2., and I have always argued that *legitimate* post-sovereign constitution making was possible in Iraq, even if it was never actually tried.

was the classical European, *single stage* model of *sovereign revolutionary* constitution making in what became its electoral version. It has great affinity for majoritarian democracy, because not being bound by any previous rule an assembly is free to choose majority rule by majority rule if it wishes. Even if the constitution making majority were to grant some other rule by majority, it could always retract it by the same simple majority as long as the constituent assembly was in existence. In a divided society like Iraq, the dangers of proceeding by such majoritarian logic would be obvious.

In any case, Sistani could influence but could not control the overall process that would have to be filtered through the Governing Council, and would remain under the legal control of the CPA. He could have his elections, but not as soon as he wanted. He could have his assembly both governmental and constitutional, but it would not be unlimited in the latter capacity. He could have a constitution at the end of the process, but before then he would have to put up with an American authorised interim constitution, even if he managed to make its status uncertain. This interim constitution, and a multistage process, initially willed by no major actor, could in principle have been the key to a process that would have allowed the generation of legitimacy and the institutionalisation of learning. The continued element of imposition, linked to a very dangerous form of political exclusion, made the generation of legitimacy impossible. It was the political bargain concerning the state that led to the severe learning problems.

As to the exclusion, at issue was the structure of the Governing Council (GC), ultimately determined by American fiat. When I say that Sistani's influence was filtered through that body, I am of course admitting that some actors other than the Americans had a say in the process of drafting. Indeed, in the GC there was a plurality of such actors. In other post-sovereign constitution-making settings, from Spain to South Africa, that plurality together with elements of public discussion and participation, legal continuity and attempts at a fair structure of compromise, and even consensual decision-making, helped to generate some initial legitimacy for processes that, for logical reasons where there was no democracy initially, could not be begun democratically. Almost all these elements of legitimacy generation presuppose an inclusive structure of participation of the main political forces of society, including the political formations representing beneficiaries of the old regimes that are likely to survive as sociological power blocks in the new ones. In Iraq, the most important consequence of American imposition was an exclusionary structure of participation. Not only the Ba'ath, but all Sunni Arab nationalist formations were excluded from the Governing Council, where Sunni Arab participation was defined in terms of personal belonging to the relevant group by particular exile politicians acceptable to the Americans. On the other hand, the Kurdish and Shi'ite representatives were there on behalf of well-organised political parties, capable of pressure also outside the negotiating chamber. Even here, the American presence introduced a major inequality: as we will see, it was possible and necessary to recognise the Kurds as a group and to negotiate with them as such, but not with the Shi'a clerics. Thus, with the exception of the Kurds, the proceedings that produced the TAL were not accepted as legitimate by Iraqi society. Whatever role Iraqi actors played in the outcome, the results were regarded as functions of almost pure American imposition.

Descriptions of the drafting of the interim constitution, by participants themselves, seem to confirm this picture.[9] Using a mostly disregarded draft, prepared by an Iraqi advisor of the GC, a five-member 'drafting committee' composed of three Americans and two Iraqi-Americans spent many weeks of intense work redrafting and drafting and redrafting the TAL, which was followed by relatively few days of discussion in the GC before its adoption. Other public discussions projected earlier never took place. Initiatives on the part of the GC itself were on the whole rejected, for the better as in the case of family law, and the worse in the case of a security agreement with weak controls at least over coalition forces. In effect, the text of the five-person drafting committee was hammered through the GC by L Paul Bremer, with the apparent exception of the supposedly last minute introduction of the ratification rule initiated by the Kurds that gave three provinces the right to veto the permanent constitution. All later efforts to reconsider and amend were totally resisted, quite unreasonably so even in the view of some of the participants themselves.[10]

The fact that these results appeared almost unchangeable did not help matters. In general, the more legitimate a constitution, the more its framers can afford to enshrine it against the will of mere majorities later. Interim constitutions, on the contrary,[11] should be playing the role that the first, often replaced constitution of a country plays in a revolutionary setting: the facilitation of experimentation and orderly change. Instead, the TAL made both its own change and the adoption of a permanent constitution, another rule of change, both very difficult, or rather possible only by meeting the exacting minority demands tailored to the needs of the Kurds.[12]

Thus, depending on the interests involved, all the amendment rules of the TAL could involve a very high level of insulation of the interim constitution, and only under some circumstances would they allow an easy adoption of a new constitution. Paradoxically, I would argue that Iraqis could free themselves from the form of the TAL only if they kept or radicalised its

---

[9] Here I am relying on L Diamond's presentation in *Squandered Victory: the American Occupation and the Bungled Effort to Bring Democracy to Iraq* (Times Books, 2005).

[10] *Ibid* 140 *et seq*, 145 *et seq.*

[11] Given inevitably non-democratic beginnings where there is a dictatorship before, they always retain a legitimacy deficit from the democratic point of view.

[12] For the details see Art 3 and Art 60 of the TAL; and Arato, above n 4.

substance. If they wanted to get rid of the TAL both in form and substance, they would fail as long as they stayed within the procedural pattern indicated by the document. This state of affairs was in violation both of international law (since the foreign-imposed TAL would not be interim after all), and of the concessions given to Sistani, since his freely elected National Assembly was being reduced to a rubber-stamp. To understand how this became possible we must move on to the state bargain that constitutes the heart of the TAL.

AN EXCLUSIONARY STATE BARGAIN

In spite of Sistani and his significant informal pressure from *outside* the formal process of making the TAL, the document is generally considered an American imposition, and the legal form of the process confirms that appearance. Nevertheless, both appearance and legal form may partially mislead, and not only because of Sistani's role. There was also political bargaining *within* the process. This happened, because given the American destruction of the Iraqi state along with the Saddam regime, constitution making had to contain a distinct dimension of state making. The genuine bargaining that dimension came to involve was between two parties only: the American occupiers and the Kurds. The immediate reason, was that it was these two parties that held something like state power in Iraq at the time.[13]

Indeed, *historically* all *modern* constitution making presupposes successful state making. In a case like Iraq, that was a state before the American invasion and occupation, it is hard to see how public power and public security and therefore the *object* for which constitutions would be made could come from any other arrangement of the polity than a state. This theoretical point has been persuasively argued by Dieter Grimm, who has further maintained, in the tradition of Schmitt's *Verfassungslehre*, that the *subject* of constitution making as well as the object presupposes a state, in other words unified public powers capable of being activated by a people or a nation as a constituent power.[14] Accordingly, if a state did not exist before constitution making, or was destroyed, the logically prior act of state making would have to proceed simultaneously with constitution making. That this is possible is shown by the historical examples of the formation of federations and federal states where a new subject (state) is constituted from

---

[13] I say something like: the Americans, while they had a right recognised by the Security Council (UN SC Res 1483, 1511, 1546) to temporarily exercise the powers of a state in Iraq, never had monopoly of the legitimate means of force, while the Kurds, who had such a monopoly in Kurdistan, never had international recognition of an independent statehood.

[14] See most recently D Grimm, 'The Constitution in the Process of Denationalization' (2005) 12(4) *Constellations* 447.

old subjects (states) in some kind of constitutional treaty.[15] Even in such contexts the perspective advocated by Grimm can be sustained, because as we see from the example of the United States both in 1776 and 1787, the units that formed the confederation and federal state in constitution making themselves had well-organised states with close enough approximations of public monopolies of the legitimate means of violence. Here both the subject and object of constitution making were public. Nevertheless, I believe in any case that the notion that private powers cannot be the source of constitutional authority is belied by the role of juridically private conventions in the American states in the period 1775 to 1780, as well as roundtables in the recent experiences of the new democracies. In these cases *only*, new forms of public legitimacy had to be generated for private organisations and agreements which had then to be approved in public political procedures. Of course, Grimm would be able to answer that even these experiments presuppose 'stateness' or public powers with the requisite monopolies either before or constituted during the constitution-making process, at least as the object of constitution making.

What the American invasion and occupation in Iraq did, however, was to introduce both serious doubts concerning the legitimacy of 'the subject' of constitution making and equally serious uncertainty about 'the object' for which a constitution would be made. This issue of legitimacy I have already discussed, but I can briefly restate it here. The foreign occupying power has no right under international law to give the occupied country a constitution. By implication, neither do its Iraqi agents, like the GC.[16] Private organisations like political parties, not organised in a public body, also have no legal right to do so, but could, as against a foreign occupier, generate political legitimacy under conditions resembling the roundtables of Hungary, Poland and South Africa. This has not happened because of the narrow, exclusionary bases of the only real negotiating process in the making of the interim constitution under the shadow and influence of foreign imposition.

The situation is, however, even worse with the 'object' for which constitutions are made: public power. The issue of unresolved state structure goes so far as to have consequences for organisational choices on almost all levels, making the writing of a constitution that could be taken seriously extremely difficult. The problem was both de-differentiation and disorganisation of the Iraqi state. The differentiation and independence of something like that state both from an *external* power, and *internal* private powers with their own armies, allows considerable doubt. The occupation forces,

---

[15] See AV Dicey concerning the formation of federal states on the bases of the American example (*The Law of the Constitution* Part I, ch III, (1st edn 1885, London, Macmillan, 1967) as well as C Schmitt, *Verfassungslehre* chapter on the 'Bund' (Berlin, Duncker & Humboldt, 1928).

[16] See Fox, below n 17. He is very persuasive on this point.

now under simply the name of coalition forces, remain a state within the 'state' not subject in any way to Iraqi law or constitutional restraints. These latter could be written into the TAL in general, but thus did not apply to the major forces of violence and incarceration in particular. With the de facto Kurdish entity that acts like a fully-fledged state within its territory, and at times elsewhere where its forces are engaged nominally under an Iraqi flag, and the assertion of various uncontrollable forms of local rule, all with their own military forces, the boundaries of state authority or authorities are extremely poorly defined, even if we forget the foreign forces. From this point of view the insurrection may be particularly ugly and violent, but legally represents more or less the same problem as the other violent non-state organisations that control people and territory, and cannot themselves be controlled. The organisations that in the modern world are called upon to enforce 'stateness', the 'national' army, the 'public' administration and the 'national' police, presently lie in shambles because of deliberate American policy. As to the issue of security and the control of violence, it is clear that at present the enforcement of any constitution in the legal sense could not focus or rely exclusively on public authorities but to an equal extent on private powers (and their goodwill) that are themselves the greatest threats to legality. The issue, however, is not only that of violence and security. Public services, enforcement of contracts and in most areas personal relations too are under the control of juridically private organisations, in the latter case religious organisations. In such a situation, Grimm's question, concerning the very meaning and possibility of a constitution, makes a great deal of sense. One makes a constitution, but it establishes or regulates only a small part of political power in the country, by no means the most important part.

As Iraq *had been* a state before the beginning of the American war to change its regime, in principle constitution making here could have followed the pattern established with the overthrow of *old regimes,* one relying on the inherited state structures. Instead, there was a set of policies, coordinated or not, whose aim or at least consequence was to destroy the Iraqi state as well as the regime.[17] By now the *mea* and *tea culpa*s regarding de-Ba'athification and the dismissal of the army are so well known that no more is needed to be said on this subject. Perhaps one long sentence though: the very same Sunni elites that were being deprived of employment in the state organs were also denied all representation in the political process, while they were being given an underground army or armies, fuelled by powerful new resentments, in a context where there were no effective military forces available to control them, or even to prevent their access to the enormous amount of ordinance stored in various parts of the country.

---

[17] Best documented by GH Fox, 'The Occupation of Iraq', (2005) (36)2 *Georgetown Journal of International Law* (April) 195–298.

The result was not only the insurrection and the collapse of public security, but the impossibility of dismantling militias and private military organisations. In short, the effort to temporarily replace the dismantled Iraqi state by the occupation state was strikingly unsuccessful: no one established any kind of monopoly over the legitimate means of violence, except for the political authorities relying on the Peshmerga in Kurdistan—the Kurdish quasi-state that was neither dismantled nor occupied, but strengthened in its autonomy, whose strengthening was a sign of Iraq's disintegration and the difficulties in the face of rebuilding its state.

State building or rebuilding in Iraq was not in principle impossible.[18] On some level a state is only the knowledge, skill and competence of a large number of actual or potential agents, and in Iraq all this is readily available. What no longer existed in Iraq was some kind of coherent set of public controls over coercive powers in the country as a whole, especially the means of violence. Bracketing the all important question of limited sovereignty because of the occupation, since a state with limited sovereignty is possible, whatever control was left to Iraqi governmental powers by the occupier could have been coherently organised only if there was either a fundamental, binding agreement over a state structure, or one power forcibly bringing all other powers under its lasting control, or a binding agreement between some of the powers capable of bringing the others under their control. The second of these options presupposed the viability of long-term compulsion against all actors but one, the third against at least one such actor. In retrospect, the Sistani-led protest shows that pure compulsion is impossible with respect to the Shi'a part of the population, and the insurrection showed, I believe (though the jury is still out) the same with regard to the Sunni. Therefore, effective state building as the object of constitution making[19] presupposed, at the time of the writing of the TAL as well as now, a comprehensive, inclusive agreement of all the major actors.[20] Before any further work on the structure of the regime, it was the working out of a state structure acceptable (not preferable) to all sides (obviously some kind of federal state, but what kind?) that would have been the top priority of such negotiation, and this should not have been tied to time limits structured by any other nation's political calendar.[21] Alternative views and possibilities

---

[18] The issue was, again, whether Iraq was one of the relatively rare situations where the logically prior act (or stages) of state making could be accomplished at the same time with (the stages of) constitution making. Consciously or not, that was the double task facing the makers of the TAL.

[19] And not only in the sense of the generation of legitimacy.

[20] I argued for this in my first article on Iraq: 'The Occupation of Iraq and the Difficult Transition from Dictatorship' in (2003) 10(3) *Constellations* (September) 408–24.

[21] Given the potential of Kurdish secession, such a negotiating forum in order to work had to be shored up by an international posture, supported by the neighbouring states, with two fundamental premises: the territorial integrity of Iraq and national but equitable control over its oil resources.

should have been considered and seriously debated. Assuming federalism, it comes in many forms and involves a choice among institutions. The same goals of one side can be achieved by alternative options that may be more or less injurious to the interests of another side.

In fact, prior or at least separate negotiations apparently did take place regarding the structure of the state. Remarkably, however, they were of the most exclusionary structure possible under the circumstances. The main sessions occurred between the representatives of the two major Kurdish parties, the KDP (Kurdistan Democratic Party) and PUK (Patriotic Union Kurdistan) and the Americans, and only subsequently were the results brought to the Governing Council as a whole, and imposed, with some concessions to the Shi'a parties. Since, no relevant Sunni actor was involved given the political, though not ethnic exclusion of that side, and since Paul Bremer refused to have any formal relations similar to the Kurds with the emerging Shi'a caucus in the GC,[22] it is fair, I think, to describe the emerging state bargain as one between the Kurds and the Americans, with the proviso that the latter probably saw themselves as negotiating not on their own behalf but as supposedly disinterested trustees of Arab Iraq.

Remarkably enough, what may have begun as an attempt to simply dictate to the Kurds on 2 January 2004, wound up as the only serious, genuine negotiation Iraq had within its political process, one whose internal logic was not deformed by the overwhelming power of the occupier, mainly over the structure of the state but inevitably touching on other constitutional matters as well.[23] According to Phillips, 'the Kurdish leadership sent Bremer packing' when he first presented his demands.[24] Who else in Iraq was then in the position to do that? Thus, in effect, two holders of sovereign or quasi-sovereign powers, the Americans (in most of Iraq) and the Kurds (in Kurdistan) conducted negotiations, that would transform (in probable violation of the Hague Convention) the future structure of the occupied state as a whole. Since the Kurds were *de facto* outside of Iraq since 1991, from their own point of view (that to be sure no one in the world recognised de jure!) they were in effect negotiating entry or re-entry into some kind of state-like structure, but they were not doing so with their potential partners, the other Iraqi political actors, whether parties or ethnic groups or regions or whatever, but with the occupying power. The latter protected itself from the charge of illegality under international law only by various covers like having a 'conversation among friends'[25] or by being involved in generating only interim regulations. Having such a powerful agent negotiating on their behalf may have seemed like an advantage, from the point of view of the

---

[22] Diamond, above n 9, at 171.
[23] *Ibid* 141, 161 *et seq*, 171.
[24] DL Phillips, *Losing Iraq* (Boulder, CO, Westview Press, 2005) 187.
[25] Diamond, above n 9, at 163.

weak Arab members of the GC. Pachachi, the most serious advocate of a united Iraq, according to Diamond[26] suggested the first meetings, and perhaps it really was, because (with 50,000 armed *pesh merga* and a disbanded Iraqi army!) only the United States could have laid down the law that there will be no Kurdish secession, and that that Kurds will not gain control over the province's oil resources that would enable them to build and finance a de facto independent state anyway. But again remarkably, they got most other things they wanted: an ethnically based regional government with important nullification powers of Iraqi law, the likely survival of the *pesh merga* as independent units under whatever cover and the absence of Iraqi Arab troops from Kurdistan, some kind of process for the reversal of the Arabisation of Kirkuk, as well as some important powers in the 'federal' state through the collective presidency, the rule of the appointment of the prime minister as well as the amendment rule of the TAL and ratification rule of the permanent constitution.

We can only speculate concerning the reasons (1) why the Americans engaged in a merely two-sided bargaining process and (2) why they conceded so much. Was it their far greater trust in the Kurds than any of the Arab factions that made them their prisoner, or was it a desire to rush the process for reasons of the domestic political calendar or did they actually aim at a weak Iraqi state open to influence and penetration? In Diamond's presentation[27] there were in any case several failed attempts from Washington to deprive the Kurds of their Kurdistan Regional Government, whose potentially negative consequences for the integrity of Iraq as a whole were obvious and this speaks for the first or second but not the third interpretation. It seems to me that ultimately the fact that the Americans did not occupy Kurdistan, and did not have the military means to force the Kurds to do anything, led to the mistaken view that they had to be treated completely differently than those who were supposedly under their full physical control and tutelage. This was the origin of two-sided negotiations which thus came to resemble a federal pact between two holders of state power in two independent units, which of course meant conceding the most fundamental point to the Kurds right from the outset. And, given such bargaining structure and the Bush administration's ever-present time constraints, the ability of the Kurds to outwait the Americans always proved decisive. But whatever the reasons, once the deal emerged among Bremer, Barzani and Talabani, to put the matter crudely, it became their consensual position, and the rest of the GC or the drafting committee of five were in no position to do much about it. At best what could still be done, if inconclusively, was to generalise some of the concessions given to the Kurds to the Shi'ites, with provisions like the ability of any three provinces, potentially, to form a region, and the firm intention to hold on to other militias under the same cover given to the *pesh merga*.

---

[26] *Ibid* 161.
[27] *Ibid* 166–7.

Most remarkably, the Americans passively accepted, until Sistani's intervention, a potentially long-term freezing of the deal as entailed by the already mentioned amendment and ratification rules of the TAL. As to the amendment rule, the Kurds would certainly have one-quarter of the National Assembly or one member of the presidency council or most likely both to block amendments (they overperformed because of the Sunni insurrection and boycott and wound up with 30 per cent and *the* president). The ratification rule was a way of freezing the agreements of the TAL, because the Kurds could always muster two-thirds of the voters of three provinces to vote against any draft that reduced their autonomy in any way. Together with the provision that the defeat of the permanent constitution entailed a return to the TAL, in principle an indefinite number of times, the formula meant that the Kurds could gain more autonomy under any new arrangements but would never have to accept less.

We now know that, despite many challenges, Paul Bremer faithfully protected this result of the American-Kurdish state bargain, along with the ratification rule. Modification of the state bargain was possible, only if it was compatible with the original structure. And certainly there had to be some concessions to the Shi'ites who had to sell the scheme to Sistani, who in turn always had sanctions at his disposal. These problems were solved by trying to generalise the state bargain, and by working out structures of government that were compatible with it. Neither effort was fully successful, but both were to have important consequences.

L Diamond represents the incorporation into the TAL of the provision that other provinces (a maximum of three) could also form regions (Article 53C) as such a concession to the Shi'ites. But even he treats this element more as an afterthought than a product of serious Shi'ite demand and genuine negotiations. So it seems that general unhappiness with the deal given to the Kurds, and the desire by the American drafters to find something to compensate the Shi'ites, increasingly vocal outside the formal process, may have been responsible. The fact that the proposal by A Mahdi of SCIRI involved a three province limit seems to indicate that he was more interested in establishing a principle that would limit the Kurds than to establish an ethnic region containing all the Shi'ite provinces, since as many as nine provinces are Shi'ite majority, 10 including Baghdad. On the other hand, and probably most importantly for the Kurds, it was not enough to gain their own confederal enclave. As we see from writings of advocates like Peter Galbraith, for the sake of their future security they continued to fear above all the re-establishment of a centralised state, and ardently wished for a 'federal' Iraq.[28] This meant for them the extension of their

---

[28] Article 52A of the TAL therefore states: 'The design of the federal system in Iraq shall be established in such a way as to prevent the concentration of power in the federal government that allowed the continuation of decades of tyranny and oppression under the previous regime'.

own confederal status to the state structure of the whole country. I see no evidence that the Kurdish parties actually advocated this position in their bilateral negotiations with the Americans. In any case, the TAL contains the option, restricted however to regions containing a maximum of three provinces. Note however, that it contains it only as an option contingent on the agreement of the majority. Article 52C makes region formation a function of not only relevant provincial referenda, but also a vote of the National Assembly, which is an incredibly cumbersome or remote or symbolic formula only if we think of the short time period of the TAL in the narrow sense,[29] but in any case left it up to the Shi'ites themselves whether they wished to exercise power through a highly decentralised scheme, or through their expected control of the governmental majority. If they wished the latter, they could under the TAL stop the Sunnis from forming their three province region in the centre of the country.

It is certainly true that the majoritarian elements in the parliamentary government given to Iraq corresponded to Shi'ite aspirations, to the extent that only they could hope to have a majority, and because almost no majority could emerge without them. This majoritarianism comes through first and foremost through the unicameral structure of the legislature provided for by the TAL, contradicting the common practice in states described as 'federal'. The TAL indeed establishes provincial self-government, with some fiscal powers, based on elected councils, and governors generated through provincial elections either in the councils or by the citizens directly. But it gives neither provinces, nor regions as such for that matter, a legislative foothold in the central government. Whatever the parliamentary majority in the single chamber decides is law, with the exception of constitutional limits provided by the TAL itself, to be enforced by the Federal Supreme Court.

There were a variety of ways the TAL tried to make this majoritarian structure of government compatible with the confederal element introduced into the state (and potentially with a confederal state under the right to form new regions). Structuring a central government around carefully defined, enumerated powers (Articles 25A–25G) and leaving all else to the region(s) with nullification powers of most federal laws (Article 54B) was to give Kurdistan protection against central government encroachment in the scheme. If the Shi'a were conceded majoritarian powers, they were not going to apply in Kurdistan. Moreover, there were supposed to be consociational checks on that power as well having to do with the appointment of the prime minister, and, as it was mistakenly assumed, the passing of laws. Regarding both issues, the consent of a (very probable) Kurdish member of the presidency council was supposed to give the Kurds sufficient protection in case of a clash of interests between the majority and their region.

---

[29] Diamond, above n 9, at 167–8.

As it turned out, careless drafting of the TAL and/or undiscovered political design on the part of some of the drafters made the consociational mediations less effective than they first might have appeared. As to the veto power of the members of the presidency council, what was established by mistake or design was a one person veto on the collective veto itself, rather than a one person veto on laws, thus making the veto power irrelevant. As to the appointment of the prime minister (Article 38A) the unanimous nomination of the presidency council, or, failing that, a nomination by two-thirds of parliament seemed to be a strong consociational check on majority rule requiring high (possibly unworkable) level of consensus in the formation of government. Less noticed, however, was the provision that, once in office, through the power of dismissal to be confirmed by only the parliamentary majority, the prime minister could reconstruct his cabinet as a narrow majority one (Articles 40A, 41). Thus, there were many imaginable circumstances in which a government of the bare majority was capable of legislating by simple majority concerning issues it interpreted as its exclusive competence, at the expense of the regions, and indeed 'unconstitutionally' as long as it could control outcomes in the Supreme Court where such issues may possibly wind up.

The over all legal character of the constitutional package of the TAL suggests that it was first and foremost a state bargain, but this appearance again may disguise an ultimately antinomic structure. It is true that both the amendment rule and the ratification rule incorporated a Kurdish veto, indicating that the state bargain could not be touched by the majority, not even the majority of the constitutional assembly, unless it was willing and able to abrogate the whole legal framework of the TAL, extra-legally. The same rigidity was transferred to all matters including the structure of government, where the Kurds themselves may have had very good reasons to seek changes. A more differentiated amendment rule, enshrining the powers of the Kurdistan region and enumerating the powers of the central government, but allowing easier alteration of other governmental powers, would have served their purpose even better. Since the consociational safeguards intended to link Kurdistan to the central state were badly designed, they either had to be extended or replaced by an entirely different federal structure (ie the main traditional federalist mediation, a second, federal parliamentary chamber) if a potential clash between majoritarianism and confederalism was to be avoided or mediated. This could not be done under the TAL, and the contradictions had to be left as they were. Under some conditions these contradictions could lead to two kinds of fundamental difficulties. The first was the governmental majoritarian invasion of the regional prerogatives, already alluded to, whose success would depend on the forces at the government's disposal. The second was a political impasse specifically during the period of government formation; a parliamentary majority may not be able to form government, but could stop any other force from doing so. The rule of the country would then revert to its provinces and region(s), demonstrating the primacy of the state structure in the incoherent synthesis. The only option the majority would then have is to repudiate the TAL itself. Thus, either before or after government formation some scenarios following from the TAL itself could have led to a clash between the majority and the state.

In fact, the unresolved tension and potential clash between majoritarianism and confederalism was not only a matter of the contents of the TAL, but had to do with the status of the whole, if we look beyond *legality* to issues of *legitimacy*. To the extent the rules of change gave a clue to the status of the whole, the rigid and consensus-requiring structure of these in the TAL indicated the *legal* predominance of confederal elements. At the same time, since the freely elected national assembly provided for by the same TAL would have far greater *legitimacy* than any of the instances that collaborated in its making, it could choose to repudiate the interim constitution once in session. Ultimately, if the TAL survived, pre-programmed clashes between the government of the majority and the regions would have their source and conflicting justification in this contradiction between legality and legitimacy built into the interim constitution. Similarly, a very destructive clash between these principles could have occurred over the making of a permanent constitution, unless there was a consensual agreement concerning the degree of adherence to the TAL's framework. Given the multiple lines of conflict, and the American occupation, there was not one force among the Iraqis capable of imposing a solution on all others. The Shi'a clerics, who won (barely) the elections of January 2005, were too weak even in their own eyes, and understood from that moment on that there would have to be a consensual agreement, both concerning the operation of the Transitional Government and the making of the new constitution. The only question therefore was the breadth and inclusiveness of that consensus.

FAILURE OF THE STATE BARGAIN AND OPTIONS OF CONSTITUTION MAKING

The focus on the state changes the way the Iraqi constitutional process should be looked at, as a whole. From this point of view, the TAL does not appear as simply externally imposed, or appears as pure foreign imposition only in the legal sense. Politically, it was a mixture of agreement and imposition. Moreover, while some of the imposition was purely repressive, other dimensions involved trade-offs. But it should be made entirely clear none of the agreements nor even the compensatory trade-offs brought into the process all the relevant actors. The agreements were highly exclusionary, and the trade-offs made up for the exclusion only partially. All this was the result ultimately of American imposition, creating a hierarchical structure among the relevant Iraqi actors in classical imperial fashion.

The fact that it was based on some agreement, and trade-offs, even if mostly involving only two sides, contributed to the survival of the TAL. The Americans negotiated of course on their own behalf, but to be successful they had to take many other interests into account. Thus, the Shi'a gained powerful positions already in the interim which allowed them to live with the system in which they hoped to get an electoral and parliamentary majority. They never accepted the inflexibility of the TAL scheme, and the idea that all they could do through a freely elected assembly was to confirm its scheme. Their numbers and the nearness of elections allowed them to take the position of waiting for their own moment to come. Wherever they could, in the South they began to impose local forms of rule in tune with their authoritarian inclinations. There emerged a tacit Shi'a-Kurd agreement supporting the survival of the TAL, perhaps even formalised before or after the 2004 elections that led to the continuation of the framework on paper, and as far as the formal procedures of the central government were concerned.[30]

But this type of arrangement did not make the state structure agreed upon by the Kurds and the Americans actually work. The Kurd deviations were at least orderly, duly legislated by the regional government and arguably consistent with one interpretation of the TAL as some kind of treaty. The massive violations of rights by the Americans in the Sunni triangle, and in one conflict in the South as well, indicate that in their presence the rights of due process (TAL Articles 15B, 15C, 15D, 15E, 15F, 15G, and 15J, none of which contain any kind of exception for coalition forces operating in this supposedly sovereign state) were a dead letter. Yet even with the massive and disgraceful violation of rights, no monopoly over the legitimate means of violence has been established in this region by the Americans, the Iraqi government, or the insurrection for that matter. The Sunni triangle is a 'failed state'. Finally, though there is only sporadic documentation, the rights of the TAL cannot be enforced against the local authorities in the South either. This has been amply shown only in the case of women's rights, but we have to assume that religious freedom is not doing any better. If the central government seems to have some genuine power in the South, this is so only after the elections when the same Islamic parties and militias are dominant in both. Given the multiplicity of the latter, and their penetration of the local police, it is a question to what extent there is a monopoly over legitimate violence in this region or Baghdad.

---

[30] Prof Brown was kind enough to tell me that, indeed there was a formal coalition agreement, in March, containing an affirmation of the TAL and of 'federalism' as understood by the Kurds.

Of course the insurrection is against the occupation, and the occupation continues, supposedly, because of the insurrection. It is a vicious circle, but is it impossible to break? The occupation is also there to police a state structure negotiated in an imposed, exclusionary bargain; and the insurrection is also against that bargain. Sunni elites are against that bargain for the formal but very good reason that they had no part in making it and did not even receive some trade-offs like the Shi'a. But they are also against it for the generally recognised, solid and substantive reason, that the arrangements are very dangerous for the Sunni provinces in particular. First of all, the ethnic cleansing needed to create the state or region the Kurds really want would be mostly at the expense of Sunni Arabs, involving a huge refugee problem for the provinces further to the South. Even more seriously, the assymetric confederal structure of the bargain already in the TAL establishes the possibility for a more symmetric one (Article 53C) with any three provinces having the right to form a region, possibly with powers like Kurdistan now or then. Assuming regional control over significant parts of the oil resources, which the Kurds have always demanded, which at least some of the Shi'a would have an interest to concede if their provinces got the same privilege, the oil poor Sunni provinces would be impoverished. They have a much better chance to fight such an arrangement now, when they still have the men, the arms and the expertise, than later. Aside from ideological and traditional Arab commitments to a more unified Iraq, which are probably very passionate for some, there are also solid material interests supporting such a politics.

I have little doubt that the problem was foreseen in Washington very early. The answer was not, however, a Governing Council with memberships arranged according to ethnic quotas. Once the United States presided over an exclusionary deal that it refused to reopen, it was this deal that had to be enforced. But enforcing this deal was not possible without the indefinite continuation of the occupation. It gives two reasons for the insurrection to continue, and the seemingly vicious circle cannot be broken: the occupation and the arrangement it guards. Since the occupation could not be ended immediately or even in terms of a realistic timetable without admitting defeat, with all its political consequences, the only thing the present government of the United States could try to do is to change somehow the deal that the occupation continued to preserve. After having negotiated a state deal with the Kurds, and given the Shi'ites the election that produced a governmental majority for them (modified of course by the results of the state deal though consociational controls), the United States now had to make a project of some kind of Sunni inclusion, real or illusory.

There were two roadblocks in the way of such a project: the interim constitution and the results of the January 2005 elections. As to the former, sufficiently discussed already, its rules allowed the Kurds to establish a bottom line that was most likely not acceptable to the Sunni, and to the Shi'a acceptable only if they would generate their own regionalism threatening the Sunni even more seriously. Thus, the factor that would allow for Shi'a acceptance would make the Kurdish position impossible for the Sunni. Assuming that the Kurds disposed over 25 per cent of the seats of the National Assembly (they had 30 per cent) and one member of the presidency (Talabani as the president, as it turned out to be) the rules that helped them to establish their bottom line could not be changed legally. However, this bottom line was not a clear one. The TAL assigns the Kurdistan Regional Government three provinces and parts of another three (including Kirkuk or Tanzim) where they presently have only partial or no control. Some of these territories were initially in Kurdish hands before Saddam's counter-attack in 1991 recaptured them, under the eyes of the allies who stopped the onslaught too late. The Kurds continue to have aspirations for the control of these territories, and especially Kirkuk for which the TAL makes special arrangements that cannot be entirely satisfactory to them because of its delays (Articles 58A, 58B and 58C). Obviously, it is unacceptable to the other communities that all or parts of Arab majority provinces be handed over to Kurdistan. Assuming that a special arrangement could be made for Kirkuk, for any solution to work, one had to get either Kurdish agreement to forego any further territorial and constitutional (right of secession!) aspirations and perhaps to give up some earlier gains, or to take them and their secession threat squarely on either by establishing a purely Arab government or by repudiating the TAL or both. No one in Iraq was able to do the latter, namely to risk secession and its likely military consequences, except the Americans, who were unwilling to do so. As a result, the Kurds could not really be threatened by being excluded from the government or the constitutional process. Thus no one, including the Americans, had a good chance to do the former-namely to get them to moderate their demands. Unfortunately, as it turned out, the Shi'a would in that case have another option, beyond what the framers of the TAL conceded and may have even imagined.

As far as the elections were concerned, the relegitimating effect of this great victory of Sistani for the process as a whole should certainly not be underestimated. Before, all political instances, the CPA, the GC and the Interim Government, all were ultimately authorised by the fiat of Iraq's conqueror. Now there was a freely elected assembly, whose election the conqueror at first resisted, an election that in most of the country generated considerable enthusiasm. As far as the Shi'ite community was concerned, it could now claim a majority position in Iraq (with 48 per cent of the votes and 51 per cent of the seats), and within that community, in terms of both local and national results two organisations that previously owed their official status also to the Americans, SCIRI with its militia and Da'wa, now had electoral legitimacy. The elections, however, only worsened, initially, the problem of exclusion. Because of the insurrection and the Sunni boycott, their consequence was a very low level of participation achieving almost no representation, and thus the further delegitimation of the whole process in that part of the country. The electoral rule formally responsible for all this was chosen by its original authors, UN officials, for both principled and practical reasons. Proportional representation (PR) is the only fair electoral system for a constituent assembly, allowing the widest possible participation even of small, dispersed groups. A one country district PR, moreover, is the most proportional variant. More pragmatically, this system did not require a census of the country and its districts to apportion seats in advance. But it was a turnout dependent system, and by the autumn of 2004 it became clear that because of the insurrection, Sunni turnout would be very low, giving their parties at best a much lower percentage of seats than they would have obtained otherwise. The system should have been changed right then and there, but the dominant forces in the Interim Government that had their origin in the old Governing Council would not hear of it.

In fact the Sunni boycott was a rational response to this situation, because a merely low turnout would have produced numbers that would have allowed claims that the Sunni were accurately represented. Only a representation that approached zero called attention to the old exclusion in a particularly powerful way, as a scandal that could not be continued. One of the major communities of Iraq, estimated at about 20 per cent, could not be simply left out of the constitution-making process as a matter of justice, and also as a matter of collective security if there was to be any chance of politically dealing with the Sunni-based insurrection. Many schemes were offered to remedy the situation, but the one eventually chosen, after intensive pre-negotiations with the new Sunni National Dialogue Council, was entirely satisfactory.[31] Fifteen new Sunni members were added to a 55-member parliamentary Constitutional Committee, plus 10 advisors, with the larger group renamed Constitutional Commission. Technically, the smaller body would still have to confirm the product of the larger one, but since a consensual structure of decision-making has been decided on, this should have been automatic. There were some fights concerning who the Sunni representatives would be, whether deBa'athification rules would be applied, but finally the decision was left to a new umbrella group called the National Dialogue Council that chose 15 delegates and 10 expert advisors from groups such as the Association of Islamic Scholars, the Iraqi Islamic Party and the Sunni Endowment and its own members. I think it is safe to say that some of the 25 new members, most likely a majority, sympathised with at least some wings

---

[31] The most accurate summary is in NJ Brown's report 'The Iraqi Constitutional Process Plunges Ahead' in Carnegie Endowment for International Peace, *Policy Outlook* (July 2005). Brown does not, however, mention the numbers. Now also see International Crisis Group, *Unmaking Iraq: a Constitutional Process Gone Awry* (26 September 2005) 2–3.

of the insurrection, with some perhaps having even political ties and certainly channels of communication to armed groups. That was very important if the whole process was to work.

Aside from the goal of making a deal around everyone's notion of a second or third best, one crucial experience of negotiated transitions has been that deals that can be made and have a chance to last are based on agreements among moderate forces on opposing sides, who can control or win the assent of radical forces on their own side.[32] Thus there are, abstractly speaking, two types of agreements required: one among the sides and one within each side. In Iraq there are three sides, four if we count the Americans, thus four necessary agreements. And it is not difficult to identify more moderate and more radical forces on each side, even if the picture would shift depending on given issues, and if not all of what we have experienced can be fitted into any such neat scheme.[33] Since in any serious deal, there are two types of agreements to worry about, and no deal will be worth much if the deal-makers on any side will be easily denounced by (all) their radical allies as traitors. At the same time, in a polarised situation the risk of some such denunciation must be accepted, even if the consequences as in Iraq can be quite deadly.[34] It is important, in other words, for the moderate partners to give each other enough in the negotiations, so they *and* the deal can survive the bargaining process.

This means that the presence of Sunni players like the ones now included should have dramatically changed the bargaining process. That presence signified two things. First, on the *procedural* level, Iraq now almost had its genuine negotiating forum for working out a new state bargain. Though not quite. While a great number of issues of detail could be handled by the new Constitutional Commission, the really fundamental questions could not be. This became a serious problem as the deadline for a possible six-month extension (TAL Article 61) approached. Strong pressure had been put on the members to come to an overall agreement within that deadline,[35] but they could not, since those belonging to hierarchical leadership parties like the Kurdish delegates did not have that kind of authority to give up anything really important. First, there were some unfortunate attempts to divide the package into two, and leave the few really important and divisive questions until later, to be decided by majority votes. But this actually would have been equivalent either to not getting the job done, and trying to replace the TAL with an inferior product, or delivering the crucial questions

---

[32] A Przeworski, *Democracy and Market* (Cambridge, 1990).

[33] There have been surprising alliances and conversations among the most radical Shi'a, al Sadr, and some moderate Sunni forces, the Association of Islamic Scholars.

[34] We still do not know who killed two of the initial Sunni members (one full member and one advisor).

[35] See Brown, above n 31, for the reasons, and his criticisms, as well as International Crisis Group, *Iraq: Don't Rush the Constitution*, Middle East Report No 42, 8 June 2005.

to a future parliamentary procedure with much fewer restrictions than the current constitution-making one. It is hard to see, for example, why even the Kurd would accept majoritarian insecurity over the security provided by the TAL. Certainly, the Sunni representatives could not accept any such 'compromise'.

Almost all roundtable settings presuppose that aside from the more formalised meetings, there is also a possibility for a meeting of political principals of the really important groups who would be capable, if anyone is, of making the fundamental decisions, right now, in one or several sessions. With the deadlock of the Constitutional Commission on the really fundamental issues, on the structure of the state and the place of Islam in it, just such a meeting of principals had been called for the weekend of 6 August 2005. To me this meant for a brief, but alas vanishing, moment that finally Iraq had the right negotiating format, that it should have had two and a half, or one and a half years ago, when the United States and the United Nations respectively should have pushed through a round-table negotiation including all the major political forces of Iraqi society, to negotiate the state deal that was in fact bargained by the Americans with the Kurds exclusively.

Thus, it appeared for that brief moment that all the elements characteristic of recent round-table type of constitution making were now established, though certainly not in their right historical sequence. Admittedly, the cart was before the horse, and sequencing is a very important matter. This meant first that Iraqis were now supposed to negotiate, very late in the game, under very unfortunate time pressures, a state structure, and all at the same time governmental institutions appropriate for these, as well as a symbolic identity in a final, and no longer a merely interim, package. Secondly, the change in sequence meant that at best an elite deal would come very late in the process with little opportunity for genuine parliamentary, not to speak of public, discussion. Once a draft emerged, there would be little opportunity to correct it, though the rejection of the draft in a constitutional referendum could supply yet another opportunity. But that rejection, with the popular choice and input reduced to a simple yes or no, would not be based on experience with malfunctioning, and the corrective would be more a function of a new electoral arithhmetic (about which more below) than constitutional learning. Finally, the temporal conjunction of a roundtable, elite leadership format with a constitutional assembly allowed the parliamentary majority freedom to manipulate among these venues according to its perceived interests. The majority was not compelled to make a deal because it reserved the right and had the contemporary opportunity to pass its own option. As against the initially dominant forces of roundtables elsewhere called early in such processes, the leaders of the Iraqi governmental parties had electoral legitimacy.

We will never know for certain whether the three-sided discussions of leaders came to exclude the third, the Sunni side, only under the extreme time pressure they were working under, or whether the purpose of the meeting of the principals from the outset was to seal a Shi'ite-Kurd exclusionary deal which the Constitutional Commission or the Committee were afraid to complete on their own. The latter more likely option seems to be the opinion of the Crisis Group, who say that the goal was to both speed up the process and to confirm that whatever the commission structure and its procedural rules, 'the real power to take durable decisions lay with the heads of these two communities'.[36] What seems, however, shameful is that all this happened in the presence of the American ambassador, Zalmay Khalilzad, who up until this point had been presumably working on the three-sided, fair deal some of his own principals in Washington considered essential.

What such a fair deal would have been like is not difficult to reconstruct. As a *second, substantive* implication of serious Sunni participation in the negotiations, the outcome, this time, in order to really work, had to favour their bargaining position to whatever extent still possible. This was so because the previous state bargain, and the subsequent political trade-offs under Sistani's pressure, favoured first the Kurds, and then the Shi'ites, and because many of the results of the earlier arrangements were now no longer reversible. Under the TAL, the Shi'ite majority of the National Assembly would not pass any arrangement that would take away the establishment of Islam as the state religion, and the majoritarian, parliamentary structure of the central government. Similarly, three Kurdish provinces would not ratify a significant dimunition of the special rights of the Kurdistan Regional Government. Thus, important compensations had to be found for the Sunni delegates to be able to play their proper role, which consisted not only in coming to agreement with Shi'ite and Kurd moderates, but convincing significant sectors of the radical Sunni insurrection that the deal was a good one, or at least the very best one that could be achieved under the circumstances. It may be that Sunni elites still hoped for a fully centralised state, and some insurrection leaders may even imagine that a new dictatorship could be erected on such foundations. This is the position continually ascribed to them as a group, in a rather self-serving manner, by supporters of the Kurds. Such a state was now, however, excluded as a possibility, not only because of the special status of Kurdistan, but because the Kurds cannot accept the rest of Iraq being so organised waiting to bring them again under Arab control. It is therefore much more worthwhile to pay attention to the bottom line of the Sunni which is that they cannot accept being an impoverished region in the centre of Iraq that the various break-up and confederal plans have in store for them. Thus, it was up to the other side to offer them arrangements that would involve guarantees against this worst case outcome. They would have to come on three levels: the organisation

---

[36] International Crisis Group, above n 31, at 3.

of the state, the organisation of the government, and the disposition over natural resources, ie oil. Substantively, it was important that the Sunni receive with respect to all three areas a perceivably better deal, and certainly not a worse one, than in the case of the TAL in whose making they did not participate at all.

There is no need to generate my own idea of a fair constitutional settlement, because, before the consensual process broke down, there were some clues in the press and in the documents of the expanded Constitutional Commission that its members were well on the way toward developing at least important elements of such solution. As to the structure of the state, it was clear that the Sunni delegates now accepted, however reluctantly, that the Kurds were not going to lose their special status, and this meant having a fully autonomous region, with a regional government, constitution and a regional militia, all in a bilingual Iraq where they would play a strong role in national government. But it was not likely that they were going to get to expand their region, with the possible exception of Kirkuk, and gain the major right, ie to dispose over the natural resources in their territory. Most importantly, they were not going to get to extend the regional formula to the rest of Iraq, under the misleading name of 'federalism'. It is true that the early draft of the permanent constitution available to me[37] contains regions as well as provinces, and allows region formations in addition to the region of Kurdistan, which in this draft is not explicitly mentioned. But there is no sign in that document of a formulation that would restrict the federal government to a few enumerated powers, and of nullification rights of the regions regarding most federal laws. On the contrary, it is the regional constitutions that must conform to the federal constitution (Chapter 4 Article 18). While the mechanism of region formation seems to be undecided, the constitutions of the regions would be produced by the National Assembly (Chapter 4 Article 7). According to press reports, the constitution was certainly going to establish a second legislative chamber, based on the geographic principle of provinces, and there is some trace of this in the draft which does not, however, provide a scheme for such a body.[38] The draft in any case has a single person presidency[39] rather than a three person council, and thus has no other place to involve decentralised units in the management of the federal government than in a second parliamentary chamber. Thus, as to the political role of the Kurds in the Federal Governemnt of Iraq, it would have corresponded to their numerical weight

[37] Text of the draft constitution, raised for discussion at the Constitution Drafting Committee, see www.iraqfoundation.org/projects/constitution/arabicconstitution_unsept 1505.doc.
[38] See K Semple, 'Constitution Proposes Some Limits on Role of Clergy', New York Times, 4 August 2005.
[39] 'Executive Authority' arts 1 and 2.

in two chambers, and not according to consociational, power-sharing arrangements within the executive. In this sense the journey from the TAL to the permanent constitution would have been, had things gone right, from consociationalism to constitutionalism, as it was in South Africa.

The direction of change regarding the structure of government seems to be parallel, though for reasons of ideology rather than demography. The changes are in the direction of a more consistent, parliamentary government, based on the rule of the majority, and that favours the Shi'ites and not the Sunni. The latter, however, are ideologically committed to all measures that have the tendency of strengthening central government. Paradoxically, in order to deny the confederalist Kurds consociational rights of participation in the executive, the Sunni must accept the consequences of that same denial with respect to their own participation. Under TAL (and in practice after the January 2005 elections) it took the consent of the Kurds (and potentially the Sunni), again assuming a Kurd (and a Sunni) in the three person presidency, to name a prime minister, making the formation of government, if not its later composition, dependent on their will. The first constitutional draft no longer contained any trace of this particular, cumbersome power-sharing arrangement that could have made government formation impossible at some point even with a parliamentary majority, an impossible state of affairs for a parliamentary government. Not only does the draft have only one president, a more ceremonial one, elected by parliament by a two-thirds majority, he *must* also first offer the leader of the largest party the position of the powerful prime minister. The overall relationship between government and state substitutes a federal state, with a confederal enclave, Kurdistan, whose centre-unit relations are mediated by a geographically based second parliamentary chamber, for the TAL's uneasy mixture of a centralised government and a confederal state mediated by badly designed consociational elements. Everything, of course, would depend on the composition of the upper chamber, its powers and its decision rules. But assuming either a purely provincial upper chamber (with three to four Kurdish provinces) or one based on a combination of regions and provinces, it would have been possible to give sufficient guarantees to the Kurds (and the Sunni) against any tyranny of the majority, at least on the level of law making. There was, to say the least, a potential here for a better federalist formula, concentrating more flexibly on the ongoing political decision making than one focusing, with great rigidity, on the very beginning of the governmental process. Amendment rules tend to indicate (cf Dahl) the nature of the state, and therefore in the case of the TAL an ultimately confederal plus consociational structure from the point of view of the Kurds. In the early drafts this was going to change. Now minor amendments would take two-thirds of the vote of one national assembly, major amendments (Netherlands style) would take two-thords of two assemblies, with an election in between. In both cases a national referendum would have to approve an amendment, by simple majority, but there was no provincial veto of any kind. While there was a need for the president to approve amendments, this again was in the place of the unanimous, ie consociational approval of the presidential council.[40] Nothing was stated to be unamendable this time around, including the rights of regions. In short, large minorities, regional or ethnic, unless they controlled over one-third of the parliamentary seats, would lose their control over constitutional change. This would be the amendment rule of a federal rather than a confederal state. From the point of view of majority and minority relations, however, note that one kind of equality has replaced another. Under the confederal or consociational rule, one group out of three, whether minority or majority could veto any amendment. Now it would have taken either two groups to pass or two to veto an amendment. From the point of view of the Sunni Arabs, they would need an ally either to amend or to block an amendment, but the same would be true for all other groups.

COLLAPSE OF CONSENSUAL PROCESS AND SUBMISSION OF A DRAFT

Given the acceleration of the process, few serious observers really believed a fair constitutional deal was possible. I, however, believed in it because I thought that Sistani would not allow the Shi'ites to agree to (or to sponsor!) a project that would risk the break-up of Iraq, and because the Americans simply could not afford to fail in sponsoring a genuinely three-sided deal that had a hope of splitting the Sunni insurgency. Why these two factors did not work as they should have probably lies in a third factor I foolishly neglected: the relative strength of Iran in Iraq with respect to America.[41] Before trying to explain this let me recount what happened.

After weeks of apparently intensive three-sided bargaining, strongly (perhaps much too strongly) supported by the Americans and specifically Ambassador Khalilzad, during the week of 22 August 2005, what should have been the conclusion of a fair negotiating process producing a consensual solution suddenly collapsed. During the final week or 10 days of negotiations, the Sunni delegates were effectively excluded, in favour of bilateral Shi'ite-Kurdish leadership meetings. Sunnis were called in only to be told results they had to take or leave; they were left to appeal to the United States, the United Nations, the Arab League, mostly in vain. No Sunni group or even a major Sunni politician previously in the GC or the Transitional Government, not Adnan Pachachi, Vice President Yawer, and certainly not the leaders of the Iraqi Islamic Party, supported the new draft. The leaders of the majority of the National Assembly, of the Shi'ite and

---

[40] Chapter 6 art 1A and B.
[41] See the brilliant *New York Times* Editorial of 25 September 2005, 'Empowering Iran'.

Kurdish parties, proceeded to negotiate bilaterally and produced a draft without Sunni agreement. It is remarkable, however, that they did not feel confident to have that assembly they controlled actually vote on their draft constitution and precipitously approved it by executive fiat. Acting entirely extra-legally, they compromised not only the consensual decision rule previously agreed upon with the Sunnis, but the prescription of the TAL (Articles 60, 61A) on which the process up to that point depended.[42] Thus, they compromised the TAL through executive fiat rather than the vote of the freely elected Assembly, though of course the executive, having a majority in that Assembly, could count on not being challenged by the legislative majority. Technically, however, they carried out a scarcely disguised coup against the TAL as well as the National Assembly.[43] Paradoxically then, while the TAL straightjacket remained constrained in substance, and specifically as regards the state bargain, the potentiality of its majoritarian overthrow had been realised as well, albeit on the procedural level.

All this was done in the name of a mediocre document, full of holes, inferior to the TAL itself, leaving some of the most fundamental constitutional questions for later majorities or qualified majorities to decide. From the point of view of the Sunni, in spite of some very late half-hearted concessions, the constitution voted in on 15 October 2005 made it extremely likely that the worst case scenario would be institutionalised.

The result was also disastrous from the point of view of the United States, because the consensual process that collapsed, and a document all Iraqis could live with, was to be a fundamental element of dealing with the insurrection currently almost fully out of control. The American authorities, from Secretary Rice to Ambassador Khalilzad, played an especially active role in both the process and its disastrous ending. They have maintained throughout both the reality, and even worse, the appearance, of an externally imposed process. To be fair, Sunni inclusion may not have happened any other way. We can now see how little interest there really was in the major Shi'ite and Kurdish parties in genuine negotiation with those they take to be inheritors of the ex-state party, the Ba'ath, and agents of the current insurrectionists. The American authorities on the other hand are the ones who have to deal with the Sunni insurrection in the face of diminishing support at home. They seemed to have reconciled themselves to the idea that after the dominant position of the Kurds, and later the Shi'ites, the

---

[42] According to the TAL, the National Assembly 'shall write a(the) draft of the permanent constitution of Iraq' but the National Assembly did not write anything, and could not, without voting. Only a committee wrote a text, without the authority to submit it to the electorate.

[43] J Cole, *Informed Comment* 23 August at http://www.juancole.com/2005/08/fisking-war-on-terror-once-upon-time.html; Arato, '[Il]legality and [Il]legitimacy'; Brown in 'Iraq's Constitutional Conundrum' puts it like this: 'the notion that the TAL's requirement for the Assembly to write a constitution could be satisfied by handing the speaker an incomplete draft a few minutes before the deadline is beyond implausible' (at 2).

Sunnis too may play for a time an important role in constitution making. So a lot of pressure was put on the Shi'ite and Kurdish leaders to expand the process, and to allow Sunnis linked to important political forces to participate. This was good as far as it went. It is not difficult to explain, however, what then went terribly wrong.

I would focus on several factors that demonstrate that in Iraq the role of the external dimension may have remained primary until the bitter end. First, even though the American government was now a sponsor of an extraordinarily complex three-way process of negotiations, it insisted on adhering to a rigid timetable in the TAL (Article 61A-61G), according to which a draft would be 'written' by the National Assembly by 15 August, a ratificatory referendum would be held by 15 October, and new parliamentary elections by 15 December. Even though the same TAL permitted a six-month extension of the process, if applied for by 1 August (Article 61F), and, even subsequently all the dates could be amended by Article 3 of the TAL, American representatives insisted, however implausibly, that the insurrection could be dealt a serious blow by the constitutional process only if all the dates were kept. The Iraqis adhered to the deadlines with the exception of the 15 August Amendment of the TAL (that would have gained them a mere week had they used it for any good purpose, which they did not) with disastrous results. The extreme time pressures confronted the parliamentary leaderships with the choice of final deadlock and majoritarian imposition, and chose, wrongly but perhaps understandably, the latter. As we saw afterwards, new avenues of compromise that may have been available were therefore not explored. Positions were hardened too soon. As to the American team on the spot, led by Ambassador Khalilzad, the same time pressure forced him to abandon in a spectacular manner the Sunni side and accept Shi'a-Kurd imposition on the question of 'federalism', and at least initially the secular side on the question of the role of Islam in civil affairs. (The only reason why in the end he did not accept pure Shi'ite imposition concerning the relationship of Islam to the state after apparently having done so, was because the Kurds went public on that issue with serious potential domestic consequences for the US government). In the end, there was no alternative left for Khalilzad and his chiefs at home than to try to spin the very results (lack of consensus and Sunni exclusion) that they previously and very publicly called unacceptable and dangerous.

Secondly, the highly public involvement of Ambassador Khalilzad, going beyond even Paul Bremer's hands on practice during the making of the TAL (that at least was kept secret for a while), was certainly disastrous. Perhaps this activity was simply a function of trying to accelerate the timetable, but it is hard to see why the parties could not have been pressured secretly and confidentially. It is possible that after free elections only public pressure with media support had a chance to influence political leaders who had their own democratic legitimacy, and parliamentary backing, not to speak of their increasing control of local affairs in the South and in Kurdistan. But many newspaper editorialists actually denounced the insistence on speed as an end in itself. Thus, it is difficult to escape the impression that the highly public role of Khalilzad was intended exactly as such, to demonstrate to the American public and the world that the US government is really in charge trying to accomplish good and important things in spite of Iraqi resistance and recaltricance. Now it is possible, but by no means certain, that at least Shi'ite if not Kurdish actors considered it important to resist American pressure. Amending the TAL in the face of Khalilzad's tantrums on 15 August, when TAL was amended to extend deadlines by one week, was such a small declaration of independence. More spectacular and decisive was the bombshell of a demand thrown in by `Abd al-`Aziz al-Hakim of SCIRI for a region of nine Southern Shi'ite provinces on 11 August when the political principals of each group had already begun to meet to iron out the remaining issues left over from the Constitutional Commission.[44] Little remembered now are two facts, connected to this announcement, that demonstrate that Hakim's demand was by no means consensual within the Shi'ite community itself. One was the immediate opposition to the idea by Prime Minister Jaffari that went absolutely nowhere. The other and much more important fact were a series of 'round robin' meetings just before Hakim's speech between the Grand Ayatollah Sistani, Moqtadad al-Sadr and Hakim. Given Sadr's attitude before and after, and Sistani's before and Jaffari's after, it is not impossible to deduce that the two were trying to convince the leader of SCIRI not to throw his idea of a nine province mega-region into the constitutional negotiations, or at least to stay with the less destructive three province version of the TAL.

Next, not many have noticed how strongly Iran supports the new constitutional draft.[45] In fact, the attitude of Iran may have counted for more in the outcome than the parallelogram of then internal Shi'ite attitudes. To the extent that the United States so publicly identified itself with a consensual solution of the constitution-making process, it was much too easy to bring that process down through the act of a proxy that introduced a new demand that made consensus impossible. The temptation to greatly embarrass the Americans was there, and it is hard to believe that the rulers in Teheran did not take advantage of the opportunity, especially, because a policy was available that presented them with a very favourable opportunity of extending their influence in Iraq without having to take responsibility for the

[44] 'Key Shiites Demand Autonomy in Southern Iraq as Deadline Nears', Reuters, 11 August 2005.
[45] 'Iran Satisfied with Iraq Charter' Tehran, 29 August (UPI): 'Iran expressed satisfaction Monday over the completion of Iraq's new draft constitution, despite Arab Sunnis' reservations on several articles of the charter. Foreign Ministry spokesman Hamid Asafi was quoted by the Iranian News Agency, IRNA, as saying, "Iran hopes the political process in Iraq will lead to a referendum on the constitution and the creation of a government as planned". ... "There is no doubt that establishing peace and security in Iraq will lead to economic prosperity and will serve the interests of all the Iraqi people", Asafi added'.

chaotic consequences of pursuing that goal. Undoubtedly, from Iran's point of view, Hakim's new demand would not only wreak havoc with American plans for a consensual solution of constitution making, but had its own independent rationale. If successful it would lead to the creation of a powerful region with all the ports, 60 per cent to two-thirds of the oil, and half the people of Iraq, where Iran would have decisive influence. If Iraq would stay together in a 'federation' of three very unequal regions, the Southern region would dominate it, because of its size and resources and since the Shi'ites would also control through their majority the central government. The South would be the Prussia of the new Iraq. And if the formation of the region demanded by Hakim led to Iraq's break-up, a high likelihood, Iran, which always argued for Iraq's unity, would easily deflect responsibility to the Americans, who indeed destroyed the Iraqi state, among other things by having encouraged Kurdish separatism in the first place.

Finally, Hakim's demand and the ability of the Kurdish and Shi'ite negotiators to wreck consensual negotiations is a function of the continued occupation that is not tied to any schedules or deadlines. Evidently, embittering the Sunni leads to the continuation of the insurrection and the possibility of open civil war. As long as the Americans are there to deal with the military consequences, the internal reasons for the Shi'ites seeking a *modus vivendi* are greatly vitiated. Had the Americans made any threats concerning their stay in Iraq, or established any timetables for leaving, the results could have been different. Of course, wishful thinking may play a role here as well, because the Shi'ites cannot really predict what the Americans will do in the face of an insurrection exacerbated by the constitutional disaster they are now causing. At the same time, the Sunni, who may also be guilty of wishful thinking of their own, do not think that the Americans can stay for ever in the face of continued losses, and therefore may think they have no reason to accept a parallelogram of forces predicated on their presence. The situation leads to imposition on the one side, and bargaining by means of the insurrection on the other side, weakening moderate and constructive forces on all sides.

In any case, once Hakim's demand, providing for the creation of a Shi'ite super-region, was introduced, all attempts to save the process were doomed, including the pointless and embarassing phonecall of President Bush to the SCIRI leader on 25 August. First, resisting Kurdish demands to weaken the central state and to extend their regional structure to the whole of Iraq had to depend on Shi'ite resistance, and their defence of the unity of Iraq, as the main beneficiaries of that unity. When Shi'ite leaders themselves championed regionalism in a more radical version, the Sunni were left alone.[46]

---

[46] Admittedly, had they received more support from the Da'wa party of Prime Minister Jaffari or from Ayattolah Sistani, the combined pressure of the Kurds and SCIRI could have been resisted. But all signs of a Shi'ite split disappeared after a few days, with even the Sadrists putting up only feeble resistance against the mega-region of the South. Again one should suspect the hand of Iran in all this.

It is not the case that Shi'ite demands could not be resisted. Their clerics were also demanding a strong constitutional statement on behalf of the role of Islam in civil and family law. The effort of getting them to compromise was, however, more successful in this area where the Americans, Kurds and secular deputies could concentrate their pressure, however inconsistently. A similar coalition was not available in the area of 'federalism'. Moreover, the timing of Hakim's monkeywrench or bombshell so late in the game meant that there was also no time to work on some complex compromise formula allowing all sides to make an input and save face. Here, the American acceleration of the process was to harvest its bitter fruit.

In the end of the official or legal process, between 15 August and 22 August, only a small unilateral concession was granted to the Sunni. The draft (Article 114) as it stood on 15 August, allowed the creation of new regions of any size both from provinces and old regions simply through the request of one-third of the provincial legislature or one-tenth of the voters and the approval of the majority in a provincial referendum. On 22 August, the implicit reference to size is gone, but the constitutional right of any province to form regions of undetermined size remains. While the request for forming a region is the same as before, what approval entails is no longer clearly specified. In a new Article 114 it is stated, however, that 'The Council of Representatives shall pass a law that fixes the executive procedures relating to establishing regions by simple majority in a period that does not exceed six months from the date of the first session'. This law, since it is not stated otherwise, would be passed by simple majority, and the mechanism of region formation it clearly has in mind also has to operate, it is clearly stated, by simple majority. It is possible now, however, that the majorities involved would operate on three levels: the provincial electorate, the provincial council and the National Assembly, as in an early proposal by Khalilzad. At the same time, since forming a region is still defined as a right of provinces (Articles 115–116), a future Supreme Court may declare any law interfering with that right unconstitutional. In any case, all that may have been objectionable in the 15 August version to the Sunni leaders, could be re-established by simple majority. There could have been one rub: as a law, the new legislation dealing with establishing regions could have been open to vetoes—in the transitional period the Kurds were able to insist on the veto of any of the three members of the presidential council (Article 134, fifth clause). But the same article explicitly exempts laws concerning the establishing of regions from the possibility of a veto.

Thus, the unilateral concessions that went into the 22 August draft were entirely unacceptable to the Sunni who assume that very likely the Kurds and the religious Shi'a would have at least a majority in the next National Assembly, and that they, the militant Sunni, will not control one member of a presidential council. The bottom line of the Sunni delegates was that it would have to be a two-thirds majority, ie the constitution amending majority that would have to work out the rules governing federalism. Since it is possible that a Shi'ite-Kurdish coalition would get two-thirds of the seats in the next parliament, even this solution carried an element of risk, admittedly for both sides in the debate. But this solution was decisively rejected.

Note that the compromise on the issue of the role of the *shari'a* in the constitutional set-up had *apparently* a far different structure, corresponding to the solution the Sunni sought on the question of federalism. Here the issue is relatively complex because both drafts make Islam as well as democracy and the rights of the constitution standards that all legislation would have to adhere to (Articles 2A, B, C). In the end these standards are likely to be contradictory and conflicts would have to be resolved by the constitutional court, the Supreme Court. That court, most dangerously from the secular point of view, is to contain both judges and experts in *shari'a* jurisprudence (Article 89). The number and the form of appointment, however, would be have to be determined by the next National Assembly (similarly to the executive rules for region formation) but by two-thirds majority. In this area, therefore, the way is open to a future consensual solution of the deferred issue (or to a hopeless stalemate!) showing quite clearly that in the area of 'federalism' deferral is intended only as a smokescreen for the same non-consensual solution on which agreement today is not possible.

The place of Islam in the state is not a function of the compromise concerning the court alone. Secular Iraqis, especially women, have been especially concerned about repeated attempts of Shi'ite clerics to change the personal status law of 1959, according to which marriage, divorce and inheritance law are legislated by the state, and are uniformly administered by secular courts. The constitution (Article 38) establishes 'freedom' of Iraqis to choose their status 'according to their own religion, sect, belief and choice' and leaves the organisation of these choices to an ordinary parliamentary law. Thus, the majority will be free, as Nathan Brown shows, to give as much or as little weight to a secular alternative and a uniform administration as it chooses, or to establish religious predominance over all cases where even one litigant or interested party may so desire.[47] The mechanism here as in the case of federalism is deferring the decision in favour of later majoritarian imposition, rather than a constitutional, consensual process.

Let us put the two major proposals concerning the relationship of Islam and law together. The Supreme Court can only be formed by a wide compromise. The status law, that could be judged unconstitutional by such a court can be established by simple majority. But a court may not be able to form at all, unless the Shi'ites get the number and type of *shari'a* experts and a mode of appointment acceptable to them. In that case a status law

---

[47] N Brown, 'The Final Draft of the Iraqi Constitution: Analysis and Commentary', Carnegie Endowment for International Peace, www. CarnegieEndowment.org.

can be enacted by a simple majority that does not have to worry about constitutional review. No wonder that advocates of women's rights and secularism are very upset about the end result of the process, and about the betrayal of their cause by the American Ambassador who wound up accepting and even praising the relevant parts of the draft. They should have nevertheless noticed that in the first parliamentary session, each of the three members of the presidency council would have veto rights over parliamentary legislation (Article 134). Thus, the election of one secular member could interfere with, but only for a single parliamentary period, the establishment of a status law that definitively decides the issue in favour of religious jurisdictions in this area.

As to the third really contentious issue, the question of resources, there was no real compromise here either. The Kurds and Shi'a were here to gain important rights as compared to the TAL. The issue is, of course, central, because even regional federalism would be acceptable if the two oil rich regions would have to fully share their wealth with the third. This could be guaranteed, however, only by central government control, which the TAL still provided among the exclusive powers of the federal government, that has to consult with the regions (Article 25E). It is true that the new constitution (Article 108) states that 'oil and gas are the property of all the Iraqi people' but it adds 'in all the regions and the provinces'. The actual dispensation comes in the next article. The federal government administers 'current fields' but in cooperation with the region, and on condition that the distribution be fair, and a quota be defined to make up for wrongs of the past (ie for the benefit of Shi'ite and Kurdish provinces). Thus, even current fields are not fully under central contol, but only under legally contestable conditions. There are, however, future fields to be explored, in terms of the brand new concept of 'current' and about these potentially much more important resources we get no clear regulation. In line with the premise that powers not defined as exclusive or shared powers of the federal government belong to the regions or to provinces (Article 111), the only conclusion to draw is that future fields would be under their, ie regional, administration. Peter Galbraith certainly draws this conclusion, but hopes to avoid it by pretending that all regions are likely to have future oil resources.[48] Oil company officials, who know better, expect nothing but contested jurisdictions, chaos and disorganisation, deeply undermining the financial capacities of the Iraqi state for a long time to come.[49]

There are finally issues we have heard little about in the press, but also of great importance, having to do with the structure of government. The TAL, as I have argued, sought to reconcile an ultimately confederal bargain

---

[48] P Galbraith, 'The Last Chance for Iraq' (2005) *New York Review of Books* 22.
[49] M Karouny and G Ghantous, 'Devolving Power in Iraq Threatens Oil Development', *Reuters*, 8 September 2005.

about the state with a centralistic version of parliamentarianism by using consociational structures, rooted mainly in the three person presidency, rather than by a bicameralism characteristic of a federal state. A move in a more federal direction in the earliest constitutional drafts would have been based on the combination of a new, second, federal parliamentary chamber and the replacement of the consociational presidency council in favour a single, more ceremonial president who *has to* offer the prime ministership to the largest parliamentary bloc. The new draft, probably because of the inability of its framers to agree on a federal formula, solves these questions by somehow combining all these competing alternatives into a single package. There will be a second parliamentary chamber, a Council of the Union including representatives of regions *and* provinces not in regions. But the definition of its rules of formation as well as powers (!) are left to the lower chamber, the Council of Deputies (Representatives), not the current one but the one elected in the next elections, voting by two-thirds majority (Articles 62 and 133). An important consequence of this very unusual delay was the restoration for a single parliamentary period the three person presidential council of the TAL, elected on a single slate by two-thirds majority, this time with a veto for each of the members, obviously as a replacement for the role of a federal chamber in national legislation (Article 134). These vetoes, as already said, do not exist in the case of region formation, but apply to the new law governing personal status, the two-thirds law governing the make-up of the Supreme Court, and indeed to constitutional amendments which require presidential assent.

The amending structure of the new constitution, though rigid enough, is in fact more flexible than that of the TAL. Initiatives for amendments can come from the president and cabinet together, or one-fifth of the lower chamber, the Council of Representatives, which is the only parliamentary chamber given a right of participation in constitutional revision. Where in the case of the TAL no amendment could be made at all that would abridge rights, here (Article 122, second clause) the basic principles of Chapter 1 and the rights and freedoms of Chapter 2 are unamendable only for the first two parliamentary cycles.[50] Subsequently, they can be amended according to the general rule that applies to most of the constitution: namely two-thirds of the members of parliament, agreement of the president plus majority support in a referendum. In the first parliamentary period, this means the presidential council, one way or the other (by either the amendment rule or the ordinary rule of legislation as now revised) has the option of a consociational veto for each of its members. Finally, and given what

---

[50] This provision was put in the place of the early draft's idea of a revision in two parliamentary cycles, that would bring up the possibility of amendments by one cycle, but would have protected basic rights better in the long term, since the new regulation does not then require that two parliaments in general approve amendments of certain articles.

is at issue today most importantly, no amendment is allowed that would lessen the powers of regions without the consent of their legislature and population in a referendum, unless one of the very few exclusive powers of the federal government is at issue (Article 122, fourth clause). This means that since the constitution already recognises the powers of the Kurdistan Region (Article 113), no constitutional amendment can touch these.[51] But interestingly enough, powers given by simple majority to new regions in the first session also would become by this clause amendment proof. If Iraq begins to break-up according to the dispensation of the current draft, for example, a duly elected parliament would be powerless to legislate any counter-measures, regardless of the majority supporting them. If the state structure of the new constitution did not work, only a revolutionary over-throw could remedy the situation.

INSTEAD OF A CONCLUSION

After the refusal to *legally* extend the process of constitution making as permitted by the TAL, the process was nevertheless extended in a manner that was most astonishing, as well as entirely illegal. The formal date of 22 August 2005, by which the draft should have been concluded and approved, came and went. The constitutional text, though never voted on, was to be sure pronounced final on that day, only it was not. Negotiations concerning changes continued and several changes were indeed made before the refer-endum of 15 October 2005, one on central control of water resources and another on having two deputy prime ministers. The most dramatic change, however, came on 12 October, three days before the referendum. Finally, a concession that appeared to be a genuine compromise was offered to the Sunni parties, and was accepted by one of them, the Iraqi Islamic Party. Relentless American pressure to appease the Sunni may have had some-thing to do with this turn of events. Fear of the failure of the constitutional referendum in three Sunni provinces could have been equally important, or perhaps the fear of being put in the position of having to openly fix the results of these referenda.

The compromise came right after the failure of an attempt to guarantee the referendum results through open manipulation of the TAL text. We were told that originally it was the Independent Electoral Commission of Iraq that decided, absurdly and certainly against the most obvious intentions of the drafters, and the plain meaning of the text itself, that the two-thirds of the voters of three provinces that would have to vote against the new

---

[51] It is this provision that enshrines a confederal state once it is formed, as against the amendment rule of the early draft that allowed ordinary constitutional amendments to change the whole regional structure.

constitution in order to reject it would have to be of the *eligible* rather than the *actual* voters. In this case, two-thirds could be mustered, perhaps in one province.[52] But when UN officials had some serious qualms about allowing this ruling to stand,[53] the National Assembly proceeded to vote by simple majority on 2 October that it must indeed be two-thirds of eligible voters in each of three provinces to vote against the constitution if the draft is to be rejected.[54] If they wished to do this, they should have amended the TAL by three-quarters of the votes, preferably when still under the veil of ignorance, and the Kurds had reasons to preserve the veto they long fought for. What the governing parties attempted to do instead, under the guise of mere interpretation of the TAL, was to 'interpret' voters in the same sentence once as actual (when it had to do with approval by majority) and the second time as eligible (when it had to do with rejection by two-thirds of each of three provinces). Most embarrassingly, under open UN and, this time fortunately tacit, US pressure, the very same National Assembly was forced, two days later, to withdraw the measure and return to *actual* rather than *eligible* voters, in the case of *both* majority approval and three province rejection of the draft.[55]

The solution, however, may have raised the possibility of rejection anew.[56] The compromise package offered to the Iraqi Islamic Party could have made a crucial difference in at least one Sunni majority province, Nineveh, we will never know for sure. But was the compromise offer a really serious one? In its most positive interpretation it reduces the constitution just passed to a provisional one once again, and makes the newly elected National Assembly yet another constitutional assembly that has been given the time extension foolishly denied to it predecessor.

What was done, technically speaking, seems more modest. The text of the draft that was subsequently voted on in the referendum was amended by a new Article 141 (not included in the printed draft already distributed to the voters), that stated:

> *First:* The parliament shall form, at the start of its work, a committee from its members, representative of the main components of the Iraqi society. The task of the committee is to present a report to the parliament, in not more than four months, including a recommendation of the necessary amendments that could be

[52] Galbraith n 48 above. This author-participant is in a good position to know that the ruling is wrong, but rather scandalously did not say so.

[53] See J Cole, *Informed Comment*, n 43 above and M Karouny, 'Sunni Arabs Seek UN Guarantees on Iraq Referendum', Reuters, 13 September 2005.

[54] RF Worth, 'Election Move Seems to Ensure Iraqis' Charter', *New York Times*, 4 October 2005 '"I think it's a double standard, and it's unfair", said Mahmoud Othman (or: Osman), a Kurdish assembly member who, like many other lawmakers, said he had not been present during the vote and only learned of it afterward. "When it's in your favor, you say 'voters.' When it's not in your favor you say 'eligible voters'"'.

[55] RF Worth and S Tavernise, 'Iraqi Lawmakers Reverse Rule Change', *New York Times*, 5 October 2005.

[56] In the actual event, 97 % of the voters of Anbar , 82 % of Salahddeen, but only 55 % of Nineveh voted against the draft.

made to the constitution. The committee is dissolved after a decision about its suggestions is taken.

Second: The amendments suggested by the committee shall be presented, in one bulk, to the parliament to be voted on, and it is considered to be passed by the approval of the absolute majority of the members of the parliament.

Third: The articles amended by the parliament according to what came in provision (second) of this Article shall be put to the people for a referendum, not more than two months after the passing of the amendments in the parliament.

Fourth: The referendum on the amended articles is successful, by the approval of the majority of voters, and if not refused by two thirds of the voters in three governorates or more.

Fifth: The effect of Article [126 related to amending the constitution] of this constitution is stopped, and its effect starts again after the amendments in this article are decided on.

Since the new amendment rule of the new constitution was suspended, everything could be changed for the four-month period and the road was in principle indeed open to a historical compromise of the main groupings. At the same time, that road was to be made very difficult by the restoration of the old three province veto by two-thirds of the voters of each. As in the case of the TAL, that veto protected most of all those who would benefit from the current constitutional draft, since a rejection of a package of amendments would not return Iraq to a condition without a constitution, or even to the TAL itself, but to the new arrangements approved on 15 October. Thus, the same text could be viewed as provisional and permanent at the same time, depending on how one judged the likelihood of it being actually transformed. The supposed compromise maintained the dramatic inequality of the Sunni Arabs with the other two main groupings, because if in principle the Sunni too could use the three province veto, it would be actually useless to them in a situation when the fall back position was represented by a constitution they entirely rejected. They were in effect delivered to the goodwill of their partners, assuming it existed, with a remote possibility that with allies they could hold government formation itself hostage to a prior constitutional deal.

It is very likely that it is the latter possibility that Sunni parties as well as most armed groups of the insurrection counted on when they urged and permitted (!) high participation in the elections of 15 December. Accordingly, if they along with possible allies like Allawi's secular list, had one-third of the seats of the National Assembly they could hold the formation of the presidency council hostage to a constitutional deal, and along with it government formation, because there is no other way that the candidate of the largest parliamentary group could be nominated as prime minister than by that council.

Unfortunately, it is now almost certain that through a combination of low electoral quotas for the Sunni in relevant provinces, possible fraud, and possibly the deBa'athification of deputies, the numerical and political weight of Sunni parties and a secular grouping led by I Allawi is not going to reach the one-third (92 seats out of 275) necessary for this strategy, for which a cosmetic Government of National Unity, without a constitutional bargain, will be no replacement whatsoever. Of course, the support of Kurdish parties for a constitutional deal would be an adequate substitute, since without them no government can be formed in any case. But most likely there already is a Barzani-Hakim deal over Kirkuk, and the Kurds are about to get what the Jaffari government denied them in exchange for support on the other major issues, namely a referendum over the fate of the city and possibly the province that will allow them to take control.[57]

Thus, there are only two factors, or their combination, that could help achieve the historical compromise that would lead to a renewal of the constituent process and significant, consensual constitutional amendments. The first is a possible split in the Shi'ite camp itself, as indicated by the earlier opposition of the Sadrists and the Jaffari government to the Hakim plan of nine province regionalism, as well as recent proposals by people as different as Sadr himself (who now should control a significant bloc of deputies) and Kanan Makiya to table the 'federalism' question for a lengthy period.[58] In effect these proposals all mean a return to the TAL's formula of an asymmetric structure of Kurdish confederal status in an Iraq whose exact nature would remain undetermined, but may involve elements of provincial federalism as well as the formation of smaller, weaker regions. So far, however, all such proposals have been swamped by the strength of SCIRI, with the probable backing of Iran.[59] Their slight chance of success is therefore dependent on what the Americans choose to do.

By this I do not mean the strength of their visible pressure, which may indeed be counter-productive. If it is true that the Americans want

[57] S Tavernise, 'U.N. Rejects Sunni Demand for New Vote in Iraq', *New York Times*, 28 December 2005. The vote for the constitution was 63 % yes in Kirkuk province. Honest or not, that percentage can be probably duplicated in a referendum concerning the political fate of the province.
[58] See 'Pact of Honor' as reported on by G Achkar in J Cole's *Informed Comment*, 9 December 2005 ; as well as K Makiya's recent op ed, 'Present at the Disintegration' in the *New York Times*, 11 December 2005.
[59] 'Abdul Aziz al-Hakim, the head of the victorious (fundamentalist Shi'ite) United Iraqi Alliance suggested Friday that Baghdad province join Kurdistan, the Middle Euphrates, and the deep south as a confederacy with special privileges, overseen by a federal government. He said that the constitution had given the Iraqi people this right, adding, "The choice of federalism is the right one, because it has strengthened the unity of Iraq on the one hand, and on the other has ensured justice. It has saved the country forever from the troika of dictatorship, racism and sectarianism".
Al-Hakim said it was unlikely that the establishment of provincial confederacies in the south would lead to a break-up of Iraq ... He called on the Kurds to work jointly with him in order to "safeguard the constitution from any attempt to alter it that might erase the gains that have been achieved by the Iraqi people". (*Informed Comment*, 31 December 2005, quoting Al-Zaman/AF).

a significant force to stay indefinitely in Iraq, the Americans have little leverage to impose a really fair bargain, though they may desperately try. The Shi'ites need not fear an insurrection more or less neutralised by a superpower, nor take its political wing seriously. The amazing thing is that at least Secretary of State Rice and Ambassador Khalilzad, if not the Pentagon, seem to understand by now that they are guarding Iran's prize, and that many of the Sunni they are shooting at are their geo-political allies. Yet they can do nothing about this bizarre state of affairs, and may even have to watch passively as the elected political leaders of these very Sunnis, like Saleh al Mutlaq, are deBa'athified and removed from the National Assembly by the commission set up by Ahmed Chalabi, the good friend of both the Pentagon and Iran. Leaving suddenly would indeed produce the chaos that would make their already very real failure visible to all who now choose to pretend otherwise. What the US government could and should do if it wished to salvage something from the whole lamentable operation is to produce a timetable for withdrawal to pressure the Shi'ites to take their own promise to renegotiate the constitution seriously, and defer to an international, Security Council authorised coalition to make sure that Iran does not take up the slack as they progressively withdraw. But is anyone going to listen to them after the fiasco that the adventure in Iraq has become?

Index

Abbasgholizadeh, Mahboobeh, 82–3
Abbasids, 16–20
'Abd al-Malik ibn Marwan, 13
'Abdul Hamid, Sultan, 46
Abdülmejid I, Sultan, 23, 25
Abdülmejid II, Sultan, 29
Abu al-'Ala' Salim, 15
Abu Musa, 17
Abu Yusuf, 17
Ackerman, Bruce, 125
Aden, 85
Afghanistan:
    1923 Constitution, 57
    1931 Constitution, 58–9
    1964 Constitution, 9, 59–60,
      150, 152
    2004 Constitution, 51
      assessment, 60–1, 160–1
      Emergency Loya Jirga, 149, 151,
        152, 156
      legitimacy, 73–6, 149–51
      power relations, 151–3
      presidentialism debate, 154–6
      process, 67–8, 69–72, 147–61
      recognition of diversity, 159–60
      status of Islam, 72, 150, 156–8
    Bonn Accords (2001), 67–8, 147,
      148, 150–1, 161
    civil wars, 148
    codification, 51, 57–8
    Cyprus Group, 149
    democracy, 60
    early 20th century constitutionalism,
      57
    ethnicity, 70, 148, 153, 158, 159
    freedom of religion, 93–4
    gender equality, 93, 157
    human rights and Islam, 92–4
    judiciary, 160
    Khost rebellion (1924), 58
    languages, 159, 160

    Loya Jirgas, 9, 60, 147, 149, 150
    national anthem, 159–60
    Northern Alliance, 148–9, 150–1, 154
    Penal Code (1924), 57
    Peshawar Group, 149
    regime change, 63
    Rome Group, 148–9
    Shinwari rebellion (1928), 58
    Supervisory Council of the North
      (SN), 151, 154
    Supreme Court, 157, 160
    warlords, 151, 152
    Wolesi Jirga, 153, 154, 156
    women, 58
Afghanistan Compact, 148
Ahmedi, 22
Ahwas, 13
Akhisari, 23
al-Qaeda, 148, 151
Alexander the Great, 15, 18, 21
Alfieri, Vittorio, conte di, 42
Algeria, 31
'Ali ibn Abi Talib, 14
Allah, Shayk Fazl, 40
Allawi, I, 199, 200
Amanallah Khan, 57, 58, 59, 147, 149
ancient Greece, 15, 16
Annan, Kofi, 149
Arab Charter on Human Rights
    (1994), 80
Arab Charter on Human Rights
    (2003), 80
Arab Human Rights Movement, 81
Arab League, 188
Arato, Andrew, 5, 10, 69, 163–201
Aristotle, 15, 18, 21
Arjomand, Saïd Amir, 1–10, 33–62, 65,
    66, 97, 99, 117, 125, 136, 138, 140
Atatürk, Mustafa Kemal, 3, 46, 113
al-'Attar, 20
Austria, 6

Lightning Source UK Ltd.
Milton Keynes UK
UKHW020341130521
383641UK00004B/158